COMPUTERS

Image Objects

Image Objects

An Archaeology of Computer Graphics

Jacob Gaboury

The MIT Press
Cambridge, Massachusetts
London, England

The MIT Press would like to thank the anonymous peer reviewers who provided comments on drafts of this book. The generous work of academic experts is essential for establishing the authority and quality of our publications. We acknowledge with gratitude the contributions of these otherwise uncredited readers.

An earlier version of chapter 1 was published as "Hidden Surface Problems: On the Digital Image as Material Object" in the *Journal of Visual Culture* 14 (1), and a version of chapter 2 was previously published as "The Random-Access Image: Memory and the History of the Computer Screen" in *Grey Room* 70 (Winter 2018).

This book was set in Stone Serif and Stone Sans by Westchester Publishing Services. Printed and bound in the United States of America.

Library of Congress Cataloging-in-Publication Data

Names: Gaboury, Jacob, author.
Title: Image objects : an archaeology of computer graphics / Jacob Gaboury.
Description: Cambridge, Massachusetts : The MIT Press, [2021] | Edited version
   of the author's thesis (Ph.D.)--New York University, 2014, under the title:
   Image objects : an archaeology of 3D computer graphics,1965–1979. |
Includes bibliographical references and index.
Identifiers: LCCN 2020031707 | ISBN 9780262045032 (hardcover)
Subjects: LCSH: Image processing--History. | Computer graphics--History.
Classification: LCC TA1637 .G33 2021 | DDC 006.609--dc23
LC record available at https://lccn.loc.gov/2020031707

10 9 8 7 6 5 4 3 2 1

Contents

Acknowledgments

This book is the product of many years, and the work and collaboration of countless people, communities, and institutions. It has benefited, first and foremost, from the patience and enthusiasm of mentors who saw this project through its earliest iterations nearly a decade ago. I would like to thank Alexander Galloway for pushing me to make big claims, Lisa Gitelman for ensuring those claims had substance, Mara Mills for her guidance and foresight, and the support and investment of Jussi Parikka and Timothy Lenoir. I am truly lucky to have had the opportunity to work with and learn from the incredible intellectual community that is the NYU Department of Media, Culture, and Communication, whose faculty and students remain my advisers, colleagues, and friends.

That this project was allowed the time and resources to mature is thanks largely to the support of key research fellowships and archives, which provided critical funding and through which I presented early chapter drafts that challenged my own disciplinary preoccupations. My first trip to the University of Utah was made possible through the ACM History Fellowship, and subsequent trips were supported by the IEEE Life Member's Fellowship in Electrical History. At Utah, I benefited from the guidance of an incredible group of archivists in the J. Willard Marriott Library Special Collections, including Elizabeth Rogers, Lorraine Crouse, Krissy Giacoletto, Sara Davis, and Molly Rose Steed. Work in the Carl Machover Papers at the Charles Babbage Institute was supported by the Adelle and Erwin Tomash Fellowship in the History of Information Technology, where Jeffrey Yost and Thomas Misa helped guide me through the collections and pushed the project in new directions. Access to the National Museum of American History and the Air and Space Museum were made possible through a

Lemelson Fellowship from the Smithsonian Institution, where Eric Hintz and Paul Ceruzzi offered invaluable guidance. I would also like to thank David Brock at the Computer History Museum and Henry Lowood at Stanford University for their invaluable assistance in navigating their institutional archives and collections.

The first draft of this project was completed in Lüneburg, Germany, during a transformative fellowship at the Institute for Advanced Study on Media Cultures of Computer Simulation with Martin Warnke and Claus Pias. A final chapter was added during a research fellowship at the Internationales Kolleg für Kulturtechnikforschung und Medienphilosophie in Weimar, Germany, alongside an incredible group of fellows, and with the expert guidance of Bernhard Siegert and Lorenz Engell. The proposal for this book was completed during a postdoctoral fellowship at the Max Planck Institute for the History of Science in Berlin, where Lorraine Daston, David Sepkoski, and an amazing community of historians pushed me to consider a much broader view of the history of science and the place of computer graphics within it. That proposal is likewise indebted to the care and attention of Raiford Guins and Henry Lowood, whose feedback and advice transformed what was a vague plan into a complete and legible project. An early draft of the final manuscript benefited greatly from a University of California Humanities Research Institute's manuscript workshop fellowship, and the patience and sage advice of Patrick LeMieux, Patrick McCray, Colin Milburn, Rita Raley, and Fred Turner in tweaking, nudging, and totally reworking key elements of what would become this book. Finally, I would like to thank Doug Sery, Noah Springer, my three anonymous reviewers, and the editorial team at the MIT Press for carrying this project through its final stages. Their patience and support made this work possible, and I am grateful to have had the opportunity to work with them.

I often tell graduate students that much of their professional career will be learning to confidently perform a series of tasks for which they have not been trained and might never be asked to perform again—a near impossible task without the guidance of horizontal communities of practice and care, without which none of this would have been possible. To the media slackers: Stephanie Boluk, Patrick LeMieux, Laine Nooney, David Parisi, and Carlin Wing, your friendship means the world to me. To the Critical Media Forms Working Group, whose annual media aesthetics workshops refined nearly all of what follows: Brooke Belisle, Stephanie Boluk, Kris Cohen,

James Hodge, Patrick Jagoda, Patrick Keilty, Patrick LeMieux, and Scott Richmond, thank you. I would also like to thank my students and colleagues at Stony Brook University and the University of California at Berkeley for the train rides, writing groups, happy hours, and phone calls that supported me and my work as I navigated the challenges and complexities of academe.

Finally: to my family—Beth, David, Bryse, Hannah, and Keith. And for Keehnan, who makes everything possible.

Figure 0.1
Ivan Sutherland's students mark and measure Marsha Sutherland's VW Beetle for digitization, 1972. Courtesy of the Special Collections Department, J. Willard Marriott Library, University of Utah.

Introduction

In order to be in a relation with the world informatically, one must erase the world, subjecting it to various forms of manipulation, preemption, modeling, and synthetic transformation. . . . The promise is not one of revealing something as it is, but in simulating a thing so effectively that "what it is" becomes less and less necessary to speak about, not because it is gone for good, but because we have perfected a language *for* it.
—Alexander Galloway, *The Interface Effect*

Doing with images makes symbols.
—Alan Kay, *Doing with Images Makes Symbols*

In the fall of 1972, Marsha Sutherland spent several weeks driving around Salt Lake City in a Volkswagen Beetle half covered in a polygon mesh. The car was a spectacle, its green exterior dotted with hundreds of numbered vertices connected to form a grid of irregular squares (figure 0.1 and plate 1).[1] Marsha had moved to Salt Lake from Cambridge, Massachusetts, just four years prior with her husband, Ivan, who left Harvard University in 1968 for a tenured position in the computer science program at the University of Utah. Each week Marsha would drive up the foothills of the Salt Lake Valley to the Merrill Engineering Building, where Ivan's students would carefully mark and measure the car for digitization. Along the way she would traverse a grid of a different sort: the lockstep raster of city blocks that make up the Plat of Zion, the plan for a city of God first devised by Joseph Smith in 1833, and dug out of the valley floor by Brigham Young and his followers with the colonial settlement of Salt Lake City in 1847.[2] By the end of the year, Marsha's Beetle would become the first real-world object to be fully scanned and rendered by a computer—the physical made digital (figure 0.2).[3]

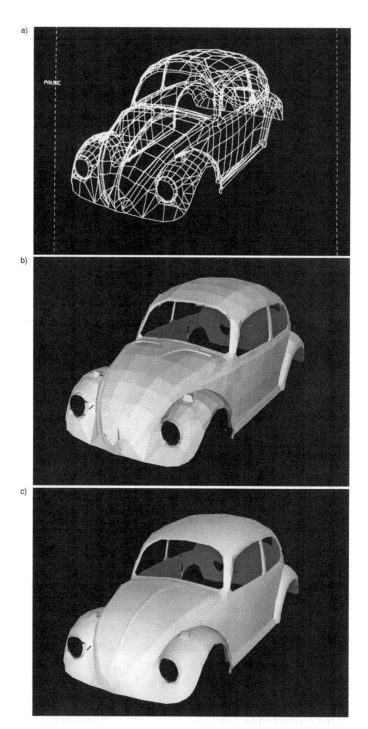

Figure 0.2
Digitized Volkswagen Beetle rendered in wireframe, flat shading, and smooth shading at the University of Utah computer graphics lab, 1973. Courtesy of the Computer History Museum and the University of Utah School of Computing.

A surprising object in an unlikely place, Marsha's Volkswagen straddles two worlds. A global symbol of 1960s' counterculture, the Beetle was near ubiquitous at the start of the 1970s. Earlier that year, in February 1972, the Beetle surpassed the Ford Model T to become the most widely manufactured vehicle ever produced, its design largely unchanged since 1938.[4] It was this iconic status that drew Ivan's students to it and made it legible as an object for simulation in the first place.[5] Yet this particular Beetle marks the beginning of a radical transformation in the shape of our lived environment—a turning point in which the physical world becomes saturated with digital objects. Think, for a moment, of the building in which you now sit, the phone in your pocket, the book you now read; each of these objects have been materially shaped by a process that can be traced to Marsha, winding her way up the hills outside Salt Lake City half a century ago. Each of these objects have, over the course of their design and creation, been touched and transformed by computer graphics.

This may be surprising to anyone accustomed to thinking of graphics exclusively as visual images produced, augmented, or transformed by computation. Likewise, for most of us computer graphics are a relatively recent invention, emerging at the end of the twentieth century as spectacular visual effects and lifelike simulations in film, television, and digital games. In fact, computer graphics are as old as the modern computer itself, and their development marks a fundamental transformation not only in the way we make images, but in the way we mediate our world through the computer, and in turn come to reimagine the world as computational. We live in a world that has been structured by the visual regime of computer graphics. Whether captured with a digital camera, designed and rendered using 3D interactive software, or simply displayed on the pixelated grid of a computer screen, almost all images we view, make, and interact with on a daily basis are shaped by computation. Yet computer graphics have largely disappeared as a legible object of analysis, and the history of computer graphics remains almost entirely unwritten.[6]

This is due in part to the phenomenal invisibility of computer graphics as a distinct technical medium. Most computational images we encounter are designed to simulate and reproduce the formal and aesthetic norms of those media that precede them, be it the photo-realistic renders of special effects and digital games, or the skeuomorphic interfaces of our laptops and smartphones. Consequently the more advanced computer graphics become, the less visible they appear to be and the less we remark on their ubiquity.[7] When graphics do register as objects for critique, they are almost always framed by discourses of realism and mimesis, or broad narratives of techno- logical development that lead inevitably toward verisimilitude.[8] Computer graphics are perhaps the only medium that is analyzed exclusively in terms of the ways it successfully produces its own invisibility. We might value and remark on the photographic, televisual, or cinematic quality of a media text, but if an image reads as computer graphics, it has failed its simulation. This is because unlike those media that claim an indexical relationship to the world they represent, the thing reproduced by computer graphics is not the world but another medium in simulation. Computer graphics are thus always already mediated, and the goal of nearly all graphical research is the accurate reproduction of the effects of this prior mediation. This mimetic quality has precluded an examination of computer graphics that takes seri- ously its historical emergence as a distinctly computational technology untethered from the long history of visual representation. Likewise, it has limited our engagement with computer graphics to only their most visible manifestations: as images on screens.

This book begins with the premise that computer graphics are much more than the images we see. They are one of the principal technologies of our historical present, and have reshaped the way we understand, relate with, and engage the material world today. To understand this transforma- tion will require a material and local history of computer graphics as it developed alongside the modern computer in the second half of the twen- tieth century. Taking up this task, *Image Objects* traces the history of com- puter graphics in the thirty years prior to the technology's emergence in popular visual culture. In this it offers two interrelated stories.

First this is a history of the computational image, and those technologies that made possible its appearance on the experimental screens of academic and commercial research centers some sixty years ago. Refusing popular nar- ratives of convergence and remediation, I argue that computer graphics is a unique medium distinct from those earlier visual forms it seeks to simulate. To understand and make visible the material specificity of computer graph- ics, I pull apart the rendered image and identify its constitutive parts: those historical objects that make up the material history of graphical simulation, and through which we might posit a theory of graphical computing. To this end, I ask not simply how computer graphics developed over the second half of the twentieth century, or who helped shape the discipline through research and innovation, but rather what historical technologies structured and limited the field as it evolved, and how those technologies continue to determine the ways we engage with computational images today. In each of the following chapters I dig out a single technical object, broadly construed, that in turn becomes emblematic of an entire practice of image making. Through an analysis of these five objects that shaped the early history of computer graphics—an algorithm, an interface, an object standard, a programming paradigm, and a hardware platform—*Image Objects* reflects on the ways that visibility, memory, simulation, relation, and history are each inscribed into the technical infrastructure of the medium of computer graphics itself. In turn these objects form the basis for my broadly materialist methodology: an archaeology of this seemingly immaterial media form, the computational image.

I adopt this term strategically as a means of signaling a set of political and methodological concerns, and as part of an effort to place this text in dialogue with a broad field of practice. Both a theory and method, media archaeology encapsulates a great number of media historical interventions. What draws me to this field is, following Vivian Sobchack, its concern for the materiality of media *objects* over the linear teleology of "realist historical representation, which attempts to fill in the absences of the past with coherent—and metaphorical—narratives that substitute for their loss."[9] Media archaeology excavates dead media objects and brings them to bear on the present through a descriptive contextualization that is concerned primarily with what an object is and how it functioned rather than what it might have been interpreted to mean. That said, media archaeology is not exclusively concerned with old and dead things, the forgotten practices associated with them, and their impact on the coproduction of past knowledge. It is also concerned with media as a mode of engaging the material world, and the ways that media act as sensory prostheses that mediate practice and experience. The primary distinction here is that of materiality over representation, and a critique of progressivist, revolutionary, and linear forms of history. I view this book as an archaeology because it looks to a neglected prehistory that has been assumed or obscured by popular discourses of graphical realism. Likewise, in focusing on a series of objects that—while deeply important to the historical function of graphics—have been largely forgotten or taken as given by contemporary researchers, this project points to the dead media of existing digital forms. Holding in tension the need for a cultural politics of technology and the desire to deprivilege human-centered narratives of technological innovation, I acknowledge the difficulty of describing and performing a fixed media archaeological method, and view it as an essential focus of my investigation.[10]

Further complicating those historical narratives that would presume the centrality of the sites and objects that dominate our contemporary media landscape, *Image Objects* frames the history of computer graphics through a unique but largely neglected site in the history of computing. At a time when the vast majority of computational research was concentrated at university and corporate research institutions on the East and West Coasts, the field of computer graphics developed largely at secondary sites that have been left out of the broader history of computing.[11] Chief among these is the research program at the University of Utah, founded in 1965 by Salt Lake City native David C. Evans and heavily funded by the Department of Defense with the goal of advancing research into "graphical man-machine communication."[12] In the period from roughly 1965 to 1980, the faculty and graduates of the Utah program were responsible for no less than inventing the very concepts that make modern computer graphics possible, and many of the school's graduates went on to become industry leaders in the field of computing in the second half of the twentieth century.[13] The founders of Pixar, Adobe, Silicon Graphics, Netscape, Atari, and WordPerfect were all students at Utah during this period, and dozens of key researchers at Xerox PARC, NASA's Jet Propulsion Laboratory, the New York Institute of Technology, and Industrial Light & Magic all began their careers in Salt Lake City. The University of Utah was the epicenter of graphical development for the first fifteen years of the discipline, and its archives and papers form the foundation of this book. Grounding the history of computer graphics in this way—at a particular historical site and through a discrete set of technologies—*Image Objects* extends a theory of computer graphics not as an ephemeral abstraction but as a physical thing: the digital image as material object.

In tracing the history of computer graphics in this way, *Image Objects* tells a second story about the emergence of a new object form, and along with it the transformation of computation as a technical and cultural practice. Prior to the 1960s, computers were machines built for the procedural calculation of numerical data. They functioned hierarchically, with large mainframes designed for solving predetermined problems or processing data according to predetermined procedures. Computing was an explicitly noninteractive process; its inputs and outputs were punch cards and paper, and its objects were logic and numbers. Computer graphics was first developed as a means of abstracting computational processes toward human readable modes of interaction—that is, of bringing the material logic of the sensible world to bear on the informatic logic of computational systems. Through computer graphics the image world was operationalized, made to compute and perform actions, to take up and simulate space. The development of computer graphics in this sense marks a reorientation of computer science toward the object world such that it could be made subject to computational forms of simulation, transforming the computer from a *tool* for procedural calculation into a *medium* structured by a distinct ontological claim. Over the past fifty years, this claim has become one of the dominant modes of engaging with and thinking through all manner of processes, such that our contemporary world is now populated by a vast number of objects shaped by their encounter with graphical systems—that is, *image objects*.

The image object here marks a theory and method for engaging the transformation of the visible world under computation. It insists first that digital images are materially structured by those historical objects that produce them—objects that have been rendered out of the visible image, but that fundamentally shape the function and appearance of computer graphics as a distinctly computational technology. From microprocessors and graphics libraries to software suites and shading algorithms, computer graphics contain a vast number of objects whose material histories are erased if we restrict our analysis to the rendered image alone. At the same time, the image object affirms the broad influence of computer images on the shape and function of the material world today, describing the historical process whereby a vast number of material objects have been taken up by computer graphics and made subject to the logic of the digital image. Over the course of this history we will find countless objects taken up and transformed in this way. From the shape of contemporary architecture and built environments, the aesthetics of digital printing and desktop publishing, the interfaces we use to engage and communicate with our world, industrial design and rapid manufacturing, the structure of cars, planes, and other vehicles, and even the design of chips, circuits, and computer hardware itself—all are mediated and informed by this dual logic: at once visual and material, representation and calculation, both image and object.

It can be difficult to see the influence of computer graphics on our lived environment. The processes that define and articulate this relationship are so diffuse that they too often appear ordinary, naturalized, and mundane, and therefore are rarely remarked on or analyzed. In order to make visible the function of computer graphics today, we must return to those early moments in the history of the technology when the gap between the physical world and its simulation is most clearly felt, when the theory of the world articulated by computer graphics was still in formation. For over two months Marsha Sutherland's Volkswagen occupied this space between worlds: an object in practice and an image in the making; one foot in the digital and another in Salt Lake; neither image nor object, but an image object trapped in an extended moment of becoming.[14] With a few clicks of my mouse, I can drop Marsha's Beetle into any modern graphical simulation, draping it in the newest texture and lighting algorithms, modeling its behavior as part of an interactive environment made from thousands of objects structured by this same logic (figure 0.3). Today the aerodynamic curve of all motor vehicles is the product of this transformation, a spline

Figure 0.3
A contemporary VW Beetle simulation in Autodesk Maya. Note the visualization of the software's node architecture on the left, in which each of the elements that make up the rendered image (texture, lighting, geometry, etc.) are displayed as a nested structure of objects. Altered. Image by the author.

function driving around Salt Lake City, materially connected to that first digital object rendered out from Marsha's Volkswagen some fifty years ago. Ultimately this book is an effort to develop a language to speak to this quality of the world we now occupy. In doing so, we will find that computational images are not pictures of the things they represent; they are pictures of the world that produced them, and they execute a theory of that world in the world.

Visible Outputs

For over thirty years, computer graphics have been synonymous with illusion and artifice. Their appearance at the end of the twentieth century marked a crisis of visibility whereby the world was refigured as an image severed from the materiality of the thing it represents. Popular accounts of this transformation were commonplace in the enthusiasm surrounding new media technologies in the 1990s, a period often characterized by theories of the postmodern and the new, the supposed dissolution of the material into the virtual, and the rise of simulation across all facets of contemporary culture. This was also the period in which computer graphics first entered the realm of popular entertainment on a large scale, with the release of the first feature-length computer-animated film, broad success of Hollywood blockbusters that prominently featured computer-generated effects, and development of the first interactive 3D gaming consoles.[15] Along with the internet, computer graphics were one of the quintessential "new media" technologies of the decade. Just as scholars and critics touted the revolutionary power of the web, distributed networks, hypertext, and cyberspace, so too did they envision a future in which computer graphics would dominate our visual field, transforming our relationship to reality itself. As science fiction author Bruce Sterling exclaimed at the start of the decade, "The seams between reality and virtuality will be repeatedly and deliberately blurred. Ontology be damned!"[16]

Yet in many ways this moment was more aberration than innovation: a dramatic flourish of visibility that seemed to erupt fully formed before receding almost as quickly as it came. While today the internet continues to be viewed as one of the most important and pervasive technologies of our current media landscape, computer graphics seem an almost improper object whose vision of total simulation appears naive at best. Instead, the past twenty years of media theory have seen a pronounced shift away from these immaterial preoccupations and toward the materiality of digital media as historically instantiated technical objects. New media, we are reminded, are not as new as they appear to be and have much in common with those older media forms they were said to replace.[17] If there *is* a radical transformation to be found at the heart of digital technologies, it lies in the procedural, algorithmic logic of computation itself, and not in the ways that computation is made meaningful to us through visualization. This materialist turn offers a valuable corrective to over a decade of enthusiastic writing on the transformative effect of the simulated image and of reading the rendered output of our machines with little regard for the means by which such images are made possible.[18] While the digital image was once thought to reveal the always already virtual nature of representation itself, under the material turn such images would seem to hide the truth of those technologies that ground all digital media, such that if we hope to understand the true function of our computers, we must look to the software, platforms, and code that structure them.[19]

This distinction implies a broadly hermeneutic critique whereby the machine conceals its function beneath the veneer of the digital image and its simulation, such that we are compelled to open the black box and look beyond mere representation.[20] Taken to the extreme, this formulation suggests that we have not simply misrecognized our true object of analysis, but have fallen victim to the illusory and seductive quality of digital images, which hide not only their material function as technical objects but likewise their role within the broader social and political circuits of computation. To imagine computational media as virtual or ephemeral erases the physical and affective labor required to build, maintain, and dismantle technical systems; their potentially catastrophic effects on the environment, human, and nonhuman life; and their political function in the lives of their users, the culture of their designers, and the shape of our societies.[21] As media scholar Tara McPherson has warned, "Our screens are cover stories, disguising deeply divided forms of both machine and human labor. We focus exclusively on them increasingly to our peril."[22]

Yet this wholesale refusal of the screen image produces its own restrictions. Despite this turn toward the mechanical interiority of technical things, our engagement with computing remains highly visual and deeply tied to the logic of simulation. It is true that our screens are not transparent windows that lay bare the act of computing itself, but they are likewise not somehow outside that act, and play a principal role in shaping our understanding of and relationship to computational technologies. Yet in our rush to correct the visual bias of digital media studies, we have largely neglected the screen image as a material object in its own right—one with a heterogeneous history that runs parallel with that of textual or purely mathematical forms of computation. Rather than dismiss the visual as mere interface for deeper material processes, we might extend this materialist critique to include the simulated image, unpacking the means by which these images are modeled and displayed. Reading the digital image in this way—as an object structured by a set of distinct material practices—allows us to move beyond discourses of immateriality and virtuality to a theory of the digital image that is not visible in the rendered output of the screen. In doing so, we will find that computer graphics are one of the foundational technologies of our modern computational culture, and that they played a central role in the development of computing over the past seventy years.

To begin, we must unlearn the way we look at computational images. It does not seem controversial to suggest that our visual and material landscape has been fundamentally transformed by computation, yet this quality often cannot be deduced simply by looking.[23] Popular discourses of realism and fidelity dominate our analyses of digital image technologies, but are derived from an uncritical appropriation of those formal qualities that have historically defined prior modes of image making. As countless scholars have argued, digital images do not hold an indexical relationship to the world they represent, such that to analyze them exclusively in terms of their ability to reproduce the aesthetics of film and photography is to willfully occlude the means by which they are produced. This does not mean we must ignore the visual altogether. Rather, we must attend to the Janus-faced nature of digital images, which are shaped not by the etching of light but by the articulation of a set of computational objects developed to enact this simulation. Computer graphics exist simultaneously as both an assemblage of technical objects and an image that has been rendered out from them. To examine computational images in isolation from these objects is to mistake the render for the thing itself, and be drawn into an uncritical and ahistorical relationship that makes one culpable in the forms of material erasure so widely critiqued by media scholars today. If we wish to understand the function of these images, we must examine those objects that surround them—objects that are the product of this distinct material history and articulate a distinctly computational ontology.[24]

Object Simulation

This connection between computer graphics and a computational theory of objects may seem counterintuitive. After all, "computer graphics" can be used to refer to any image produced by computer processing, from a single digital photograph to a fully interactive 3D environment. Not all graphical images are the product of object simulation in the sense that a digitized Volkswagen Beetle so clearly is. Nonetheless, nearly all contemporary computer graphics are structured by a theory of objects that emerged alongside these early experiments in the mid-twentieth century, in which the world is understood as a relational system of objects capable of discrete forms of interaction.

This distinction is visible in the first documented use of the term "computer graphics," formalized in 1960 by Verne Hudson, chief of preliminary design at the Wichita Division of the Boeing Airplane Company.[25] In 1964, a member of Hudson's team named William Fetter was the first person to model the human figure using a computer, crafting a three-dimensional object model out of vector lines that formed the shape of a sitting man (figure 0.4).[26] The figure appears as a transparent mesh of curves and angles, woven together with seven joints for basic movement and articulation. Its form was derived from United States Air Force anthropometric data, modeled by an engineer and transferred onto punch cards, and then fed into an IBM 7094 mainframe computer to produce a reel of magnetic tape that could be read by an automated plotting tool for paper output. The purpose of Fetter's model was to approximate the human body and provide adaptable representations for use in ergonomics and design. Its principal use was to model a pilot's ability to reach and grasp the various switches and dials found in the cockpit of the Boeing 747, designed from roughly 1964 to 1970 using a range of computer-aided techniques. The figure is commonly known among graphics researchers as "Boeing Man," and it is one of many origin stories in the history of computer graphics.[27] Fetter himself referred to the figure as First Man, implying a kind of archaeological lineage: the dawn of a new species form.[28]

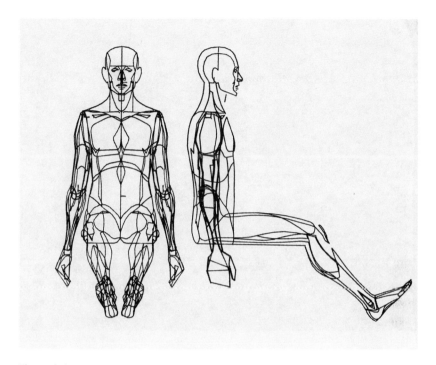

Figure 0.4
William Fetter, *First Man*, 1964. Courtesy of the Boeing Company.

Of course, Fetter's sitting figure is by no means the earliest example of what we now call computer graphics. Arguably the most visible graphical application in the history of early computing was the Semi-Automatic Ground Environment (SAGE) for air defense, commissioned and developed over the course of the 1950s after the US Air Defense Systems Engineering Committee recommended computerized networking for radar stations guarding the northern air approaches of the United States as a response to the threat of nuclear attack from the Soviet Union.[29] The SAGE system was a hugely ambitious sociotechnical apparatus made up of computers, network technology, radar, aircraft, and weaponry mobilized in the service of a global system. Designed to allow human operators to determine possible threats from long-range bombers, it required the complex cooperation of data transmission, calculation, and display. While SAGE was not exclusively or even primarily graphical, its visual interface was key to its operation. Using graphical consoles equipped with light guns, operators

Figure 0.5
Frame capture from IBM's short film "Freeing Man's Mind to Shape the Future" (1960), showing the graphical terminal of the Semi-Automatic Ground Environment air defense system.

could track two-dimensional representations of airplanes as they moved across a screen overlaid with a map of the part of the country under the defense of a given station (figure 0.5). When an operator identified a potential threat, the system would calculate an intercept path for fighter pilots or surface-to-air missiles before a decision was made whether or not to destroy the target.[30]

While SAGE was one of the earliest applications of large-scale interactive computer graphics, the image of the world that it articulates is fundamentally different than the one pictured by Fetter some ten years later. For SAGE, an enemy airplane is a blip on a screen, a target meant to be identified, part of a global system to be commanded (figure 0.6). Its visuality is two-dimensional and cartographic; its images functioned as symbols designed to elicit a response from a technical operator.[31] The SAGE system was a product of the Cold War environment that produced it, and articulated a

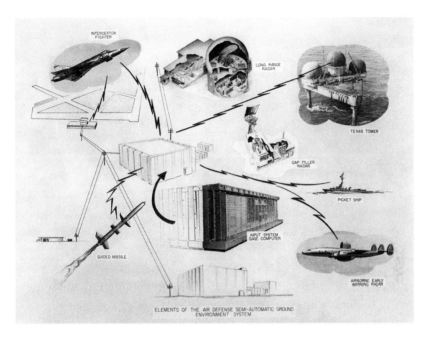

Figure 0.6
Diagram of the SAGE system as a complex sociotechnical apparatus. MITRE Corporate Records and Archives, SAGE collection, M0-139.

theory of that world as a system to be directed and controlled—a vision that would have long-standing repercussions for the development of communication technologies over the subsequent seventy years.[32] Fetter's airplanes are quite different. Here the plane forms the ground of a relational environment in which a human operator is situated (figure 0.7). This plane is not symbolic but rather mimetic, used to model or simulate a three-dimensional space comprised of a discrete set of interactive objects that includes this human figure, this First Man. The figure serves a standardizing function, its size and shape derived from what is called a 50 percentile figure, built to approximate the average size of 50 percent of air force pilots.[33] The shape of this model thus forms the basis for the design of a technical system—the 747 cockpit—and the assumption that its pilots' bodies will not vary widely from this presumptive norm.[34] In standardizing its human model and designing for that standardization, Boeing Man is shaped by a particular image of the world, and in turn comes to refigure the world

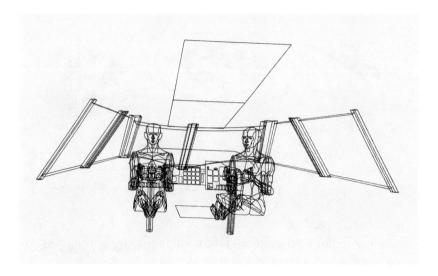

Figure 0.7
Fetter's Boeing Man as an interactive object within a simulated environment, 1964.
Courtesy of the Boeing Company.

according to that image—a fact made evident in the thousands of Boeing 747 airplanes in operation today.[35] Understood this way, Fetter's image is a model for the primitive simulation of a physical object, designed to approximate and standardize the complexity of real-world interaction. It is as much a theory of the world as it is an image of it, and in the subsequent decades that theory would be made actionable.

In the ten years that separate these two moments, we find a pronounced transformation, and along with it a change in how computer graphics were understood to relate to the world that grounds them.[36] While the SAGE system treated graphics as *images* that visually represent numerical data to its operators, Fetter used graphics as a medium for the simulation of graphical *objects*. This is a subtle but deeply meaningful distinction, and one that is lost when we treat the history of computer graphics exclusively as a history of images produced through computational calculation.[37] It is a logic that emerges alongside computer graphics, growing to become altogether diffuse across the field of computer science as it begins to take up graphical systems and develop novel uses for computational images. As early as 1961, Ivan Sutherland was using object-oriented structures in the development of his widely influential Sketchpad program for computer-aided design

(CAD). Likewise, Steven Russel's *Spacewar!* (1962)—considered by many to be the first graphical, interactive digital game—was designed using object-oriented principles in this same period.[38] One of the earliest modern graphical user interfaces, developed from 1972 to 1979 at Xerox for use with the Alto computing system, was predicated on the object-oriented structure of the Smalltalk programming language to such an extent that the language is inextricably tied to its interface and requires it in order to function.[39] While each of these object forms cannot be made commensurate, as they do not all adhere to a single, fixed theory of object relation, they are nonetheless exemplary of a broad transformation in which object simulation becomes a principal structuring logic for computational systems.

In this way, the act of computing is refigured from a set of procedural calculations into an interactive environment, understood as a spatially embodied field of discrete computable objects. In short, computing is transformed from a *process* into a *medium*.[40] Today this object logic has grown into one of the dominant forms of our contemporary media environment, transforming the ways we model and represent the world, and in turn reorienting our understanding of that world as a structure of computable objects.[41] In exploring the transformation of computer science and its adoption of object simulation across a range of technical practices, this book proposes that to understand this reorientation, we must look to those sites from which it emerged, both as a moment in the history of computing and as an articulation of a distinct culture of practice.

Other Places

Just off the main campus of the University of Utah sits Fort Douglas, a military garrison founded in 1862 to protect the overland mail route and telegraph lines running from Salt Lake City to San Francisco. The site was strategically chosen in the foothills of the Salt Lake Valley, as the US military was concerned with secessionist activity in the area and wanted to keep an eye on the territory's Mormon population.[42] For nearly a century, the fort played a strategic role in the economic, social, and political stability of the region, but by the mid-1960s, much of the land had been transferred to the ownership of the university, and its buildings were frequently delegated for research projects run by Utah faculty and staff. It was in this context that in late 1968, an abandoned bunker in this former military garrison was transformed into the home of one of the first commercial computer graphics firms in the United States (plate 2), known as the Evans and Sutherland Computer Corporation (E&S). In many ways the site exemplifies this early period in the development of computer graphics, with its proximity to military resources and isolation from the larger field of computer science. As is likely apparent, this was no place to start a computer hardware company, and for the first year researchers struggled to keep out dirt and drafts while working to maintain a stable electric grid. Yet this site marks the beginning of this strange history, if not the beginning of the computer graphics industry itself.

The 1960s were a transformative period in the history of computing. At the start of the decade, computation was still an expensive and highly limited resource, enabled by massive mainframes shared by dozens of researchers working asynchronously. Computing was a fundamentally noninteractive process: tasks needed to be programmed in advance onto physical media that could be submitted to a computer operator for calculation, and researchers would have to wait hours or even days for their calculations to be processed. These were industrial machines used for processing numerical data—more calculator than computer in any modern sense. Over the course of the decade this began to change, due in large part to the development of key technologies designed to interface human and machine.

The motivation for this shift was both technical and institutional, and involved the coordination of public funding with large-scale research initiatives driven by a strong vision for what the future of computing could be. In the United States, the principal player in this transformation was the Department of Defense and its Information Processing Techniques Office (IPTO), founded in 1962 and housed within the Advanced Research Projects Agency (ARPA).[43] Under the directorship of psychologist and computer scientist J. C. R. Licklider, the IPTO put forward a vision for the future of computing as a tool for "man-computer symbiosis," imagining a future in which "human brains and computing machines will be coupled together very tightly, [such] that the resulting partnership will think as no human brain has ever thought and process data in a way not approached by the information-handling machines we know today."[44] Investing heavily in time-sharing, network technologies, artificial intelligence, and computer graphics, the IPTO pushed a vision of the computer as a device that would not only connect humans to one another but likewise connect human and machine, allowing for new forms of communication and collaboration.[45] Far from the gatekeeping model of early mainframes, this new computer would be immediately accessible to individuals through real-time graphical interaction.[46]

It was in this context that David Evans was approached by University of Utah president James Fletcher to return to his alma mater in Salt Lake City and found a computer science division within the College of Engineering.[47] At the time Evans was an assistant professor at the University of California at Berkeley, having joined the College of Engineering in 1962 after a decade working in the computing division of the Bendix Corporation in Los Angeles. Evans was also a Salt Lake City native and received both his BS and PhD in physics from the University of Utah in the early 1950s.[48] At Berkeley, Evans had served as co–principal investigator for Project Genie—an early time-sharing system funded heavily by the IPTO—developing connections with government funders, and earning a reputation as a competent and effective research lead. Then in 1964, with the free speech movement erupting on the Berkeley campus, Evans made the decision to accept Fletcher's offer and return to Utah, taking with him a network of university and government connections that would be instrumental in establishing the Utah program.[49] The offer came with the full backing of the university to help shape a program in whatever way he saw fit, appointing him the director of computer science and computer operations in 1965 (figure 0.8).[50] Initial funds from the university were limited, but were supplemented by a $5 million grant from the IPTO that Evans was able to secure immediately following his hire. Paid out over the course of four years, the ARPA contract was devoted explicitly to "Graphical Man/Machine Communication," channeling Licklider's vision through the lens of graphical interaction.[51]

The program was deeply unconventional, recruiting graduate students that no other school would take, and fostering a kind of intellectual proving ground where students were encouraged to form their own collaborations with faculty and develop expert solutions that could be deployed broadly across multiple applications.[52] It is telling that despite the futurist aspirations that define much of today's culture of computing, many of these projects produced technologies that remain the de facto solutions for computer graphics, and are still widely used by researchers and artists today. Over the subsequent fifteen years, Utah became the epicenter of graphical research in the United States, attracting faculty from around the world and

a)

b)

Figure 0.8

David C. Evans (top) and researcher in motorcycle boots (bottom) working in the
University of Utah computing center, ca. 1968. Courtesy of the University of Utah
School of Computing and the Special Collections Department, J. Willard Marriott
Library, University of Utah.

launching the careers of dozens of researchers who would go on to define much of the commercial computing industry in the second half of the twentieth century.[53] In this sense, Utah served both as a test bed for early research that continues to shape the function of modern graphical systems, and as a network for early researchers who distributed that work to dozens of research programs as they moved out from Utah and into the emerging computing industry over the course of the 1970s and early 1980s.[54]

That the Utah program is at once so central to the history of computing and so absent from popular narratives of innovation reflects the contradictory role of computer graphics itself as a discipline within computer science. Even in this early period, graphics were considered by many to be a frivolous use of computing technology. Computational resources were a limited and extremely expensive commodity, and making pictures seemed to many a waste of time.[55] As several of its graduates recalled during a panel on the history of the Utah program at the ACM's SIGGRAPH conference in 1994,

> They knew that they were "onto something big" while outsiders at other universities disparaged the work in computer graphics as an illegitimate application of computing machinery. Computing research at that time involved computer languages, operating systems, and data processing. Graphics research required manipulating so much data to display images, that it pushed the envelope in computing technology.[56]

Computer graphics research was objectively impractical and unrealistic. The technologies that it required did not yet exist, and the computers themselves were not powerful enough to manipulate the massive amounts of data required for interactive graphical communication between a computer and user. Despite these challenges, IPTO directors viewed graphical interaction as central to the future of the field, and Evans was given the resources to develop the technologies to make these systems possible.[57] The Utah program benefited greatly from this hands-off approach, which by many accounts fostered a culture of research that operated largely independent of any broader consensus of what an appropriate object for computational research might be.[58]

By 1968, Evans had established Utah as a key research hub in an expanding network of ARPA-funded "centers for excellence" and looked to develop this work beyond the university by establishing a commercial venture. Evans had met Sutherland several years prior during his work on Project

Genie at Berkeley, and Sutherland later provided the initial ARPA funding for the Utah program during his two-year tenure as the IPTO's director. As the most prominent graphics researcher in the country and a close family friend, Sutherland was the obvious choice for a partner in a new commercial graphics venture, and while the Evans family initially planned to move to Cambridge, Massachusetts, to found the company in proximity to the funding and institutional partnerships of Boston's Route 128, ultimately it was Sutherland who moved to Salt Lake City in 1968 to cofound E&S in an abandoned military bunker just off the University of Utah campus.[59]

Plate 3 shows that same bunker five years later. The man on the left is Evans, and standing next to him is Shohei Takada of Hitachi Electronics. I found this photo inside a holiday greeting card sent in 1973 following a visit by Hitachi executives earlier that year to see the work being done in Salt Lake.[60] Taken together with plate 2, this image is emblematic of the dual role that Utah plays in the history of computing: at once isolated and experimental, yet simultaneously central, connected, and highly influential. Ultimately the same can be said of computer graphics. While making pictures with computers has been historically viewed as peripheral and inessential to the "real work" of computing, an examination of the history of computer graphics shows its key role in the growth of the modern computer, and along with it the transformation of our computational culture.

Image Objects

To understand this transformation, we must turn to those objects that enabled the emergence of computer graphics to begin with. Following this methodological imperative, each of the following chapters is structured around a distinct technical object: its history, the conditions of its emergence, its influence, and its afterlives. Through this object-oriented approach, I frame computer graphics as a structure of objects grounded in the historical conditions of their formation, but that continue to restrict and inform the ways we produce computational images today. To this end, the book follows a broadly chronological narrative, beginning with the earliest challenges of the then-nascent field of computer graphics at the start of the 1960s and focusing primarily on the role of the University of Utah as a cultural site from which the field is first articulated. Over time these clear distinctions will begin to dissolve, mirroring the historical transformation of computer graphics as it grows across an ever-expanding range of technical disciplines and practices.

Chapter 1 explores early efforts to produce an algorithmic solution to the problem of visibility in a medium divorced from the physical restrictions of sight, optics, and light—what was known to computer graphics researchers as the *hidden surface problem*. In doing so, I critique attempts to fold computer graphics into a broad genealogy of the visual by mapping it onto existing techniques such as perspective projection, or the production of tricks and illusions, arguing instead that while computer-generated images offer the successful simulation of existing media forms, they construct vision in materially distinct ways. To examine the specificity of this construction, I look to early research into hidden surfaces for graphical display from 1963 to 1978, suggesting that the diverse and highly variable solutions to the problem of constructing visibility clearly separate computational vision from the optical regime of film and photography. Through the hidden surface problem, I contend that computer graphics are structured not by a logic of the visible but rather by processes whereby data are culled or erased such that the computer may more successfully interface with human vision. Here visibility becomes an algorithmic process of withholding whose specificity articulates a distinct theory of computer graphics as simultaneously screen image and simulated object—a tension that persists throughout this book and into the present.

In an effort to further distinguish computer graphics from the material specificity of those visual media they simulate, chapter 2 offers an analysis of memory and materiality through the history of the *computer screen* as a heterogeneous object that shifts and transforms in response to changes in the field of computer graphics from 1946 to 1975. Starting with the shift from calligraphic to raster graphics that begins in the late 1960s, I examine the affordances of early screens in order to identify those challenges that prevented computer graphics from adopting the scanline technology of early television displays. Ultimately the chapter identifies a single hardware object that structures and distinguishes the computer screen from other screen media: a piece of random-access computer memory for graphical display known as the frame buffer. This focus on the frame buffer introduces an additional set of questions around computer memory and its relationship to the visual image, the random as distinguished from the sequential, and memory as both a human and computational practice. The chapter concludes by looking to the origins of the stored program concept along with the first experiments in computer graphics at MIT and Princeton in the late 1940s in order to make explicit this relationship between the screen and the random-access memory (RAM) of contemporary computing systems.

Having established the unique function of computer graphics as both visual representation and object simulation, chapter 3 explores the standardization of graphical objects in the mid-1970s, with an emphasis on questions of computational ontology. This period marks the moment in which computer graphics begins to actively digitize objects from the physical world, and in which new methods for simulating irregularity allowed for the creation of increasingly realistic images. From an examination of early techniques for the simulation of curved and shaded surfaces, I reflect on processes of standardization in computer graphics broadly, taking up perhaps the most famous graphical standard in the history of the field: an object known as the *Utah teapot*. Through an analysis of the teapot's history as a material object, research tool, and cultural practice, I look to identify how computer graphics understands, represents, and reproduces the world through simulation. Using the teapot as a foil, I ultimately argue for the materiality of simulated things and their wide-reaching influence beyond the field of computer graphics.

Moving through the 1970s, the strict focus on the University of Utah will begin to fall away as I follow the program's graduates and faculty as they enter the growing computer graphics industry. Likewise, the objects that make up the book's second half will become less representational, suggesting the diffusion of the structuring logic of computer graphics in ways that exceed its connection with the visual. Turning to language, chapter 4 argues for the primary role that graphics played in the reorientation of computer science toward the simulation of objects, with particular emphasis on the *object-oriented programming paradigm* developed by Alan Kay while a graduate student at the University of Utah in the late 1960s. Through an analysis of two early CAD systems, I demonstrate the influence of graphical paradigms on the structure of object-oriented systems generally. In doing so, I trace the afterlife of the Utah program through the circulation of this object logic in early graphical user interfaces and the rise of desktop publishing, documenting the history of the Adobe PostScript language in an aircraft carrier simulation built by E&S in the mid-1970s. In deploying textual and linguistic objects, I suggest that computer graphics has had a structuring effect on the culture of computing that is not always legible as visual image, demonstrating the influence of the Utah program throughout the field of computer science in the second half of the twentieth century.

In examining the thirty-year prehistory of computer graphics, *Image Objects* ends where most histories begin. Arriving at the period in which computer graphics emerge in popular media over the course of the 1980s, chapter 5 pushes back against narratives that presume the inevitability of computer graphics' widespread adoption. Asking instead what technical and cultural shifts allowed for this rapid growth in the visibility of the medium, I suggest that the development of the *graphics processing unit* (GPU) by Utah graduate James Clark in the early 1980s allowed for the rapid proliferation of computer graphics across a range of applications and industries. In the GPU, each of the objects of the previous chapters is miniaturized and embedded within a single metaobject: a computer devoted exclusively to the task of graphical calculation. In this sense the GPU mirrors the object logic of this book itself, a metonym for the history of computer graphics as a whole. Tracking the emergence of the GPU as a set of conceptual shifts scattered throughout the history of computing, I assert the technology's principal contribution is its transformation of the algorithmic logic of software and memory into a physical object, formally fixing it for the purpose of acceleration and specialization. Ultimately the chapter argues that through the GPU, we can see an articulation of the historical claim of computing itself, whereby the complexity of computation as a cultural and historical practice is formalized and flattened through the crystallization of a procedural logic.

Computer graphics today are ubiquitous and invisible, as all manner of objects are produced, reshaped, and transformed by their encounter with computational images. Yet we have no language to describe this relationship, which exceeds the logical binaries we so often use to make sense of the world: the material versus the immaterial, the physical versus the digital, the natural versus the designed, the real versus the virtual. Each pair embeds different valences and represents different attempts to parse an image on a screen from a physical object in one's hand. And yet neither option sufficiently captures the tension inherent in the image object, which is neither material nor immaterial, neither natural nor designed, neither physical nor digital, but rather all of the above simultaneously. In examining the world in this way, my hope is not to reveal some hidden ideology that sits beneath the veneer of the digital image, or propose some imaginary sense of the relation between the material and computational, but rather to make visible an operational continuity that stitches together distinctions we presume to be categorical yet have become coextensive under computation. Analyzing computer graphics in this way asks us to account for this and/both quality of our world, bringing it into being as an analytic and practical category in the hope that it might transform the ways we attend to how our world is articulated.

1 Culling Vision: Hidden Surface Algorithms and the Problem of Visibility

$$(x_s \quad y_s \quad z_s \quad w_s) = (X_e \quad Y_e \quad Z_e \quad 1)\begin{bmatrix} 1 & 0 & 0 & 0 \\ 0 & 1 & 0 & 0 \\ 0 & 0 & 0 & 1/f \\ 0 & 0 & -1 & 0 \end{bmatrix}$$

$$X_s = x_s/w_s \quad Y_s = y_s/w_s \quad Z_s = z_s/w_s$$

—Ivan Sutherland, Robert Sproull, and Robert Schumacker, "A Characterization of Ten Hidden-Surface Algorithms"

Picture a pair of white and gray spheres suspended midair against a black background.[1] Intersecting these spheres is a triangular plane cutting across but not through each faceted surface. This is one of the earliest complete three-dimensional images ever rendered, produced on March 28, 1968, at the University of Utah in Salt Lake City (figure 1.1).[2] A small, four-inch square in black and white, it seems in many ways an image out of time—twenty years before the widespread use of computer graphics in popular film and television, ten years prior to the development of graphical user interfaces for personal computing, and five years from the start of the commercial video game industry. Not only out of time, but perhaps out of place—Utah in the late 1960s, rendered as part of the foundational efforts of the first government-funded initiative into graphical human-machine communication.[3] Yet despite its distance from our historical present, in many ways it is immediately recognizable. As an early media object, it fits neatly into a narrative of technological development—a picture that leads to better and more realistic pictures, marking the start of what is known in the computer graphics community as "the quest for realism": that pursuit for the receding horizon of perfect simulation.[4]

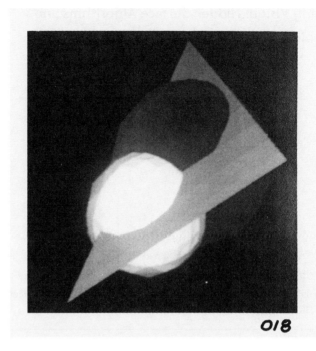

Figure 1.1
Hidden surface test image, University of Utah, 1968. Courtesy of the Special Collections Department, J. Willard Marriott Library, University of Utah.

One need only look to the technical papers of the annual SIGGRAPH conference on computer graphics to see how this "quest" remains a seductive
aspiration for researchers today. From hair movement to skin translucence,
cloth draping, and object collision, contemporary researchers are explicitly
concerned with improving the visual realism of graphics one object at a
time. Much like the progressivist narrative that drives the development of
technology more broadly, this quest operates under the tacit assumption
that total simulation is possible and a belief that we might one day produce
a perfect image of the world. Indeed, this is one of the animating fantasies
of the field. In his 1965 address to the International Federation for Information Processing, Ivan Sutherland outlined his vision for the future of computer graphics and visual displays, concluding that

> the ultimate display would, of course, be a room within which the computer can
> control the existence of matter. A chair displayed in such a room would be good

enough to sit in. Handcuffs displayed in such a room would be confining, and a bullet displayed in such a room would be fatal. With appropriate programming such a display could literally be the Wonderland into which Alice walked.[5]

Later published as "The Ultimate Display," Sutherland's essay has become one of the most influential works of early graphics literature and a rallying cry for the industry's development over the subsequent fifty years. Its vision of total simulation has since been taken up by science fiction writers and virtual reality CEOs alike to sell a vision of the future in which the material world might be fully simulated, customized, and controlled. This foregrounding of realism as the principal effect of graphical simulation likewise produces the assumption that visual mimesis is the locus from which graphical images should be read and interpreted, and that this mimetic ability makes computer graphics the logical or necessary outgrowth of indexical visual media, such as film and photography. Under this rubric, the digital image is the mere extension of some enduring visual technique, be it illusion, perspective, or representation itself.[6] Certainly visual technologies offer us a lens through which to view the long arc of historical perception, but such genealogies likewise collapse the meaningful distinctions that mark the digital image as explicitly computational. Put another way, while so-called new media are often much older than they first appear, it is a mistake to dismiss the fundamental transformation that computation brings to the material form of our contemporary visual culture. What would it mean to take seriously the newness of new media—its unique historical articulation?

Return now to the image in figure 1.1. How did it physically come to be? Holding this picture in the special collections department of the Marriott Library at the University of Utah, I took for granted its status as a digital image, not unlike the hundreds of images I interact with on a daily basis. It depicts a virtual object programmed and rendered by a computer, and yet its physical presence as a material thing to be held in my hands, turned, and examined seemed to speak to the strange materiality of this supposedly immaterial practice. At first glance it appears to be a screenshot, but in 1968 there were no image files, JPEGs, or photo printers. One could not easily extract and preserve an image from the screen of a computer, as there was no computational mechanism to do so. This image is in fact a Polaroid taken with a light-tight camera that was physically attached to the screen of a slow-scan cathode ray tube (CRT) (figure 1.2). The image was etched

Figure 1.2
Students Alan Erdahl, Chris Wylie, and Gordon Romney in the University of Utah's graphics lab, ca. 1968. At the lower left of the image is an oscilloscope with a light-tight camera attached to its face for screen documentation. Courtesy of the Special Collections Department, J. Willard Marriott Library, University of Utah.

in a long exposure over the course of several minutes, line by line, as a mainframe computer calculated the position and shade of each part of the image to be displayed. Researchers couldn't actually see the image directly without the mediation of long exposure photography, such that producing this image was a process of exhaustive preparation, and to a degree, trial and error. While this image may resemble computer graphics as we use and understand it today, the apparatuses that enabled its production are wildly different—a fact that is nowhere apparent in the image itself, and cannot be derived from visual analysis alone. It is an image that straddles the analog and the digital, a visual cluster held together by an assortment of media technologies equally visual and invisible.

But what of the object? What was the purpose of such a simple simulation? Unlike the experimental images produced by artist researchers in this early period, this is not a principally aesthetic object. Likewise, while this image may be historically significant, it is not unique or exceptional. Its purpose was to assist in the testing of visualization algorithms developed for these early graphical systems, and its historical value is the way it indexes the everyday labor of graphical research at sites like the University of Utah. In this early period, computer graphics researchers were only just beginning to work out the question of how to produce a visual simulation. Indeed, the primary concern for researchers was not how to realistically simulate any *particular* object but rather how to simulate *any three-dimensional object at all*. How is an object constructed, what is it made of, and how does it interact with the world around it? These were the questions that most interested the field, and they display an equal investment in both form and representation—that is, in both what an object is and how it appears, its status as both image and object. Looking back at our image, it becomes clear that there is more going on here than simple visualization, something that concerns the intersection of objects, this contact between things.

From roughly 1963 until at least 1978, one of the key concerns for the field of computer graphics was the solution to what is known as the "hidden line" or "hidden surface problem."[7] It is, in effect, a crisis of visibility. Whereas photographic visibility models itself on our phenomenological perception of the world, following a camera obscura tradition whereby objects are made visible through the interaction of light with an aperture, computer graphics do not function in this way. For computer graphics, each object must be described in advance if it is to be rendered visible. In other words, graphical objects exist in their totality—as a collection of coordinate points, image files, and object databases—prior to their manifestation as a visible image. Graphical objects are in this sense nonphenomenological, known in their entirety prior to our perception of them. In order to simulate our perception of objects, graphics must not only calculate that which is to be seen but also anticipate and hide that which is known yet should not be shown, that which must be made hidden and invisible. This is what our image seeks to simulate with its intersection of object and plane: the removal of that which cannot be known through sight alone. In refusing the apparent similitude of our image, we find an object held together by a complex topology that little resembles our contemporary visual culture. While this image may be novel as one of the earliest of its kind, it is also exemplary of the struggles and challenges of this early research field, and a failure to solve for something we simply take as given in other media forms: visibility. As such, it speaks directly to this moment in the history of computer graphics—a period defined by the challenge of making the digital visible.

Problem Solving

By the mid-1960s, researchers had already succeeded in producing interactive three-dimensional computer graphics. At MIT, Bell Telephone Laboratories, Boeing, and General Motors (GM), research teams had developed systems for rendering pictures that bear a striking resemblance to modern graphical images. Yet while these images are compelling, their appearance masks significant constraints and limitations. In this early period, computer graphics was a broad field with widely varying approaches to the display of graphical images. From the SAGE system for air defense to the experimental computer animations of John and James Whitney, these early systems were highly idiosyncratic with little application beyond the research or artistic context in which they were developed.[8] Much as with early experiments in protocinematic visualization at the end of the nineteenth century, in which multiple visual forms competed with and functioned alongside what would become the cinematic image, this period is marked by a multiplicity of solutions to the problem of computer graphics.[9] If the field was to develop as an area of scientific research, it would need a shared vision of what the future of graphical computing might look like and a set of explicit goals that could begin to move research closer to that vision.

Central to this effort was the cultural, financial, and institutional apparatus of the IPTO, and the ambitious research programs developed by its various directors over the course of the 1960s. Under the directorship of J. C. R. Licklider from 1962 to 1964, the IPTO had focused funding primarily on applications in time-sharing and artificial intelligence.[10] When Licklider stepped down, he was replaced by Ivan Sutherland—only twenty-seven years old at the time—who quickly funneled the office's $15 million research budget toward programs in computer graphics. This work extended Sutherland's field-defining research as a graduate student at MIT, where he developed one of the earliest and most influential CAD programs on the TX-2 mainframe computer, discussed in chapter 4. Sutherland's overarching vision was to produce systems that would allow a human operator to communicate with a computer through drawings, solving graphical problems with graphical methods. Such a system would allow researchers to produce new pictures of the world that would not be possible without a computer. As he argues in the program plan for the first major government-funded initiative into computer graphics,

> an ability to construct, manipulate and observe complex pictures of computed phenomena may radically change our ability to grasp complex ideas. If we make computers produce projections of four dimensional objects, for instance, we may reach a new understanding. Pictures of social structures, abstracted from data about the society, may bring a new understanding to human behavior. Pictures of computer program structures will assist in getting programs to work. The need for computer graphics is great. We do not propose in the present project to solve all the world's problems through computer graphics. What we need *now* are additional ways to couple computers to humans through drawings.[11]

For Sutherland, visual images were essential tools for understanding complex problems, serving as a critical interface between human operator and computing machine.[12]

At the heart of this work was the funding of the Utah program, first by Sutherland and later by his successor, Robert Taylor, who pushed David Evans to build a "center of excellence" for graphical research in Salt Lake. This framework of the center of excellence was a key part of ARPA's funding model at this time. First implemented in its Material Science Program, directors would identify individuals with strengths in a particular field and funnel research funds into that program with the goal of creating a hub of expertise and collaboration. In effect the IPTO would invest money in a field through a single institution by way of an individual scholar. By distributing money and resources in this focused way, the IPTO was able to concentrate efforts in a particular field and create long-lasting collaborations and connections.[13] While Utah was not the only site for graphical research in this period, its position as an ARPA center of excellence and the significant financial support that entailed made it arguably the most prominent.[14] In examining the research program at Utah we can therefore identify many of the principal investments of the broader field of computer graphics at this time, drawing out the ways a concern for visibility intersects with the technical limitations of computational systems.

Unlike earlier applications in architectural rendering and CAD, at Utah the primary research objective was nothing short of photo-realistic simulation. The program's goal was to develop "a means to produce photograph-like pictures of complex illuminated objects at a reasonable cost."[15] As Evans describes in his first ARPA report from 1966,

> A major objective of the project is to develop a method which will produce synthetic video signals representing two-dimensional projections of three-dimensional objects described only in the data structure of the computer. It is considered that such a representation of the object is of basic value, because it corresponds to the representation of the real world on the human retina.[16]

What Evans is describing are the base conditions for any contemporary graphical system; but what might sound simple enough by contemporary standards was a massive undertaking at the time, as it presented a number of challenges that had never before been addressed by computer science. Evans outlines these challenges explicitly in an early report on the computer science department, suggesting that to accomplish the basics of photo-realistic rendering, three important problems needed to be solved:

1) A good means must be found so that only visible surfaces are displayed in the picture.
2) Half-tone shading determined by instant light must be provided. More information beyond that provided by line drawings is given by this means.
3) A good model must be found for representing arbitrarily-shaped surfaces.[17]

Visibility. Surface. Light. Complexity. By positing technological development and change in terms of actionable problems, researchers at Utah created a motivational structure in which otherwise-abstract goals such as visual mimesis were understood as identifiable problems that were always progressing toward a more accurate or realistic solution.[18] Identifying specific problems in this way underscores both the technical limitations of early graphics and the way institutional structures focused the field in an effort to produce workable solutions.

Looking at the challenges articulated by Evans, it seems the most glaring problem for early researchers was less how to render a visible image than how to restrict that image into displaying only that which is sensible to a viewing subject. Absent is a preoccupation with the formal apparatuses that have historically defined and united earlier visual forms, namely the simulation of depth through perspective projection. Yet these frameworks for the analysis of visual media have dominated scholarly discourse on the digital image, which often looks to imbricate computer graphics with prior modes of visual representation rather than consider the many ways such images negotiate or refuse a preoccupation with visuality altogether.

Simulating Vision

In his widely influential *Techniques of the Observer* (1990), art historian Jonathan Crary opens not with a historical anecdote on the development of early visual technologies in the long nineteenth century but instead by reflecting on the reconfiguration of vision in his own time by the technical regime of computer graphics. Drawing parallels between the transformation of vision under industrialization and our own historical present, Crary suggests that "the rapid development in little more than a decade of a vast array of computer graphics techniques is part of a sweeping reconfiguration of relations between an observing subject and modes of representation that effectively nullifies most of the culturally established meanings of the terms *observer* and *representation*." This transformation, he asserts, is "probably more profound than the break that separates medieval imagery from Renaissance perspective."[19] Writing in the late 1980s, Crary could only speculate on the radical reorganization of our visual culture that would take place over the subsequent decade, but he clearly suggests that the site of this transformation will be vision itself as a historical mode of perception tied to the production of human subjectivity. Today this link between computer graphics and the long history of visual perception would seem undeniable, such that it is no surprise that the vast majority of scholars working on computer graphics take up Crary's call to engage with the use and application of computer graphics in the context of this history. This connection has become so conspicuous that computer graphics are taken as a given in discussions of new media technologies such as computer animation and digital gaming, while scholars working in visual disciplines from film studies to art history often presume a narrative whereby computer-generated images serve as a logical extension of the visual function of optical media, even as they displace the formal materiality of these media with simulation.[20] And yet the computer is not a visual medium. We might argue it is primarily mathematical or perhaps electric, but it is not in the first instance concerned with questions of vision or image. As media theorist Friedrich Kittler simply states in his lectures on optical media, "Computers must calculate all optical or acoustic data on their own precisely because they are born dimensionless and thus imageless. For this reason, images on computer monitors . . . do not reproduce any extant things, surfaces, or spaces at all. They emerge on the surface of the monitor through the application of mathematical systems of equations."[21] In practice, this means that in order to simulate our perception of objects as fixed in a perspective projection, a graphical program must first produce a simulation of that scene in its entirety, and then extract from that scene those parts that should be rendered visible. This process by which graphics simulates existing visual media purposefully belies the means by which this sense of mimesis is achieved. Computer graphics is a medium engaged in a disavowal of its technical apparatus, which has led to an undertheorization of its material functionality. This mapping of computer graphics onto the long history of visual representation masks a number of significant differences between the way visuality is *constructed* by computer graphics and *captured* by a camera, and has limited investigations into the technical materiality of the algorithms that produce computer-generated images.[22]

One of the few theorists of the past twenty years to examine this relationship in detail is Lev Manovich, whose pivotal work in *The Language of New Media* (2001) attempts to place new media technology within a broader history of visual culture, marking those points of distinction where computational media break from earlier models and become unique technical processes in their own regard.[23] For Manovich, computer graphics are part of a long and ongoing transformation of vision through technology, from painting and photography to radar and virtual reality.[24] In his writing throughout the 1990s, Manovich frames this evolution as a kind of visual nominalism whereby visual media have historically functioned to capture the identity of individual objects and spaces through the recording of distances and shapes.[25] Central to this transformation was the development of linear perspective as a technique for the automation of visual relations through the application of a fixed method. Tracing the development of this perspectival mode through painting, photography, and the cinema, Manovich argues that visual nominalism finds its apotheosis in the mass automation of perspectival representation made possible by computer graphics. Manovich's work here is exceptional in its treatment of computer graphics as a distinct media technology grounded in a set of principles that run parallel with but are historically distinct from those of film and photography. Nevertheless, the work is marked by an insistence—found in almost all historical writing on computer graphics and digital imaging—on a narrative of inheritance across visual media that obscures a detailed historical account of computer graphics as computational ab initio.[26]

The single most pervasive technique in this effort to stage continuities between distinct media forms is *perspective*, as it has formed the basis for the production of realism across a wide range of media technologies since at least the fifteenth century. Its adoption by computer graphics therefore clearly links graphical images to the realist visual traditions of painting, photography, and the cinema, allowing for a broad historical claim that grounds computer graphics in a legible tradition of representation. In this perspectival tradition, the world is refigured as a system of relations that center the subjectivity of an all-seeing individual, giving rise to a perspectival subjectivity grounded by an optical regime that privileges this fixed perspective. As Kittler argues, "Representational thinking delivered being as an object for a subject . . . [and] linear perspective and the *camera obscura* were precisely the media of this representation."[27] Of course, the perspectival mode of Renaissance painting and the camera obscura clearly differ in technique and form, but in examining its articulation across a range of media technologies, it becomes apparent that this relation is transmutable, shifting to accommodate the formal specificity of a given medium. Taken in isolation from those media forms that employ it, what perspective offers is a structuring system whereby space is mapped and displayed in relation to a viewing subject. As Jacques Lacan notes in "On the Gaze as *objet petit a*," "What is an issue in geometric perspective is simply the mapping of space, not sight."[28] It just happens that we tend to privilege sight in the way we map space technologically. Perspective is only one potential solution to the question of object relationality; it is one particular relational technique with a long cultural history adopted by computer graphics in the production of a culturally situated realism.

This is not to suggest that perspective is a monolithic or unified system of representation. As art historian James Elkins has suggested, there is "no coherent history, no connected tradition beneath the word [perspective]."[29] Nonetheless there is a cultural significance in its deployment across a broad range of visual media. Indeed, its prevalence as a structuring logic for visual media indicates that it operates as a kind of deeply embodied cultural technique (*Kulturtechnik*)—that is, a condition whereby "signs, instruments, and human practices consolidate into durable symbolic systems capable of articulating distinctions within and between cultures."[30] It is a form that has been naturalized through its adoption by a variety of media since the Renaissance, but whose primacy as a means of producing and reflecting the world is historically bound and exists alongside other techniques.[31] While many art historians have identified the cultural relativism of perspective, it is perhaps more useful to think through perspective as a set of culturally and historically situated practices that are maintained precisely through their adoption and transformation by emerging media technologies.[32] It is this malleability of perspective across its multiple cultural and historical forms that maintains it as a governing structure.[33] As such, it is of no surprise that perspective has become the operative relational mode for a great deal of computer graphic visualizations, but that adoption is by no means essential to the way graphics produces visualization. The perspective that computer graphics offers is algorithmically rendered by a virtual camera decoupled from any connection with the embodied position of a viewing subject, let alone optics or the physical properties of light. Indeed, an investigation into the earliest use of perspective projection in a simulated image reveals little concern for this centuries-old technique. In its place we find a new set of relations structured not by vision but instead by a theory of the nature of objects, a computational ontology for which the rendered image is only one of many possible expressions.

Computing Perspective

How then does computer graphics first approach the simulation of perspective? The earliest model of three-dimensional perspective comes from the graduate work of Lawrence Roberts, whose dissertation project—titled "Machine Perception of Three-Dimensional Solids"—is a foundational text in the history of the field.[34] Along with Sutherland, Roberts was one of several graduate students working on applications in computer graphics and machine vision using the MIT Lincoln Laboratory's TX-2 computer at the start of the 1960s. Building on Sutherland's Sketchpad software, Roberts developed a rudimentary technique for producing opaque three-dimensional models in perspective projection.[35] For architect and historian William J. Mitchell in *The Reconfigured Eye* (1994), this is a critical moment in the history of the algorithmic image, an event "as momentous, in its way, as Brunelleschi's perspective demonstration."[36] Like Filippo Brunelleschi and Leon Battista Alberti some six hundred years prior, Roberts's work would seem to make possible an entirely new form of image making—one that leads directly to today's computer-generated images in film, photography, and digital games. But while the simple graphics produced by Roberts's program bear a striking resemblance to contemporary computer-generated images, we should not assume a direct lineage of inheritance. If we set aside the rendered image and look to the structure of the program itself, we find a system for producing images that bears little resemblance to contemporary graphical modeling. What's more, this excavation suggests Roberts's use of perspective projection is largely incidental to the program's objectives, creeping in under the guise of an earlier visual form.

The stated goal of Roberts's dissertation research was to enable "a computer to construct and display a three-dimensional array of solid objects from a single two-dimensional photograph."[37] That is, rather than construct a virtual object, as is common in contemporary modeling software, the program was intended to digitize objects from two-dimensional photographic representations. To construct a three-dimensional model, a simple object would be photographed and processed by Roberts's program, which would attempt to identify the edges of objects as a set of feature points. It then would try to connect those edges, and calculate the volume and shape of the object whole (figure 1.3). Objects could then be transformed,

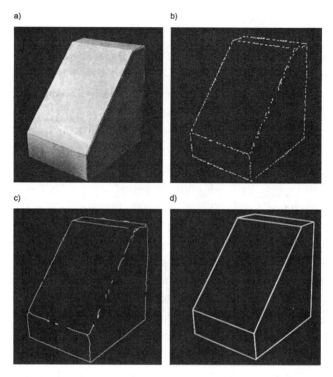

Figure 1.3
Processing a photograph into feature points and applying complexity reduction to
produce a perspectival line drawing. Lawrence G. Roberts, "Machine Perception of
Three-Dimensional Solids" (PhD diss., Massachusetts Institute of Technology, 1963).

or the perspective projection shifted and manipulated, in effect rendering
the two-dimensional photograph as a fully actualized three-dimensional
scene. It is unsurprising that the program adopted the perspective model of
photography since photographs served as the primary source of visualization for the program. That said, the goal of the project was largely one of
computer graphics by means of computer vision, and not the simulation of
a particular visual form.

By introducing embodied perspective—or its mechanization through
photography—Roberts's program adopted a set of psychological assumptions about how perception functions and might be procedurally modeled.
To this end, he drew heavily on the work of psychologist James J. Gibson,
whose *The Perception of the Visual World* (1950) he found instrumental in

formulating vision as diagrammatic and discrete.[38] Gibson's theory of vision was developed largely over the course of World War II through his research on airplane pilots and, along with the work of the mathematician Norbert Weiner, marks a shift toward theorizing vision as explicitly *machinic*.[39] Contrary to earlier theories, which understood vision as the perception of an object or array of objects in the air, Gibson formulates a *ground theory* structured by a continuous surface or array of adjoining surfaces. This leads him to a simplified model of perception, in which "the elementary impressions of a visual world are those of surface and edge."[40] For Gibson, vision is derived not from an embodied sense of place or location in space but rather the perception of the relational boundaries of objects in a visual array, reduced to a discrete set of primitive forms. Vision in this formulation is no longer concerned with accurate mimesis; it is instead engaged in the capture and replication of an external relationality.

Roberts used Gibson's theory of vision to rationalize a shift in computer vision away from its earlier preoccupation with alphanumeric recognition, and toward a world of objects comprised of lines, edges, and surfaces.[41] From Gibson he derived those qualities that he believed were most important to our perception of the world, and therefore privileged them in constructing his program. These principally included object size, texture gradient, and shape perception, among others. Significantly, Gibson's philosophy of vision argued strongly in favor of direct perception and direct realism—that is, the belief that we are capable of perceiving objects in the world directly as they are, and not as representations or abstractions. Roberts's program models itself on these tenets, "seeing" and capturing those essential, perceivable qualities of objects for digitization.

The solutions Roberts derived in his dissertation research were significant, and pushed the field forward toward the simulation of three-dimensional objects. In fact, most contemporary 3D systems still use Roberts's calculations for the simulation of perspective. Nonetheless, his system for capturing vision to produce virtual objects bears little resemblance to contemporary graphical software, derived as it was from the fields of pattern recognition and computer vision. Likewise, while Roberts's program was the first to introduce a theory of perspective into 3D graphics, this is arguably not the project's most important contribution.[42] Much more significant, in both Roberts's research and Gibson's theory of vision we can see the beginnings of a larger translation of the visible world into quantifiable parts or primitives that may be made legible to computation. As with Gibson's theory of direct perception, the algorithmic construction of three-dimensional objects is less concerned with the presentation of a visual array for the perception of a singular viewing subject than with the reproduction of an internal relationship between objects themselves—those lines and surfaces that set the limits and conditions of what is and is not perceptible.

Rather than focus on the successful introduction of perspective in Roberts's graphical research, a more instructive method would be to examine its critical failures. In order to extrapolate the dimensions of an object, the program first had to calculate its volume so that those features not visible in the source photograph might be inferred. As such, Roberts's program restricts the environment to convex objects whose volume may be calculated in such a way. The algorithm is also limited in the kinds of objects it can display, relying on simple geometric solids in various combinations to form complex shapes (figure 1.4). Most telling of all is the program's inability to scale with object number or complexity, such that the computational power required by Roberts's algorithm grows roughly as the square of the number of objects in the scene, making it an impractical system for real-time interactive graphics or complex rendered scenes. While each of these may seem like unrelated problems, in fact they are all exemplary of a single structural challenge. In order for a given program to render a visible object, it must account for what parts of that object should be visible to a viewer, and what parts should be hidden or obscured. The more complex an object, the more difficult it is to calculate an object's visibility, such that in order to produce an accurate three-dimensional model, Roberts's program had to restrict the objects that were legible to it. In doing so, Roberts developed what is quite possibly the first algorithmic means of accurately rendering visible surfaces—a task that was by his own admission a far more difficult and technically significant accomplishment than the simulation of perspective.[43] Nonetheless, it would be over fifteen years before researchers would settle on a scalable solution to this particularly challenging problem.

In interrogating the failures of Roberts's program, we find that one of the primary concerns for computer scientists at this time was not how to reproduce a particular way of *seeing* but rather in how to algorithmically account for the structure of objects themselves. Roberts's algorithm

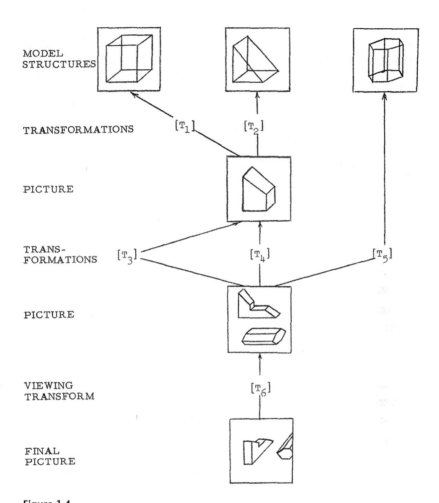

MODEL STRUCTURES

TRANSFORMATIONS $[T_1]$ $[T_2]$

PICTURE

TRANS-FORMATIONS $[T_3]$ $[T_4]$ $[T_5]$

PICTURE

VIEWING TRANSFORM $[T_6]$

FINAL PICTURE

Figure 1.4
Visualization of the list structure of Roberts's algorithm, showing the construction of models from geometric primitives, followed by their transformation and rotation in three dimensions, demonstrating clear hidden line removal. Lawrence Roberts, "Machine Perception of Three-Dimensional Solids" (PhD diss., Massachusetts Institute of Technology, 1963).

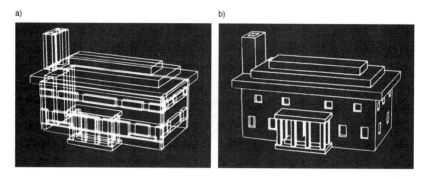

Figure 1.5

A perspective rendering of a house with and without hidden lines removed. The program for this image was written by Lawrence Roberts. Published in Ivan E. Sutherland, "Computer Inputs and Outputs," *Scientific American* 215, no. 3 (September 1966). 96.

transforms the photographic image into an array of points in Cartesian space connected by lines to form surfaces that may be extrapolated into three dimensions. In delimiting the world in this way, Roberts's algorithm makes objects from the visible world legible to computation—a process that includes much more than the reconstruction of something analogous to Renaissance perspective. While a desire for realistic images that simulate the visual appearance of film and photography was a critical concern for researchers from the beginning, this realism was predicated on a relational mode with no basis in earlier visual media.[44] In examining the material history of these forms we can begin to decouple computer graphics from the regime of visuality that so easily contains it, and in doing so, identify a broader technique at play.

Hidden Surface Problems

For any graphical system to calculate the appearance of an object, it is first necessary to understand the structure of that object. That is, in order to simulate our perception of an object as fixed in a perspective projection, graphics must both calculate its visible surfaces while preemptively removing any nonvisible surfaces so that they will not be calculated or displayed.[45] Prior to the mid-1960s this was not the case, as graphical objects were produced largely as wireframe models with no surfaces, from which all edges were simultaneously visible (figure 1.5). While such images are suitable for certain tasks, the more complex an image becomes, the more difficult it is to identify and differentiate the object at hand. What's more, even simple objects can create illusions when viewed from certain angles as lines overlap and collapse the image into an abstract form (figure 1.6). Outside these practical concerns, there is the desire for realism. As Sutherland notes in an essay from 1966 on the critical problems facing early graphical research,

> When we look around the world we see opaque objects and we don't see what is behind the opaque objects. It is hard to make objects displayed by a computer look similarly opaque. It is easy to make a perspective presentation of any individual point in space. It takes a few multiplications and a division or two to implement the coordinate transformation from the three-dimensional space coordinates to the two-dimensional display coordinates. By programming this transformation you can easily display transparent or "wire frame" views of your object. . . . It is much harder to decide whether a point ought to show or not. It is a major task to eliminate hidden lines from the complexity and variety of solutions to the problem, but also to the processing limitations of the drawing.[46]

While the elimination of hidden lines may seem trivial, it was one of the most significant challenges for the field of computer graphics well into

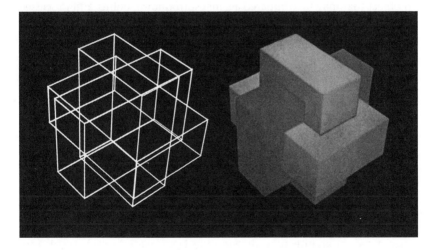

Figure 1.6
Computer-generated image without hidden lines removed, obscuring its shape (left). The same image with hidden surfaces removed and shading added using the Warnock algorithm (right). Image rendered with a program developed by Gary Watkins. Published in Ivan E. Sutherland, "Computer Displays," *Scientific American* 222, no. 6 (June 1970): 56.

the 1970s. This was not only due to the processing limitations of computers in this period; indeed, it is conceptually easy to eliminate hidden lines by brute force calculation—point by point, line by line. But as with Roberts's algorithm, this task becomes exponentially more difficult as objects increase in number and complexity. As such, the field required a scalable solution for the elimination of invisible data, a means by which it might preemptively omit the calculation of that which should not be seen. This came to be known as the hidden surface problem.

The hidden surface problem is significant not only because it is such a crucial challenge for the nascent field of computer graphics but because it also forms the basis of a much larger set of concerns for computational visualization. Without an understanding of the opacity of an object, the shape of its surfaces, and their relation to one another, it is impossible to accurately model their interaction with a given environment. Shading, lighting, shadow, collision, and any number of additional effects are dependent on a suitable means of identifying and describing the structure of an object, and a hidden surface algorithm is the first step in calculating a reasonably efficient means to do so since it produces data for each significant point of an object that may be compared against surrounding points and processed through additional visualization algorithms. As Sutherland observes in an extended article for *Scientific American* in 1970,

> Once the hidden-surface problem is solved, shading and color are relatively easy to introduce. The hidden-surface computation develops information to tell which surface is visible at each point on the screen. Since each surface in the computer includes a color, as well as other properties, the program can compute precisely what hue, saturation, and brightness to display. In the simplest pictures the surface is simply displayed in its appropriate color. It is only slightly more difficult to compute the shade, or brightness level.[47]

It is the linchpin of any functional graphics system, and forms the basis for the solution to many related visibility issues from shading and color to lighting and texture. Every 3D rendered image in a contemporary film, video game, or architectural drawing has been made subject to this process, an algorithmic articulation executed thousands of times to form a structure on which the rich and complex photo-realism of visual simulation is built.

Beginning in 1963 with Roberts's algorithm, dozens of researchers developed independent solutions to the hidden surface problem, each with their own methods and limitations. Their solutions are in fact so remarkably varied that in 1974, a team of researchers headed by Sutherland produced a coauthored essay with the explicit intention of constructing a taxonomy of hidden surface algorithms in order to identify the fundamental root of the problem.[48] Taking into account over ten years of work on hidden surfaces, the research team created a schema for categorizing these algorithms as a function of the way they sort a given scene, arguing that the primary difference between each algorithm lay in how it conceived of and handled the thing undergoing simulation: as image, object, or something in between (figure 1.7). In categorizing the algorithms in this way, their taxonomy draws out the function of computer graphics as both designed object and rendered image, irreducible to either one or the other. It is here we might begin to derive a theory of computer graphics that accounts for this dual logic: at once both structure and simulation, database and display, image and object.

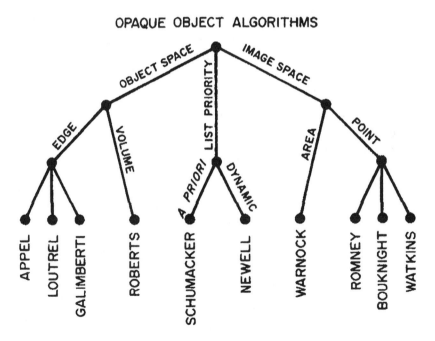

Figure 1.7
Schema for sorting hidden surface algorithms by object space, image space, and list priority. Ivan E. Sutherland, Robert F. Sproull, and Robert Schumacker, "A Characterization of Ten Hidden-SurfaceAlgorithms," *Computing Surveys* 6, no. 1 (1974): 19.

The earliest solutions to the hidden surface problem generally fall under the schema of "object-space" algorithms in that they perform computations "to arbitrary precision, usually the precision available in the computer executing the algorithm. The aim of the solution is to compute 'exactly' what the image should be; it will be correct even if enlarged many times."[49] Object-space algorithms ask whether each potentially visible item in the environment is visible, treating every object component as a potentially significant aspect of the object or environment as a whole. Algorithms that function under this schema include Roberts's algorithm for "machine perception of three-dimensional solids," discussed above. Object-space algorithms have built into them a set of material limitations, tied primarily to the processing power of the hardware at hand, but also to the potential complexity of the object to be rendered. As such, they do not scale well and cannot efficiently render complex scenes.

In an effort to increase the efficiency of this computationally intensive task, later solutions to the hidden surface problem utilized "image-space" algorithms, which only calculate that which is visible to the raster of a given screen.[50] The goal of these algorithms is to simply calculate an intensity for each of the resolvable dots or pixels on the display screen, and as such, they do not scale beyond the interface at hand. Perhaps the most significant example of an image-space algorithm is the one developed by John Warnock in 1968 for his doctoral dissertation at the University of Utah, commonly referred to as the "Warnock algorithm."[51] The Warnock algorithm functions by breaking a given screen into subregions and applying a standard procedure to each one. For each region, the algorithm identifies all possible surfaces and attempts to determine whether they are entirely outside, surrounded by, or intersect a given subregion. The algorithm then eliminates any surfaces that it finds to be behind another surface. The most significant contribution of the Warnock algorithm is its response to a subsection that is too complex for it to calculate hidden surfaces. In such a case, it simply subdivides the region into smaller regions and begins again with the new divisions, working its way back out to the larger section. If at its smallest division—the contemporary equivalent of a single pixel—a section is found to be too complex, the algorithm simply picks a value from an adjacent subregion and moves on. The result of the Warnock algorithm is a fractal effect that scales with object complexity, limited of course by the resolution of a given screen (figure 1.8). It is representative of the image-space

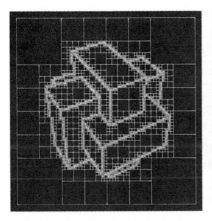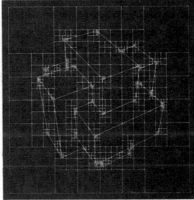

Figure 1.8
A visualization of Warnock's solution to the hidden surface problem (left), and a similar algorithm that avoids subdivision when only a single edge appears in any subregion (right). Image rendered with a program developed by Gary Watkins. Published in Ivan E. Sutherland, "Computer Displays," *Scientific American* 222, no. 6 (June 1970): 73.

subclass of hidden surface algorithms in that it calculates the visibility of an object only within the limitations of a particular viewing position and the screen technology used in its display.

The most contemporary solutions to the hidden surface problem fall under a third category that functions somewhere between the object and image space. These "list-priority" algorithms are designed for high-quality interactive simulation, an application that requires real-time speed alongside visual realism. As such, they split the task of determining visibility based on a process of object categorization. In a given interactive scene, some aspects of the world—such as the sky or a distant vista—do not change much, and hence can be calculated using static image-space algorithms. Other objects in the scene may move and change—such as other players, enemies, or obstacles in an interactive game or simulation—and therefore it is to the advantage of the algorithm to calculate them with greater precision and be aware of any changes in position that might obscure an object from view—concerns that require an object-space calculation. Thus in this last instance, the question of hidden surface calculation becomes a matter of the ordering of algorithms and proper categorization of a given scene.

While Sutherland's taxonomy is concerned primarily with uncovering the technical challenge at the heart of the hidden surface problem, it is perhaps more useful as an unintentional reflection on the first ten years of research into three-dimensional computer graphics. In his paper's description of the ways these algorithms transform and come to replace one another over time, we can trace a broader transformation in the use and application of three-dimensional computer graphics in these early years of experimentation. Far from a clear genealogy, whereby Roberts's development of perspective projection ushers in an era of realistic simulated images, what we find is a liminal period in which researchers struggle to grasp at the challenges of a new kind of technical image. By examining their solutions, we find a set of concerns that reflect the disciplinary biases of the field: object-space algorithms function best when applied to simple objects and line drawings with a high degree of accuracy and scalability, well suited to the architectural, engineering, and technical diagrams of early research institutions like GE or IBM; image-space algorithms were designed to produce visually stunning images with less regard for their technical accuracy, and as such were often used to produce animated films and rendered images at sites like Bell Labs; and list-priority algorithms were best suited for interactive environments that required degrees of both utility and mimesis, and therefore were developed for research into interactive flight simulation at sites such as the University of Utah. Computer graphics is each of these things at once, equally image, object, and something in between. Not only do the different uses for graphics help structure the types of images they produce, they structure the means by which they produce visual absence through hidden surface removal. While the final rendered image produced by each of these algorithms may appear to fit into the broad category of computer-generated images, in fact each is materially distinct from the other, the product of a unique set of concerns.

Making the Present Absent

For computer-generated images, the visibility problem lays bare the surprising challenge of simulating the inaccessibility of the invisible. For well over a decade, graphics researchers struggled to find an accurate and efficient algorithm for this problem—a calculation that could be made in *software* to quickly account for the spatial relationship of objects in a given scene that was scalable and did not restrict the form and type of objects it could simulate. Ultimately, however, it was *hardware* that provided a lasting solution.

In his PhD dissertation at the University of Utah in 1974, future Pixar cofounder Edwin Catmull proposed a graphical workstation with a built-in grid of RAM that could be used to store the depth value of all visible objects in a scene. He called this object a z-buffer, named after the depth axis in three-dimensional image space.[52] Rather than try to calculate the relational position of all objects in a scene for every image or frame of a simulation, the z-buffer stores its depth as a numerical value along the z-axis to be compared with the depth value of other objects in a scene (figure 1.9). As an object or camera moves and transforms, the buffer makes a simple numerical check, adapting to display whichever surface is most proximate the viewing position.

While Catmull's z-buffer solution was extremely effective, it was also out-rageously expensive, made possible only by virtue of Catmull's access to the most recent developments in computer memory and graphical workstation design at the University of Utah. As the price of memory fell, however, it became both feasible and practical to crystallize the material logic of depth into a hardware object devoted exclusively to this task. The z-buffer now serves as the de facto solution for the visibility problem and has remained relatively constant over the past forty years.[53]

Through the z-buffer, at last we can begin to address the transformation that interactive graphics has brought about, whereby perspective shifts from a static property to a dynamic simulation, such that graphical systems must

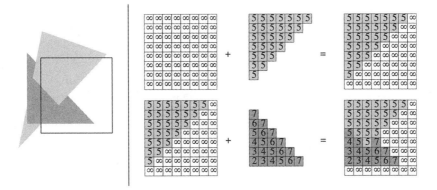

Figure 1.9
Representation of depth value in a z-buffer where each square is one pixel. Note that the closer an object is, the lower its pixel value in the buffer.

store, exploit, and negotiate depth in an effort to produce a kind of visual realism that may *appear* analogous to earlier methods, but is in fact radically transformed. Indeed, the z-buffer is only the start of this much larger transformation. While its initial value was hidden surface removal, over the past forty years the z-buffer has become an important tool for 3D imaging as a whole—one of many essential visual passes that an image undergoes as it makes its way through the rendering pipeline. This "depth pass" (resulting in a corresponding "depth map") functions like a radar image or MRI scan, interpreting objects according to their relative distance. For digital rendering in film and visual effects, this depth map is an essential tool for manufacturing depth effects in postproduction. If an artist wishes to blur an image to simulate depth of field, or rack focus a shot from the foreground to the background, they require an accurate map of a scene's depth. For film and photography this is a property of the optical device itself, with the aperture of a camera producing depth of field in a way that reads as analogous to that of human vision. In a computer this must be simulated after the fact, as there is no physical lens to modify. For this, depth mapping is used.

Unlike most computer-generated images, these depth maps are not meant to be seen or interpreted by a viewing subject, and are not representational in the strictest sense. While we can view these images, they are not functionally for us—indeed, their visualization is incidental to their function. Their characteristic gradient shading is not an abstraction or interpretation produced so that we can better understand the function of the buffer but rather an index of the data stored in the buffer itself, with a number for every pixel corresponding to the object proximity within that pixel scaled from the darkest black to the lightest white (figure 1.10). This is data visualization in the purest sense, where the image we see corresponds directly to what is stored in the bitmap itself—an incidental image that once again negotiates a tension between the visible and invisible. In the depth map we find that while the telos of computer graphics may be perfect realism and total simulation, much of what concerns the field is the restriction of visual information, a culling of vision such that it corresponds to the perception of a human subject paired with the limitations of a given computational system.

This focus on the hidden surface problem may seem counterintuitive. It is, after all, that which is meant to go unnoticed, those parts of a world that should remain unseen. And yet it is in the solution to this problem that

a)

b)

Figure 1.10
Z-buffer depth map image (top) used to calculate depth of field (bottom). Dominic
Alves, 2011. CC BY-SA 3.0.

computer graphics reveals the specificity of its construction: it produces vision by constructing absence. Rather than capturing the world through the indexical trace of light on a surface, computer graphics simulates our knowledge of the world by constructing objects for visual interaction. It is a simplification that necessitates the removal of that which is irrelevant or unknown: a making absent. Much as with Gibson's theory of vision, the world is reduced to a set of legible primitives—point, line, vertex, and surface—that can be made meaningful in the last instance as a rendered image. In this sense, the hidden surface problem functions as an analogy for computational materiality itself, or more accurately the computer's disavowal of its own materiality through the black boxing effect of the interface. Here the rendered image serves effectively as an interface for vision, configured to conform to the limitations of that vision, though not reducible to it, structured as it is by an excess of data that must be removed and restricted in order to be rendered legible. This world of graphical objects exists prior to the rendered output of the screen, and the image is only one of many meaningful forms the data might take. By focusing exclusively on the visual in our analysis of computer graphics, we limit ourselves to this restricted image, this black boxed object.

2 Random-Access Images: Interfacing Memory and the History of the Computer Screen

A memory is a means for displacing in time various events which depend upon the same information.

—J. Presper Eckert Jr., "A Survey of Digital Computer Memory Systems"

A paint program needs a canvas. The frame buffer provides one.

—Alvy Ray Smith, "Digital Paint Systems"

When we speak of graphics, we think of images. Be it the windowed interface of a personal computer, the tactile swipe of icons across a mobile device, or the surreal effects of computer-enhanced film and video games— all are graphics. Understandably, then, computer graphics are most often understood as the images displayed on a computer screen. This pairing of the image and screen is so natural that we rarely theorize the screen as a medium itself, one with a heterogeneous history that developed in parallel with other visual and computational forms.[1] What then of the screen? To be sure, the computer screen follows in the tradition of the visual frame that delimits, contains, and produces the image.[2] It is also the skin of the interface that allows us to engage with, augment, and relate to technical things.[3] But the computer screen is also a CRT phosphorescing in response to an electron beam, or a liquid crystal display (LCD) modified by a grid of randomly accessible memory that stores, maps, and transforms thousands of bits in real time. The screen is not simply an enduring technique or evocative metaphor; it is a hardware object whose transformations have shaped the material conditions of our visual culture.

The computer screen is a relatively recent invention and is by no means essential to the concept of computation itself. Some form of output is necessary to make meaningful the calculation of a computational machine, but the screen is only one of many possible media forms that output can take. Yet in our contemporary digital media landscape, the screen is ubiquitous—so much so that it is frequently taken for granted in all forms of computational interaction.[4] This ubiquity has led to a "screen essentialist" assumption about computational systems, whereby the screen stands in for and thereby occludes the deeper workings of the computer itself. Yet while we should not assume the screen exists as a pervasive feature of all machines in the history of computing, we similarly cannot discount the multiple and changing roles screens have played in the development of computational media over the past seventy years, as well as the diverse forms the screen takes as it moves through the history of computing.

Prior to the 1970s, there were no computer screens as we know them now, and until the 1980s, the vast majority of computational output was in the form of print terminals and teletypewriters.[5] What few screen-based computer-generated images did exist had to be rigged for display using a variety of cathode ray technologies, given that standard methods for interactive display did not yet exist. Despite the prevalence of screen technologies for televisual and cinematic images, these could not be readily adapted for use with computational technology because computer graphics, unlike film and television, do not begin as images.[6] Rather, they begin as numerical data sets consisting of simple geometric primitives: coordinate points connected by vector lines to form simple wireframe objects. As such, the first screens for computer graphics were adapted from radar or oscilloscope tubes, and modified to function as vector-based calligraphic or random-scan displays.[7] Experiments into raster displays did not begin until the late 1960s, driven by a desire to simulate realistic opacity in computer-generated objects for real-time interaction.[8] While the need for raster displays in the production of shaded graphics was one of the earliest concerns at experimental research centers like MIT and the University of Utah, the hardware of the 1960s was not capable of computing and translating the massive amount of graphical data needed for real-time interaction.[9] Real-time graphics would require new hardware forms that could supplement the general-purpose computer in its handling of graphical data, augmenting its calculations with the addition of a randomly accessible grid of graphical memory that contained a modifiable bitmap of each individual image frame—what would come to be known as a "frame buffer."

What may at first appear a minor technology in the history of computing is in fact one of the most significant visual technologies of the twentieth century, as it allowed for the first time the interactive manipulation of individual points of light on a screen. In doing so, it triggered an industrial-scale shift from vector to raster graphics over the course of the 1970s, leading to the familiar pixel-based computer screens used in all contemporary digital displays. More important perhaps, the frame buffer reveals a material connection between image and memory in digital systems, offering new insights into the temporality of computation as a visually mediated practice. If the screen is the site at which a wide range of graphical traditions meet and the object through which all graphics are mediated, then the frame buffer is the graphical object that made possible a new form of screen image. The frame buffer thus comes to transform the material and ontological basis of the screen as a platform through which graphical data are filtered and understood, and demonstrates how the formal qualities of the screen affect the aesthetic and material shape that computer graphics come to take.

Line

In 1950, Ben Laposky of Cherokee, Iowa, began experimenting with the display screen of a cathode ray oscilloscope in an attempt to capture the pulsating abstract forms produced through the generation and manipulation of sine waves (figure 2.1). Laposky, a trained mathematician, artist, draftsman, and World War II veteran, described this practice alternately as a form of "painting with light" and kind of visual music produced through the orchestration of electronic pulses across the screen of the CRT.[10] He named the resulting forms "oscillons," and over the course of the 1950s, his work evolved into a complex technical practice involving "as many as 70 different settings of controls on the oscilloscope and of other combinations of input waveform generators, amplifiers, modulating circuits and so on" (figure 2.2 and plate 4).[11] Laposky not only manipulated the settings of the oscilloscope to produce these desired effects, he also designed and constructed a wide range of electronic instruments to supplement and augment the oscilloscope's signal. While Laposky's oscillons clearly differ from later graphical image practices in his use of analog signals to construct abstract forms, his swirling images anticipate the three-dimensional graphical objects that would be developed almost two decades later. As Laposky suggests,

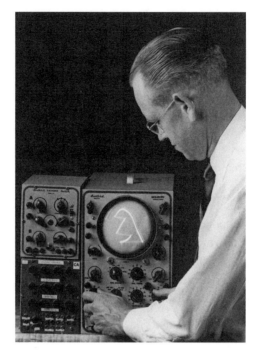

Figure 2.1
Ben Laposky with a modified oscilloscope, 1952. Courtesy of the Sanford Museum
and Planetarium, Cherokee, Iowa.

> While giving impressions of sweeping rhythms, the pulsating trace of the oscil-
> lating electron beam reveals their formation. Like other types of kinetic art, they
> involve the factor of time, in addition to giving an illusion of three dimensions
> on a two-dimensional surface. Some of the Oscillons have an almost sculptural
> quality. Because of the highly-contrasted, nonilluminated background of an oscil-
> loscope screen . . . they may seem to be images of luminescent moving masses . . .
> suspended in space.[12]

In 1952, Laposky debuted his oscillons at the Sanford Museum in Cherokee to great acclaim, and the show went on to tour the United States and
Europe from 1952 to 1961.[13] These images are a compelling predecessor
to later research into computer graphics, and are part of a long lineage
of artistic experimentation with computational technology beginning in
the immediate postwar era.[14] But the formal and technical structure of
Laposky's oscillons differs wildly from that of contemporary computer-
generated images, in large part due to the material specificity of the screens

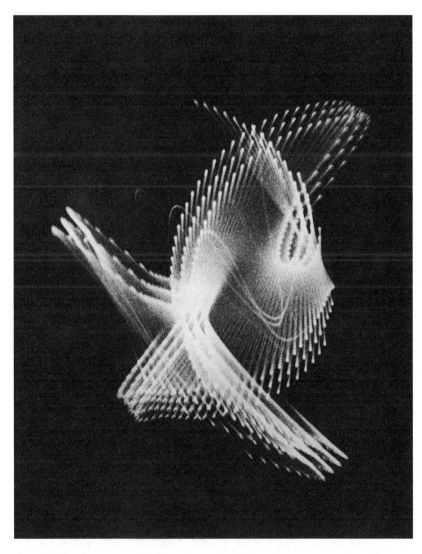

Figure 2.2
Ben F. Laposky, *Electronic Abstraction 4*, 1952. Courtesy the Anne and Michael Spalter Digital Art Collection (Spalter Digital).

on which they were produced and the medium in which they were captured. Unlike contemporary graphics, these are not the result of the precise calculation of clearly defined geometries suspended in Cartesian space but rather etchings of the interplay of analog electrical signals moving and transforming over time.

To record his oscillons, Laposky utilized a much older visual form: photography. Using a camera stand attached to the base of an oscilloscope frame and adjusted to the desired distance from the viewing screen, Laposky would photograph the waveforms in a darkened room, adjusting the exposure time to produce the desired effect (figure 2.3). The resulting images straddle multiple media forms, at once electronic and mechanical, material and ephemeral.[15] These swirling masses of light were formed at the intersection of photography and the cathode ray oscilloscope—an old medium capturing a glimpse of the new. Yet as strange and distant as the resulting oscillons may seem, they are exemplary of an extended period from the late 1940s to the mid-1970s in which a bizarre patchwork of techniques and technologies formed the material and historical condition for

Figure 2.3
Oscilloscope with camera attachment. From Ben F. Laposky, "Oscillons: Electronic Abstractions," *Leonardo* 2, no. 4 (October 1969): 346.

the development of contemporary computer screens and digital imaging technologies.

Screen

The visual logic of this early period is dominated by the vector line. Until the 1970s, few computers could produce graphics more complex than simple line drawings, and early graphics were thus largely composed of simple shapes traced onto the screen of a CRT (figure 2.4). In many ways, the CRT is one of the most emblematic and widespread visual technologies of the twentieth century: conceived and developed in its first thirty years, commercialized and widely distributed in the postwar era, and reaching near ubiquity by the close of the century.[16] Yet the rapid technical obsolescence of the CRT brought on by the popularization of LCD and plasma displays in the early 2000s revealed these screens as much more than an inert platform whose transformations were limited to progressive changes in scale and definition.[17] No longer state of the art, CRTs have become emblematic of the cycle of technological obsolescence, crisis of electronic waste, and challenge of technological preservation for media that rely on the material specificity of their form.[18] Increasingly scarce, the CRT has become a dead media artifact whose specificity must be accounted for if we are to understand its influence on our visual culture.[19]

In a CRT, an electron gun fires patterns or shapes at the face of the tube, which is coated on the inside with a layer of phosphors. These phosphors glow in response to the electrons, thereby creating a visible light for a moment before fading or being refreshed by another pass of the beam. The image on the screen is not drawn all at once but instead refreshed in a continuous pattern. By far the most common CRT display was the television screen, whose image is structured by hundreds of individual scan lines drawn by the electron gun as it slides from side to side across the screen. After each line, the beam is turned off, and the gun resets its position at the start of the next line, continuing this process until it reaches the bottom of the screen, at which point it returns to its initial position to begin its scan again.[20] Yet this is not the only form the CRT takes, nor is it the only visual tradition from which we might draw the origins of the computer display. As should be clear from Laposky's oscillons, there are many screen media that utilize CRT technology, including oscillography, radar, and ad hoc devices built for various forms of scientific visualization.[21]

Figure 2.4
John Warnock and an IDI graphical display unit, University of Utah, 1968. Courtesy
of the University of Utah's School of Computing.

To give but one example, the most common CRT used throughout the 1950s for computer visualization and display was the Charactron tube (figure 2.5). Developed by Consolidated-Vultee Aircraft (Convair) in 1952, the Charactron was designed to display alphanumeric characters using a technique known as shaped or extruded beam projection. Unlike the regimented scan lines of a television CRT or continuous curves of oscillography, the Charactron displayed images and text by deflecting its beam through a matrix mask with an array of sixty-four apertures in the shape of alphanumeric characters. In this way, it could "punch out" the shape of the desired character onto the face of the tube using only a single beam of light.[22] This system was originally designed for textual display since the combinatory logic of alphanumeric systems allowed for most any word or number to be easily displayed, but was adapted for more explicitly graphical purposes by the early 1960s before falling out of use at the start of the 1970s.[23] Many of the images produced by artists and researchers in this period were the product of this unique screen technology—one that bears no more resemblance to our modern computer screens than do Laposky's oscilloscopes.

Given the multiple and heterogeneous forms the CRT takes, it can be difficult to identify a single technohistorical tradition from which to draw out the origins of the computer screen. The technology behind the CRT display was first conceived of in the late nineteenth century by Karl Braun and subsequently developed by Vladimir Zworykin for use in television in the first three decades of the twentieth century.[24] Zworykin's legacy looms large over the early history of the television set and the move toward commercialization begun in the 1930s. These early origins of the CRT and its development as a televisual technology have been well documented by film and television scholars, yet existing histories tend toward biography and often foreground television's strained relationship with cinematic media in the struggle over cultural dominance in the twentieth century.[25] Missing is a larger discussion of the CRT as a technical object that functioned within a much broader media landscape—one whose significance is perhaps less cinematic than it is scientific or, at the very least, electronic. The CRT is not only the material object that makes possible the first fifty years of televisual images, it is also the basis for a wide range of media built around the display and manipulation of electrical currents, the most significant of which are cathode ray oscilloscopes like those used by Laposky.

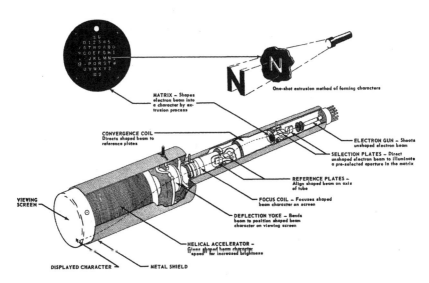

Figure 2.5
Charactron extruded beam CRT diagram. From "Programmers Reference Manual: S-C 4020 Computer Recorder," Document No. 9500056, Stromberg Datagraphics, Inc., New York, October 1964.

The oscilloscope is a type of electronic test instrument meant for the observation of constantly varying signal voltages. It serves to visualize electrical waveforms such that they may be analyzed for amplitude, frequency, and other properties.[26] Like the CRT itself, oscillography is one of many technologies born out of the massive growth in the electrical sciences during the nineteenth century, beginning with the development of electrical telegraphy.[27] These techniques for understanding and manipulating electricity—mediated as they are by the electron beam of the CRT—intersect with computer graphics at multiple points throughout its history, marking several transformations in the emergent medium's visual logic. Here the oscilloscope is of particular interest for the significant ways it mechanically differs from the television CRT. Unlike the regimented sweep of the television scan line, the electron beam of an oscilloscope can be modified to trace lines of any shape or angle onto its screen (figure 2.6). When used in the testing of constantly varying voltage signals, the oscilloscope deflects its electron beam using electrostatic force in a continual pattern, although its display could also be modified to draw noncontinuous lines following a "calligraphic" pattern. In such a system the electron gun is pointed at

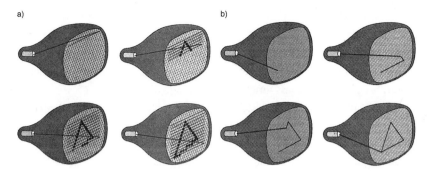

a) b)

Figure 2.6
The raster scan of a television display (left) and calligraphic scan of a vector display (right) like those used in oscillography.

a certain location, turned on, and moved from that (x, y) coordinate to another point along a line or curve, where it is then turned off again. In this way, an image can be painted or drawn on the face of the display.[28] By modifying the computer's output into a signal that can be read by the oscilloscope's calligraphic display, researchers could take advantage of the continuous movement of the waveform to draw out simple shapes and letters using varying electrical signals.[29]

The advantage of these vector displays was their simplicity. Vector images comprise little more than a collection of vertices on an x-y coordinate plane and, as such, can be modified and transformed easily and with relatively little calculation. Vector graphics can also display smooth curves, and have no difficulty with aliasing and other visual challenges that plagued raster graphics for decades.[30] Yet vector graphics were extremely limited in other ways. The most glaring limitation of vector-based systems was their inability to scale in number and complexity without noticeably affecting the visibility of the image to be displayed. One of the main benefits of the oscilloscope was that unlike a television screen that quickly scans the entire face of a CRT in a sequential line, the oscilloscope could move to draw and transform images at any point on its screen in real time. The principal drawback to this method was that it limited the speed at which the beam could operate. All cathode ray technology requires the image to be constantly refreshed in order to remain visible. If the electron beam does not refresh an image in time, the light of the screen will fade, producing a noticeable flicker. In early screens, the speed at which an image could be refreshed scaled downward proportional to the size and complexity of the image. The more the electron beam had to write on the phosphor of the screen, the longer it took and the greater the delay before it could return to refresh the image. The more one tried to draw on the screen, the more pronounced the flicker would become and the less functional the image would be.[31]

While calligraphic displays were ideal for simple shapes, the oscilloscope CRT could not scale to accommodate the needs of graphics researchers or the emerging graphics industry.[32] To accomplish complex, fully shaded, three-dimensional images, researchers would need to find a way to adapt the raster scan technique of television—a goal that would prove no simple task given the unique structure and function of computer-generated images and the challenge of moving from a visual system based on the sweeping vector line to the regimented grid of the raster and its pixelated display

Grid

The grid is the operative visual technique of contemporary digital media technology. Found everywhere, it is most visible in the pixelated face of the contemporary computer screen. Of course, the grid is nothing new. Like so many mediating techniques, it can be traced back millennia, and has been repeatedly engaged by scholars invested in its material and aesthetic form.[33] Art historian Hannah Higgins, for example, follows the grid's appearance across a range of artistic, technological, and architectural practices, reaching back as far as the development of bricklaying and fishing nets during the eighth century BCE.[34] As she shows, the grid can be found in the structure of maps, tablets, notation, type, and even in the network architecture of the modern internet. The impulse behind this genealogy is in part a refusal of the supposition that the grid is an explicitly modern phenomenon, as Rosalind Krauss suggests in her 1979 essay "Grids." For Krauss, the grid of modernist art is a pointed refusal of the naturalism that defined centuries of earlier artistic traditions. In contrast to earlier visual forms, the grid is "flattened, geometricized, ordered . . . anti-natural, antimimetic, antireal. It is what art looks like when it turns its back on nature."[35] Channeling Krauss, Higgins observes that "the modernist grid is an emblem of industry. It reflects standardization, mass production, and the newly smooth mechanics of transportation. In the modern imagination, in other words, the grid pits culture against nature and the body."[36] The raster grid of the computer screen would appear to follow in this tradition, emblematic of the standardization of the image form by digitization.

In contrast, media theorist Bernhard Siegert argues that the grid's primary function is in fact an ordering of the world. Following Martin Heidegger, he presses that beyond its familiar perspectival, cartographic, or mathematical functions, the grid serves a third aesthetic and deictic function:

> The grid serves to constitute a world of objects imagined by a subject. To speak with Heidegger, it is a *Gestell* or "enframing" aimed at the availability and controllability of whatever is thus conceived; it addresses and symbolically manipulates things that have been transformed into data. The grid, in short, is a medium that operationalizes deixis. It allows us to link deictic procedures with chains of symbolic operations that have effects in the real. Thus the grid is not only part of a history of representation, or of a history of procedures facilitating the efficient manipulation of data, but also of "a history of the different modes by which, in our culture, human beings are made into subjects."[37]

Yet not all grids function equally in this regard (or at minimum, the particularity of each grid form enacts its own kind of ordering). The raster of the Stone Age fishing net differs in substantive ways from that of the distributed network, much as the grid of the Renaissance painter's screen differs from the grids of Piet Mondrian or Jasper Johns. We must distinguish the specificity of the technical forms that the grid takes even as we acknowledge its continuity as part of a larger cultural technique that structures or orders the world. This is not to be pedantic or abstruse but instead to draw out how techniques are reproduced over time through means both technical and cultural, in which seemingly universal structures come to reflect the specificity of a historical moment through a kind of transformative endurance. Nowhere in the history of graphics is this distinction more apparent than in the relationship between the television and the computer screen.

The primary obstacle in any effort to modify a raster scan television to accept computational data is one of time or sequence, and along with it, memory. The television, as it functioned in the 1960s, was an immediate, linear medium designed for the procedural transmission of image-based input scanned from the target plate of a television camera. It adopted the serial or sequential structure of film, though it did so not through the procession of photographic images on a strip of celluloid but rather through the procession of an electron beam across the face of a CRT. Unlike film, what most distinguished the television was its ability to transmit and display images and sounds in real time and without storage.[38] Televisual images were not captured or calculated; they were scanned as signals and transmitted in a linear stream, line by line, appearing for a moment and then disappearing altogether, replaced with the next pass of the electron beam. While this served the function of television well, it did not lend itself to the display of computational images, which were produced through complex calculation, had no external temporality per se, and needed to be stored in memory to be accessible for interaction. Unlike all other screen media, computational images must linger, idle and accessible, until they are transformed through an interaction that may begin at any point on the screen. At its heart, the incompatibility of the television's grid form with the demands of interactive computation marks the basic ontological concern for all computational systems—that is, the conversion of continuous or analog information into discrete and thereby actionable forms. Put simply: digitization.[39] Thus a mediating technology was necessary to modify the procedural logic of the analog television to accommodate the digital logic of random access.[40] The solution was the development of a dedicated memory capable of storing and transforming graphical information apart from the memory of the general-purpose central processing unit (CPU): the frame buffer.

Buffer

A frame buffer is nothing more than a piece of computer memory specialized for holding pictures. When using a frame buffer, the computer writes a single frame of video into memory as a bitmap.[41] It then begins to compute the next frame while, independently, the display device reads the current frame out of the buffer to display it. In this way the computer can separate calculation from display, storing visual data in memory as needed until it is changed or transformed through interaction.

The memory in a frame buffer differs from other forms of computer memory in that it is arranged as a two-dimensional array that maps directly onto the bits of the raster screen image. Ordinary RAM stores everything in discrete pieces—bits at the lowest level. But pictures do not fit well in one-dimensional lists, so a frame buffer stores the picture divided up into rows and columns of what we now call pixels—a 2D array of memory locations (figure 2.7).[42] By mapping the image in this way, the frame buffer enables the rapid processing of graphical information that is, in turn, ordered

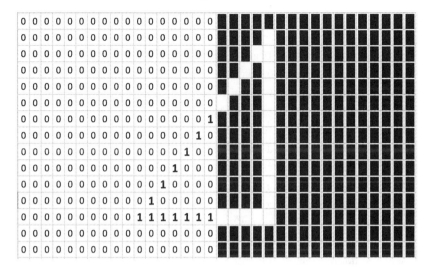

Figure 2.7
A visualization of a bitmapped image of a triangle stored in a framebuffer, where 0 corresponds with black and 1 with white. Image by the author.

for display, pushed into memory, and output onto the screen. By using a random-access form, the frame buffer models the calligraphic display without the material structure that enables the random movement of the electron beam across the screen of an oscilloscope CRT. It can thereby display shaded or halftone images in the same manner as a television set while also allowing for quick and interactive access to that display via a light pen, mouse, or other input device. Since the bitmap of the screen is randomly accessible, it is not necessary to recalculate the entire screen when interacting with or transforming an area of the image, as the computer need only calculate new values for those pixels that must be changed while ignoring the remaining bits in the buffer. Thus the frame buffer allows for random access to the procedural image, mapping the control structure of the grid onto the linear flow of the television screen through memory. As Friedrich Kittler notes,

> The discrete, or digital, nature of both the geometric coordinates and their chromatic values makes possible the magical artifice that separates computer graphics from film and television. Now, for the first time in the history of optical media, it is possible to address a single pixel in the 849th row and 720th column directly without having to run through everything before and after it.[43]

This is the image made digital: the random-access image.

As is often the case with the development of computational technologies, the frame buffer concept has no single origin. By the late 1960s, several research institutes had begun to develop experimental memory devices for graphical display on a raster screen, but the earliest functional frame buffer was likely a simple 3-bit paint program developed by Joan Miller at Bell Labs in 1969.[44] Working from Miller's program, Bell engineers developed several functional raster systems under the direction of A. Michael Noll, and by 1970, they had a modified PICTUREPHONE system capable of producing real-time halftone images on a raster display.[45] The system used a technique known as drum storage, in which the writing of new graphical data into memory was contingent on the sequential speed and rotation of a physical drum that stored the raster grid. As such, the system could not truly be considered randomly accessible, but Noll saw little benefit in a separate addressable digital core storage for display data, believing that exponential growth in storage capacity would more than make up for the future needs of buffer storage.[46]

Thus the first true frame buffer was not developed until 1972, when a young researcher at Xerox PARC named Richard Shoup began work on Super-Paint, an 8-bit paint system complete with interactive software interface and hardware frame buffer.[47] Shoup called his system a "picture memory," and it allowed an artist to change the individual bits of a frame buffer at locations specified with a simulated paintbrush, creating a direct and immediate correspondence between electrical bits in memory and the physical phosphors on a TV screen (figure 2.8 and plates 5–6).[48] In this sense, SuperPaint can be understood as the technical and intellectual predecessor to all modern paint and photo-editing software, from Microsoft Paint to Adobe Photoshop. The system itself was not limited to illustration, and could be used to produce and manipulate low-resolution photographic images. One of the first images successfully produced by the frame buffer, in April 1973, was a black-and-white photograph of Shoup holding a notecard that reads, "It works! (sort of)" (figure 2.9).[49]

Shoup's SuperPaint marked a brief period of experimentation with digital paint systems and artistic applications for frame buffer technology at PARC. Working with a research team that included computer scientist Alvy Ray Smith and artist David DiFrancesco, Shoup considered the frame buffer a new artistic medium to be explored, and saw PARC as an experimental space in which artists and technologists could meet to create new media

Figure 2.8
One rack of Richard Shoup's SuperPaint system, containing the frame buffer, Xerox PARC, 1972. Courtesy of the Richard Shoup Papers, Carnegie Mellon University Archives.

forms. This period would be short lived, however, as Xerox decided to abandon color graphics altogether in 1974, envisioning black and white as the future for the commercial office.[50] Soon after, Smith and DiFrancesco were let go as contractors at PARC, and the pair immediately began a search for the next working frame buffer.

By 1975, the University of Utah had developed the first commercially available frame buffer system, which was produced, marketed, and sold by the program's spin-off enterprise, E&S.[51] The E&S buffer marks an important moment in the transition toward a commercially viable graphics industry as hardware systems became available beyond university and government-sponsored research centers. Nonetheless, by the time of the buffer's release in the mid-1970s, researchers in Salt Lake City had been experimenting with raster graphics for almost a decade. As early as the Fall Joint Computer

Figure 2.9
Early digital image of Richard Shoup, rendered on the SuperPaint system, April 4, 1973. Courtesy of the Richard Shoup Papers, Carnegie Mellon University Archives.

Conference of 1967, Chris Wylie, Gordon Romney, Alan Erdahl, and David Evans had published a paper describing methods for producing shaded halftone perspective drawings by computer using an oscilloscope modified to accept data as horizontal scan lines from a FORTRAN IV algorithm called PIXURE. This system could produce simple shaded drawings of geometric shapes rendered at varying resolutions (figure 2.10).[52] The PIXURE hardware predates the concept of the frame buffer as a stand-alone object, but the images the system produced are nonetheless some of the earliest examples of shaded three-dimensional graphical objects.

As with Laposky's oscillons, these images could not be viewed in their entirety without the use of long-exposure photography, which in a sense functioned as the memory of these early displays, separating the act of calculation from the process of representation. The amount of time each image took to be calculated depended largely on the complexity of the object along with the desired resolution of the image. Yet despite clear limitations

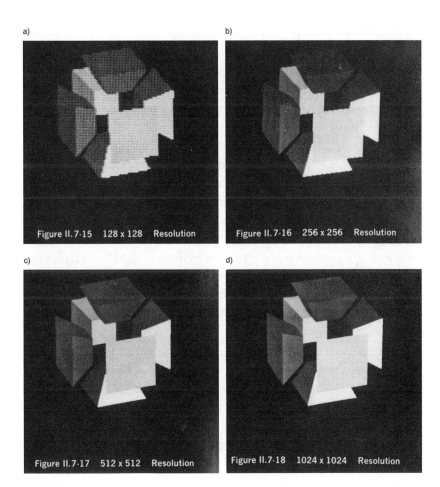

a)

Figure II.7-15   128 x 128   Resolution

b)

Figure II.7-16   256 x 256   Resolution

c)

Figure II.7-17   512 x 512   Resolution

d)

Figure II.7-18   1024 x 1024   Resolution

Figure 2.10
Early resolution tests at the University of Utah developed using the PIXURE system, 1967. Courtesy of the Special Collections Department, J. Willard Marriott Library, University of Utah.

in render speed and processing power, the research team believed that real-time movement and display for three-dimensional graphics was not far off given the rapid development of efficient algorithms for hidden surface removal and the use of parallel computing to accomplish calculations for display.[53] Thus while the frame buffer concept was not clearly articulated until 1972, it had been in development alongside research into hidden surface removal, geometry, shading, and color at the University of Utah since the mid-1960s. With the development of the E&S frame buffer system, interactive images could finally be produced on a television screen in real time.[54] Here, for the first time, was a system for interactive shaded graphics built for general-purpose computing and available for purchase through the commercial market (plates 7–8).

On hearing of the E&S system, and with the goal of finding new institutional sponsors, Smith and DiFrancesco set out on a road trip from Silicon Valley to Salt Lake City in hopes of continuing their research. What they found in Utah was a university with deep ties to the Department of Defense and little interest in funding artistic applications of their hardware.[55] After one meeting with Evans, the two were quickly turned away—but not before being given the name of Alexander Schure, a wealthy businessman from New York who had purchased "one of everything in sight" on a recent trip to E&S, including the not-yet-delivered frame buffer. "He had animators from Hollywood making an animated film," Smith was told. "You can talk art with him."[56] Smith and DiFrancesco were soon on a plane to visit the New York Institute of Technology (NYIT) in Old Westbury on the North Shore of Long Island, where after an initial meeting with Schure, they were quickly hired. Over the next five years, NYIT served as the test bed for what would ultimately become the commercial computer animation industry. Driven by Schure's enthusiasm and generous funding, NYIT had already attracted prominent researchers from Utah and PARC, most notably Edwin Catmull.[57] Schure's dream was to create the first fully computer-animated feature film, and the team worked for years developing custom software called TWEEN, which it hoped would digitize the cell animation process and revolutionize the animation industry.[58] Ultimately the system proved too costly and ineffective, and the dream of a feature-length computer-animated film went unrealized for almost twenty years. Nonetheless, NYIT served as an important test bed for Catmull, who would go on to lead the computer graphics division at Lucasfilm in 1979 and, with Smith, found Pixar Animation Studios in 1986.[59]

As the history of the NYIT computer graphics lab makes clear, the development of commercial frame buffer–enabled systems created new markets and uses for digital imaging technologies over the course of the 1970s and 1980s, leading to a large-scale transition to raster display technology and along with it the rise of the modern computer screen. This transition from simple lines painted onto the face of a CRT to the pixelated bitmap that now structures almost all computer and television screens was thus made possible through the interfacing of image and memory that is the function of the frame buffer as a technical and visual medium.

Pixel

This brings us at last to our contemporary screen and that individual unit of screen memory: the pixel. Though nearly all contemporary screens comprise pixel-like elements arranged in a raster grid, the word itself was not widely used in computer graphics until the late 1970s (figure 2.11).[60] The term has many origins and can be traced back as far as the late nineteenth-century German *Bildpunkte*, or "picture points," used in reference to photography and early cathode ray technology for television.[61] The phrase "picture element" appears as early as 1927 in reference to television, and its abbreviation as "pixel" emerges in 1965 as a reference to digital image processing for video and photography. The challenge in tracing the origin of the pixel as both a graphical object and technical term lies in its broad undifferentiated use across a wide range of imaging practices. Indeed the pixel has become an overburdened term for contemporary digital images as well—one that often obscures the specificity of the widely varying means by which digital images have been structured and produced. Perhaps more significant than any such genealogy, then, would be to clarify the function the pixel serves. As the smallest addressable element in an imaging system, the pixel functions as the most basic unit of that system. The pixel's clearest corollary in the computer itself is the binary digit or *bit*—the most basic unit of information in computing and digital communications. In fact, at the earliest moment in the history of the modern computer, the two are one in the same. This is where the history of the computer screen begins, with a display known as the Williams-Kilburn tube.

In 1945 and 1946, the English engineer Frederic Williams paid two visits to the United States to assess the radar circuitry being developed there.[62] On his second trip he made a visit to Bell Labs, where he saw several early experiments using CRTs for radar display. Bell technicians were seeking new ways to remove the ground echoes that occur in all radar systems, but Williams saw a different potential use for the CRT: as an electronic storage device for digital computing.[63] At this early moment in the history of computing, the field was undergoing dramatic changes in the theory and

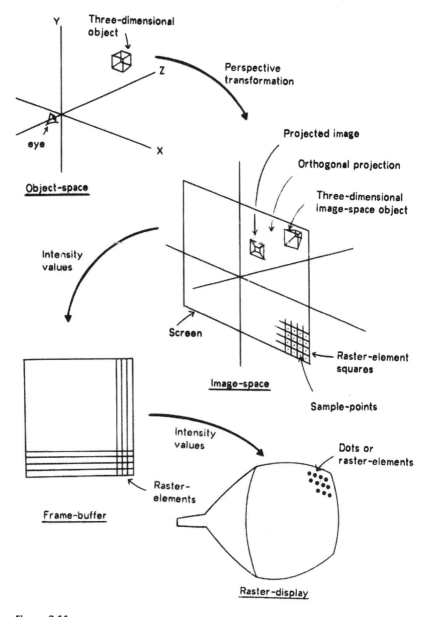

Figure 2.11

A diagram from 1974 by Edwin Catmull, laying out the terminology used in the computer graphics field at that time and covering a number of concepts that today all fall under the term "pixel." Edwin Catmull, "A Subdivision Algorithm for Computer Display of Curved Surfaces" (PhD diss., University of Utah, 1974), 6.

architecture of computational machines. While Alan Turing had developed the concept of universal computation in 1936, John von Neumann's foundational "First Draft of a Report on the EDVAC" was not published until nearly a decade later in 1945. Drawing on the work of J. Presper Eckert and John Mauchly, von Neumann's text was the first to propose the stored program concept, which would allow computers to be programmed and reprogrammed in memory.[64] Prior to this moment, all computing machines were relatively fixed, in that they were capable of executing only the single computational program that was built into the design of the machine itself. Even those early computers that were programmable used physical forms of data storage such as punched tape or cards, and had to be physically reprogrammed through switches or patch cords that took several days or weeks to complete.[65] The key to von Neumann's stored program concept was its flexibility—allowing for the transformation of instructions stored within the memory of a computer—but in 1945, it was little more than a theory. His report was explicitly ambiguous in describing the actual hardware required to make this theory function as part of a working machine, which led to several competing techniques for stored program computation, along with several competing claims for the first successful implementation of the stored program concept.[66]

In this early period most computers relied on relays, mechanical counters, or delay lines for their main memory functions, each of which had significant drawbacks in the efficient storage and retrieval of information due to the sequential and fixed nature of their storage techniques. The delay line, for example, was developed in the 1920s as a technique to delay the propagation of analog signals, and was used widely in radar technology during World War II. In the mid-1940s, Eckert modified delay lines to be used as computer memory, storing information in the delay through signal amplification. These sequential methods for computer memory functioned through repetition and were in this sense akin to the now-antiquated technique of repeating a phone number to oneself from the time one finds it in the phone book until one has dialed it.[67] The challenge of delay line memory was that reading or writing a particular bit required waiting for that bit to circulate completely through the delay line into the electronics. Thus the ability for the device to access and transform information stored in the delay line was limited by the recirculation time—a matter of microseconds.

For a computing machine that sought to scale upward in both the speed of access and size of storage, this was a significant limitation.

Williams believed the CRT could be used to develop a quicker and more efficient means of storing and transforming programs in computer memory for random access. To prove the viability of this method, a team of researchers at Manchester University began to build an experimental computing machine in late 1947. Some six months later, they had developed the Manchester Small-Scale Experimental Machine (SSEM)—also known as "Baby"—which successfully ran its first program on June 21, 1948, making it the world's first functional stored program machine (figure 2.12). While the SSEM computer is most recognizable as the earliest successful implementation of the stored program concept, it was built largely to test the efficacy of Williams's theoretical CRT storage method. After proving their storage theory with the SSEM, researchers went on to transform the machine into a more usable computer in the Manchester Mark 1, which in

Figure 2.12
Tom Kilburn (left) and Frederic Williams (right) with the Manchester Small-Scale Experimental Machine and its cathode ray output display, University of Manchester, 1948. Courtesy of the University of Manchester.

turn became the prototype for the Ferranti Mark 1, the world's first commercially available general-purpose computer. In this sense, one possible history of the modern general-purpose computer begins with the screen, though it is a screen that was never meant to be seen. Instead, this screen was one of the earliest devices for RAM, using a series of dots and dashes projected onto the screen of the CRT to store electric charges that held binary data—a technique known as electrostatic storage.

The key to this electrostatic storage is a pair of otherwise-undesirable properties of the phosphor used to coat the screens of a CRT. When electrons fired from a CRT's electron gun strike the phosphor coating of its screen, some electrons "stick" to the tube and cause an electric charge to build up. This phosphor gives off additional electron particles when struck by an electron beam—a phenomenon known as secondary emission. The rate of release for these secondary particles is significantly nonlinear—that is, the rate of emission increases dramatically when a voltage is applied that crosses a certain threshold. This causes the lit spot of electrostatic charge to rapidly decay, releasing any stuck electrons in the process. This effectively allows the screen of the CRT to store two distinct electrostatic charge states controlled by the intensity of the electron gun: positive and negative, or 0 and 1. In this way, the tube can be used to store binary data. In the case of the Williams-Kilburn tube, this appears as a grid of dots and dashes blinking across the face of its display (figures 2.13–2.14).[68] Each dot is the result of a slight positive charge in the immediate region of the beam where there is a deficit of electrons, and a slight negative charge around the dot, which acts as a charge well, where those electrons land. The dot can be erased by drawing a second dot next to the first or by extending the dot into a short dash, thus filling in the charge well.

Importantly, these pixel-like dots and dashes are not the *representation* of binary data but rather the visible electrical state of the binary storage device itself. While screen images today may be thought of as surface-level abstractions of some deeper technical language—be it code, binary, or even electrical signals—in this early moment, the storage and representation of data are one in the same. Here the image does not simply represent the processing of data; it is that data in 0s and 1s. As with the depth pass images produced by the z-buffer described in chapter 1, what we see on the screen of a Williams-Kilburn tube is not only an image but also data itself; or rather it is image and data, indistinguishable and inseparable. Thus the first

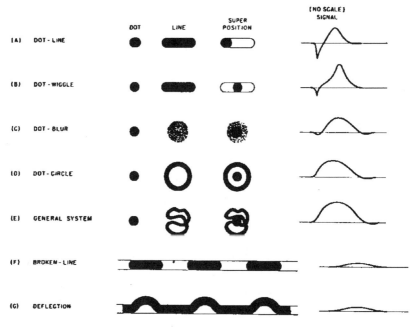

Figure 2.13
A range of electrostatic storage patterns for binary storage. From J. Presper Eckert Jr., "A Survey of Digital Computer Memory Systems," *Proceedings of the IEEE* 41 (October 1953): 189.

example of a screen technology used in the history of computing is entirely nonrepresentational and even nonvisible, as these screens were meant to be covered or hidden from their operators by a special detector used to output data from memory (figure 2.15).[69] In this sense, the Williams-Kilburn tube is exceptional in that it does not map onto the logic of interface or representation in the way that all subsequent screens do. In another sense, however, it is emblematic of all contemporary screens for its prototypical use of the pixel, the grid, and—most significant—the mapping together of image and memory.[70]

While the Williams-Kilburn tube was the most successful and widely implemented electrostatic storage device, several other systems were simultaneously developed at research sites in the United States.[71] As early as 1946, Zworykin and Jan Rajchman began development of a working CRT memory at the Radio Corporation of America for use by von Neumann at the Institute for Advanced Study in Princeton, New Jersey. Known as the Selectron

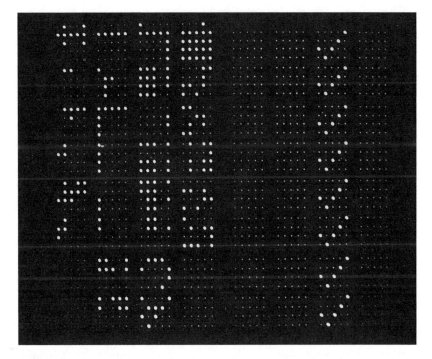

Figure 2.14
The face of a Williams-Kilburn tube with dots and dashes of electrostatic bits, ca. 1948.
Courtesy of the University of Manchester.

tube, it struggled in development and failed to be commercialized, such that its only use outside the institute was in the RAND Corporation's JOHNNIAC computer.[72] At MIT's Lincoln Laboratory, researchers began experimenting with the construction of stable electrostatic grids for use in the Whirlwind I computer as early as 1947, and by 1948, had constructed a 16×16 grid of dots.[73] This number increased rapidly over the next three years, and by 1950, the lab was experimenting with 4,096 bits displayed as a massive grid of light on the screen of the CRT.[74] To test the functionality of the Whirlwind storage tubes, researchers developed a program called Waves of One, which ran through each storage point on the screen, checking to ensure it was properly displayed. Norman Taylor, then the associate head of the computer division at Lincoln Lab, recalls this process of identifying individual points of light as the key moment in the development of graphical interaction. Referring to the Waves of One program, he notes,

Figure 2.15
A Williams-Kilburn tube with open-face panel, ca. 1948. Courtesy of the Computer History Museum and the University of Manchester.

> If we read a one, the program continued, and if it didn't, it stopped. We were asking how we can identify the address of that spot. So Bob Everett, our technical director, said "we can do that easily." All we need is a light gun to put over the spot that stops and we'll get a readout as to which one it is. So he invented the light gun that afternoon and the next day we achieved man machine interactive control of the display—I believe for the first time.[75]

This affordance of the electrostatic storage tube to randomly access individual bits in memory also allowed for interactive manipulation with the light gun, switching on and off each point of light without recalculating the entire storage array. Taylor's anecdote demonstrates how—even at this early stage—RAM was essential to the graphical manipulation of a raster grid.[76]

This brief but meaningful moment of contact between the visible image and its physical storage was quickly abstracted. As early as 1947, Williams and Kilburn began experimenting with their display as a representational interface, publishing a set of images alongside Kilburn's initial progress

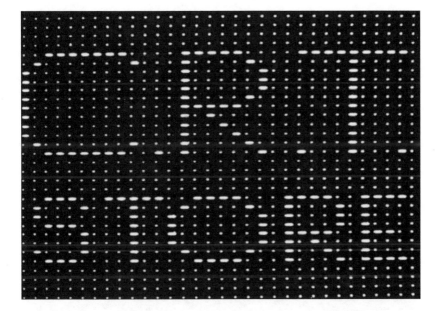

Figure 2.16
Williams-Kilburn tube with a 1,024-digit store image, University of Manchester, 1947. Courtesy of the Computer History Museum and the University of Manchester.

report to the Telecommunications Research Establishment on December 1, announcing "CRT STORE" in dots and dashes at 1,024 digits or bits (figure 2.16).[77] Likewise, researchers at MIT went on to perform graphical experiments using the storage tube, including carving out the letters *MIT* from the grid of lights (figure 2.17).[78] While these images were not intended for broad application, they nonetheless hinted at the technology's potential futures.

RAM

While the modern interactive screen with its pixelated raster and 32-bit color display is largely the outgrowth of a set of technologies developed in the 1970s, the use of screens for computation reaches back decades further to the origins of the modern computer itself. One can say the modern computer begins with the screen, but as a device for memory and storage rather than as a representational display or interface. These early screens were a means of mapping the bits of the earliest digital computers in the phosphorescent glow of electricity and light, securing a connection between

Figure 2.17
Carving out the MIT logo with an experimental electrostatic CRT, Massachusetts Institute of Technology, 1952. Reprinted with permission from the MITRE Corporation.

the screen and the material structure of the stored program computer that would repeat and reemerge throughout the history of computer graphics.

These early cathode ray techniques for electrostatic storage are important predecessors of modern-day graphical displays, but they represent a brief and largely failed experiment in the design of computer memory systems. Electrostatic storage was quick, but it was not stable or reliable over long periods of time. After only a few hours of use, any electrostatic system would produce memory errors and need to be reset. Frustrated by the failure of their storage tube design, MIT researchers working on the Whirlwind I started experimenting with magnetic forms of storage, leading to the development of magnetic core memory in 1951. Magnetic core was the first reliable form of RAM, and remained an industry standard until it was displaced by solid-state memory in integrated circuits beginning in the early 1970s. With magnetic core, the bit state of a core memory plane was held on magnetized toroids woven into a grid of conductive wire.[79] These wires formed contacts on each side of the plane, allowing for rapid and stable random-access manipulation of each toroid bit (figure 2.18). While the material function of magnetic core systems diverges wildly from the electrostatic screen technology that preceded it, they notably adopt the grid form used in all previous random-access systems. Even contemporary integrated circuit RAM chips, found in almost all computational devices, are arranged in a grid pattern on a microscopic level that mirrors these early random-access systems. This similarity is not incidental given that the grid's function is uniquely tied to the logic of random access—a logic that maps onto and can be traced through a variety of computational technologies

Figure 2.18
A grid of magnetic core memory. Konstantin Lanzet, 2009. CC BY-SA 3.0.

that appear in the immediate postwar period, and materially differentiate computer graphics from those screen technologies that precede it. The grid of computer graphics offers an ordering of the visible world such that it is made discrete and randomly accessible—transforming screen into memory, and image into simulation.

Far from an inert surface on which the digital image appears, the computer screen is a unique media form as old as the modern computer itself. It is a deeply heterogeneous object, which undergoes multiple transformations in its long history—at once line, grid, and pixel. Looking beyond these visual distinctions, what is most apparent is the endurance of memory as a structuring category that distinguishes computer graphics from earlier visual forms. By mapping the image into memory, computer graphics allow for random access to procedural vision, transforming the image from something that is captured and displayed into something that can be changed and manipulated, computed and interacted. Through the grid of RAM, a new image form takes shape—one that continues to dominate our visual culture some fifty years after its development.

Plate 1
Ivan Sutherland's students digitize Marsha Sutherland's VW Beetle, 1972. Courtesy of the University of Utah School of Computing and the Computer History Museum.

Plate 2

An abandoned bunker at Fort Douglas, future home of the Evans and Sutherland Computer Corporation, ca. 1968. Courtesy of the Special Collections Department, J. Willard Marriott Library, University of Utah.

Plate 3

David Evans (left) and Shohei Takada (right) of Hitachi Electronics on a visit to Salt Lake City, 1973. Courtesy of the Special Collections Department, J. Willard Marriott Library, University of Utah.

Plate 4
Ben F. Laposky, *Oscillon 1049*, 1960. Museum no. E.1096-2008. © Victoria and Albert Museum, London.

Plate 5
Fritz Fisher, *Black Girl*, 1973. Painting produced using SuperPaint graphics.

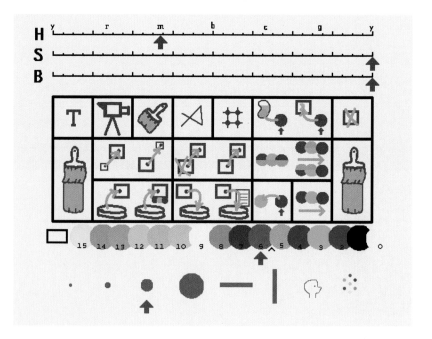

Plate 6
SuperPaint menu by Richard Shoup, highlighting the skeuomorphic paint and canvas logic of the frame buffer, 1977. Courtesy of the Richard Shoup Papers, Carnegie Mellon University Archives.

Plate 7

The video frame buffer (right) and an E&S Picture System (left) being used to display a Klein bottle. In this application, the lower half of the video frame buffer is being used as ordinary memory to store the range to the nearest surface behind each picture element. The resulting hidden surface picture is seen in the upper part of the screen. Courtesy of the Special Collections Department, J. Willard Marriott Library, University of Utah.

Plate 8

Artist Duane M. Palyka using the E&S Picture System and frame buffer to create a self-portrait, 1975. Courtesy of the Special Collections Department, J. Willard Marriott Library, University of Utah.

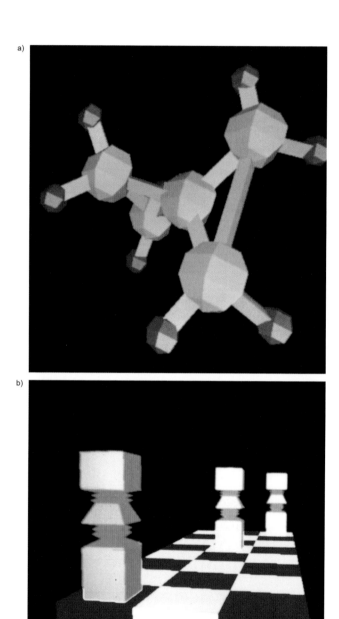

Plate 9
Molecular model (top) and chess board simulation (bottom) assembled from geometric primitives, University of Utah, 1968. Courtesy of the Special Collections Department, J. Willard Marriott Library, University of Utah.

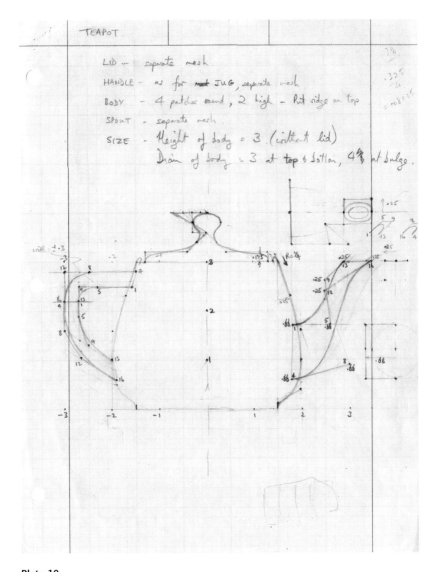

Plate 10
Martin Newell's initial drawing of the teapot on graph paper, 1972. Courtesy of Martin Newell.

a)

b)

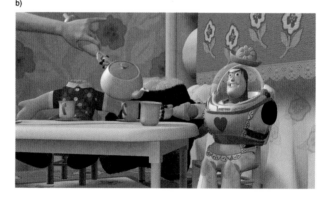

c)

Plate 11

Frame captures of various Easter egg appearances by the Utah teapot, including in the Windows NT 3.5 "pipes" screen saver (top), the 1995 film *Toy Story* (middle), and the October 1995 "Treehouse of Horror VI" episode of *The Simpsons* (bottom).

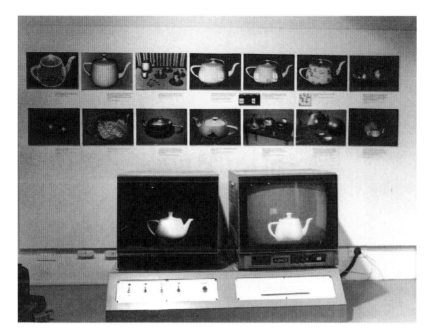

Plate 12
Snapshot of the Utah teapot lighting rig demonstration at the 1989 SIGGRAPH convention in Boston. Courtesy of Steve Baker.

Plate 13
Engineer using the DAC-1 graphical workstation at the General Motors Research Laboratories, 1966. Courtesy of General Motors.

Plate 14
View from the Wheelhouse of the CAORF simulator. Courtesy of the Special Collections Department, J. Willard Marriott Library, University of Utah.

Plate 15
Graphics from the completed CAORF, 1975. Courtesy of the Special Collections Department, J. Willard Marriott Library, University of Utah.

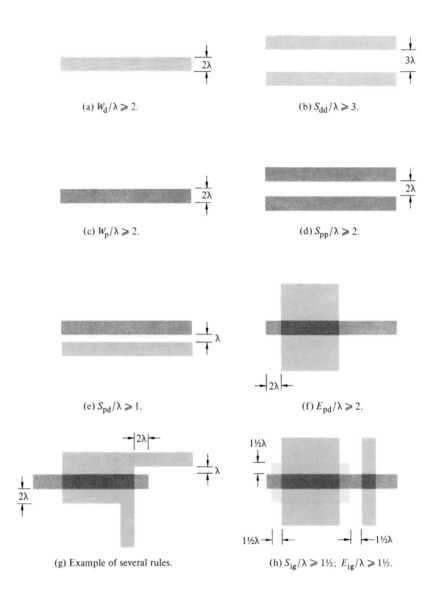

(a) $W_d/\lambda \geqslant 2$.

(b) $S_{dd}/\lambda \geqslant 3$.

(c) $W_p/\lambda \geqslant 2$.

(d) $S_{pp}/\lambda \geqslant 2$.

(e) $S_{pd}/\lambda \geqslant 1$.

(f) $E_{pd}/\lambda \geqslant 2$.

(g) Example of several rules.

(h) $S_{ig}/\lambda \geqslant 1\frac{1}{2}$; $E_{ig}/\lambda \geqslant 1\frac{1}{2}$.

n MOS design rules

Plate 16
Page from *Introduction to VLSI Systems* demonstrating several of Lynn Conway's rules and the use of the λ unit.

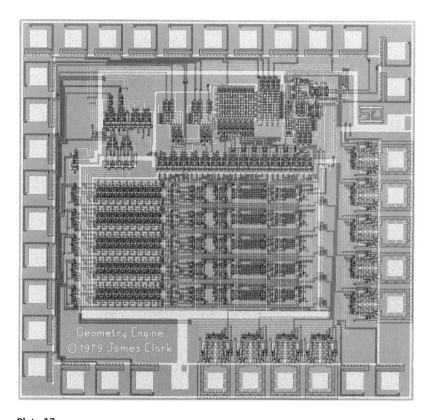

Plate 17
The first iteration of James Clark's Geometry Engine, arguably the first modern GPU, 1979. Courtesy of Lynn Conway.

Plate 18
The angular desk and custom cubicle dividers built for SGI in the mid-1990s, still in use at the Computer History Museum in 2012. Photo by the author.

Plate 19

SGI IRIS workstation in the Computer History Museum's permanent collection. Altered. © Mark Richards. Courtesy of the Computer History Museum.

Plate 20
Artie Vierkant, *Image Objects*, 2011–ongoing. Print on aluminum composite panel.
Altered documentation images. Courtesy of Artie Vierkant.

3   Model Objects: The Utah Teapot as Standard and Icon

The objective of most computer-graphics programs is easily stated: to represent objects of some kind and to provide a means for manipulating them.
—Ivan Sutherland, "Computer Displays"

To learn what nearness is we examined the jug nearby.
—Martin Heidegger, "The Thing"

What is a digital object, a simulated thing? Simulation lies at the heart of computation, as the computer may be understood most simply as a machine built for the simulation of any process that may be described procedurally. It is a tool built for the simulation of other tools, a technical object par excellence. But what then is the materiality of *digital* objects, alienated as they are from the things they seek to simulate? While this question may seem beyond the scope of an investigation into the history of computer graphics, in fact it speaks to the basic assumptions of researchers and scholars in this early moment—assumptions that in turn, come to shape the ways this technical discipline conceives of and standardizes the world itself. As computer graphics began to materialize as a field of research at the start of the 1970s, it became clear that while the realistic display of objects and environments was a primary concern, this concern necessitated a theory of the nature of objects themselves. In other words, in order to simulate an object, one must first understand and define what an object is. Over the course of the decade, computer graphics researchers began to standardize the means by which simulated objects are constructed and displayed. Objects became geometries onto which processes could be applied and algorithms could be tested—material simulations that could communicate and interact with one another in specified ways, imbued with a unique set of assumptions about what an object is, is for, and can do. This standardization brought with it broad implications for the display and construction of objects through simulation, but it also marked the beginning of a much larger reorientation in the nascent field of computer science toward the object world and a concern for the nature of objects themselves. While this is a shift that emerges alongside computer graphics, it comes to have a wide-reaching effect on a range of technologies across the second half of the twentieth century, fundamentally transforming the way we understand, model, and interact with the material world today, infused as it is with computational objects.

Over the course of the 1960s and early 1970s, the process by which objects are produced, replicated, and digitized by computer graphics was standardized. No longer exclusively concerned with geometric construction, researchers could focus on specific objects and processes, improving on the realism of individual properties through simulation. This deep and narrow focus defines nearly all graphical research today, invested as it is in the simulation of discrete and identifiable objects and properties of the material world, be it the clumping of snow, the movement of water, or the translucence of skin.[1] This emphasis on a small subset of parts in any given world produces a highly uneven quality to computer graphics, whereby realism is unequally distributed in any given simulation.[2] Yet paradoxically, this inequality is predicated on a historical flattening of the object world. While only a comparatively small number of processes are made available for simulation, that simulation may be enacted equally on any object. That is, while we may consider certain properties to "belong" to certain objects—the shattering of glass, the movement of fur, or the texture of paper—with computer graphics we may simulate these processes on any object, due to its standard form broadly resembling that of any other object. While a materialist methodology might seek to understand the specificity of the object itself—its production, use, or transformation over time—for computer graphics all objects are equal in their construction, and their unique properties may be alienated and applied to any other object—as a texture, class, or algorithm. In this way the same simulated object may be blown up like a balloon, shattered into a thousand pieces, or liquefied down to a viscous puddle with a simple change of presets, and with no regard to what we might understand as the material specificity of the object itself. Objects are no longer bound to their material form and may take on the properties of any other object.

Yet while all objects become alike in that they are subject to the same set of conditions for their construction, a small subset of objects have become particularly salient to the field. These objects are often used as tools in the everyday practice of computer graphics research, deployed in the testing of new graphical algorithms, and built into graphical software as both a visual shorthand for any generic object and a kind of nod to the history of the field. They operate, in effect, as proxy objects.[3] Like a television test card or film leader "china girl," these objects reproduce and test for the generic qualities of a given medium.[4] Unique to the case of graphical standards is that the generic quality these objects contain is precisely "objectness" itself. The most famous of these objects is known as the Utah teapot (figure 3.1). First developed at the University of Utah in 1974, the teapot has become the single most rendered object in the history of computer graphics. At once singular and generic, the teapot stands in for the history of computer graphics and the theory of objects it enacts, such that by examining the history of the teapot, we can map the process by which computer graphics came to

Figure 3.1
A modern rendering of the Utah teapot. Doug Hatfield, 2009. CC BY-SA 3.0.

standardize the object world. Over the past fifty years the teapot has been shaped and reshaped countless times, transformed by tests and algorithms for shading, illumination, material, texture, motion, and more. For each of these transformations we might imagine a teapot, and indeed for each of these a teapot could be rendered. The teapot is in this sense the principal historical object of modern computer graphics: at once everything and nothing, a thing both entirely unremarkable and the most famous object in the history of the field.

Simulating Complexity

By the early 1970s, graphical research was beginning to move away from the challenges of visibility and display. The problem of how to present wireframe models with hidden lines removed had been solved to a reasonable degree of accuracy, but the shapes and forms available for simulation were severely limited. Basic geometric solids were relatively easy to calculate, and a large number of objects could be made through the combination of these simple forms, but simulating objects from the physical world required a range of shapes whose behavior was not yet well defined. Prior to the 1970s, almost all rendered objects were artificial geometries constructed within a line drawing program. While these images often resemble objects from the material world—buildings, chess pieces, circuits, or atoms—they are not derived from any physical object or material. Instead, they are designed or drafted using basic shapes or primitives, such that the range and complexity of objects that could be rendered was extremely limited (plate 9).[5] Then, in the early 1970s, an important shift begins whereby objects are no longer simply constructed ex nihilo but are instead scanned, recorded, and extracted from the material world for digitization. This period likewise marks a shift in both form and function, as computer graphics research moves from a general concern with the display of three-dimensional objects toward the mimetic representation of the physical world through simulation. This shift toward mimesis brought with it a host of new technologies and methods for the construction and calculation of digital objects, as well as new concerns over how to render forms that do not begin their lives within a computer.

The key challenge in rendering the material world is finding ways to produce a functional representation of its complexity within the limitations of a given medium. For computer graphics, the shift from abstraction to mimesis would require an expansion of the techniques used to formalize this representation. Of particular concern was the display of curved and irregular surfaces, as the introduction of curves meant a dramatic increase in the complexity of an object as understood by existing visualization algorithms.[6] As a mathematical system for the visual simulation of digital information, the rendering of irregular forms required a precise and standardized system of calculation—one that would be scalable across a wide range of machines and calculable within the processing limitations of these comparatively early computers. Put another way, in order to simulate material objects as they appeared in the physical world, researchers would need to devise a mathematical solution for parsing complex geometric shapes using relatively simple and highly generalizable methods.

Of course, this challenge was by no means unique to computer graphics. The study of irregular curvature has a long history in both mathematics and design, where the calculation and standardization of complex forms developed alongside standardized techniques for material production. Most notable among these techniques are those used in the design of ships, aircraft, and other slipstream vehicles, whose shape must be both precise and symmetrical if it is to properly cut through water or air. Prior to the 1940s, designers who needed to employ a curved symmetrical surface would draft a line by hand, but in order to transfer that curve evenly from a drawn surface to a ship or model, a particular set of tools was needed.[7] Craftspeople would use a long thin strip of wood known as a "spline" that could be bent to the shape of the desired curve using the drawing as a guide.[8] The wood would be held in place via the tension of the rod, and the shape was maintained through a number of lead weights known as spline ducks, so named for their distinct shape, which resembles the head of a duck (figure 3.2). These ducks would push or pull on the spline at precise points to create the desired curve.[9] The elasticity of the spline material combined with the constraint of the control points, or knots, would cause the strip to take the shape that minimized the energy required for bending it between the fixed points, this being the smoothest possible shape. The curve could then be transferred to a full-size plan and shaped using traditional woodworking methods in a process known as "lofting," so named for the space in which the practice took place, in the upper chamber or attic of a building where there was sufficient room to produce a one-to-one model of these massive streamlined objects.[10]

Figure 3.2
A Boeing engineer drafts a diagram using a spline and spline ducks, 1960s. Courtesy of the Boeing Company.

Beginning in the 1940s, a number of mathematicians worked to understand the function of the curves created by these mechanical splines, culminating in several publications in the late 1950s and early 1960s from researchers at GM, Boeing, and the British Aircraft Corporation who sought to standardize and mechanize the construction of irregular curvature for aircraft design.[11] The technique was quickly imported into other fields of practice, most notably by the French automakers Citroen and Renault, where French engineer Pierre Bézier popularized their use in CAD and computer graphics.[12] Bézier curves, as they would come to be known, are produced by a set of control points that can be manipulated to transform the shape of a curve, functioning as the digital analog to a spline duck to pull a curve in a desired direction (figure 3.3).[13] Unlike earlier wireframe models, which approximate curvature as a series of angled line segments, Bézier curves produce curvature through the simulation of natural processes—that is, the mathematical approximation of multiple forces on a line. In this way, Bézier curves and other spline calculations provided a mathematical model for the construction of irregular forms, and by the late 1960s, Bézier had put these theories into practice with the development of a computerized system for the design and manufacture of cars called UNISURF, which allowed engineers to produce models in miniature that could then be divided into patches, reproduced through numerical control, and assembled into functional prototypes.[14]

Over the past fifty years, Bézier's calculations have become ubiquitous. Because of their flexibility and scalability, Bézier curves are used in almost all CAD programs to model the curve of smooth objects, from cars to toothbrushes, but they are also used for 2D applications in any software that relies on vector graphics such as Adobe Illustrator. In one of their most prominent applications, Bézier curves have radically transformed the

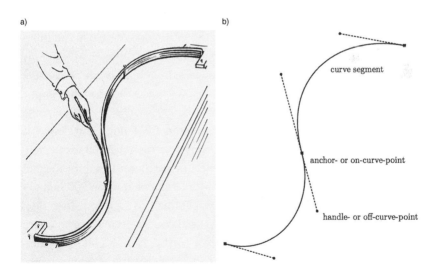

Figure 3.3
A wooden spline fixed with nails and framing squares (left), and a Bézier spline made from two cubic Bézier curves each consisting of two on-curve and two off-curve points (right).

production of fonts and typefaces, with modern desktop publishing systems like PostScript using cubic Bézier curves to draw the curved shapes and lines that make up all digital letterforms.[15] In computer animation, the shape of smooth or curled forms such as hair are often modeled in this way, though one of the most prominent uses of Bézier curves is to model the smooth movement of objects through space, like the bounce of a ball or tactile drag of an icon as you move it across your screen. In digital games Bézier curves are built into the simulation of irregular object movement that must change and adapt, from the flight path of a bird to the patrol of an enemy guard. While these widely varying applications may appear quite different, each shares an investment in the simulation of smooth irregularity in the broadest sense, from shape and form to movement over time. In this sense, the Bézier curve marks an important historical break in the mathematical modeling of irregularity for the purpose of simulation—a transformation that begins with computer graphics.[16]

Of course in order to model a shape in three-dimensions, a curve needs to be interpolated into a surface.[17] The principal figure in this transformation is Steven Coons, considered by many to be the originator of the concept of CAD.[18] Coons was a highly unconventional figure. He held no formal degree, having dropped out of MIT in 1936 after one year as a mathematics major. Working at Chance Vought Aircraft in the 1940s, Coons developed an innovative solution to the problem of surface representation using nonparametric interpolation that would come to be known as the "Coons patch." Following World War II he was hired as an assistant professor at MIT, where he became a founding member of the CAD Project in 1959. While in Cambridge he worked to formalize his mathematical solutions for drafting and design as computational models, including the Coons patch as a method for the representation of irregularly curved surfaces.[19] The patch was first implemented by Timothy Johnson in his dissertation work building on Ivan Sutherland's foundational Sketchpad software, and was formalized by Coons in a 1967 text that came to be known as "The Little Red Book" for its massive influence on the emerging field of geometric design.[20] Titled "Surfaces for Computer-Aided Design of Space Forms," the report presented the notation, mathematical foundation, and intuitive interpretation of a concept that would ultimately become the basis for a number of contemporary methods for surface description, including b-spline and NURB surfaces. In order to construct an object surface, Coons's technique pieced together a collection of adjacent patches with a set of continuity constraints that allowed the surface to hold the curvature expected by the designer. Each patch was designed from a set of boundary curves along with blending functions that defined how the space between each curve was constructed through the interpolated values of the boundaries. Beginning with any number of connected Bézier-style curves, one could use Coons's method to construct a surface patch by interpolating the space between them (figure 3.4).[21]

Significant here is the prevalence of a largely automated mathematical interpolation for the description of surfaces. No longer handcrafted or even hand calculated, objects become shaped by inferences drawn from the edges that bind them, producing a distinct aesthetic form. While the designer is free to modify the constraints of an object to increase its complexity, this aesthetic of interpolation comes to define the shapes of all digital objects derived from this algorithmic tradition. As Coons himself noted in the abstract to his report, this technique for the design, delineation, and mathematical description of bounding surfaces is derived from the design of airplanes, ships, automobiles, and other "sculptured parts."[22] Given the military funding of this research, along with its genesis in the design of military aircraft during World War II, it is unsurprising that some of the earliest digital objects produced using computer-aided techniques were vehicles designed for slipstream movement.[23] Yet from these origins, we can begin to trace the transference of this slipstream aesthetic and its irregular curves into the design of all manner of contemporary built objects, made possible through the growth of CAD in the period immediately following the work of Coons, Bézier, and others. This aesthetic manifests in the smooth

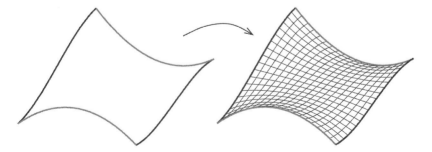

Figure 3.4
A Coons patch produced through the interpolation of a surface connecting each of four boundary curves. Ag2gaeh, 2018. CC BY-SA 4.0.

edges of injection molded plastic and ergonomic curves of objects designed to be gripped and held, such that the blob-like appearance of your water bottle or video game controller marks the digitized curve of a World War II ship's bow cutting through water. For computer graphics, all curves become bounding surfaces shaped by this interpolative mode.

Smooth Surfaces

In standardizing the construction of irregular forms, Bézier curves, Coons patches, and their descendants opened up a new world of shapes to computer graphics.[24] At the same time, this moment marks a split in the field of graphical research, in which two distinct traditions emerge. Prior to the 1970s, much of the research into computer graphics served the dual purpose of construction and simulation. That is, the issues that most interested the field were productive for both researchers who hoped to find new and more efficient ways of building material objects, and researchers interested in finding more realistic ways to simulate the appearance of objects on a computer screen. These fields began to diverge by the early 1970s, with computer-aided geometric design transforming into a distinct discipline around 1974, and research into simulation moving toward rendered images and interactive systems for use in military training, flight simulation, and other fields.[25] Here, *construction* and *representation* become discrete practices with unique interests and investments. Geometry, form, and function remain central to CAD, whose work is the construction of objects within a computer to be built or manufactured in the material world, while representation, appearance, and mimesis remain central to visual simulation, with researchers looking to digitize objects from the physical world to be rendered as computer-generated images. Certainly there is a great deal of overlap in both fields, but it is significant that this period marks the rise of new visual techniques largely disarticulated from the concerns of geometric construction, designed for the mimetic visual representation of physical objects through a new set of algorithmic processes.

Arguably the earliest work in this newly articulated subfield was research into the shading of object surfaces such that they could respond to the simulation of color, light, and shadow as they interact with an object's surface or skin. While a number of techniques for object shading and opacity had been developed in the 1960s, each relied on an early form of flat shading, whereby each visible polygon of a three-dimensional object is shaded with a single color or tone based on the angle between the polygon's surface normal and the direction of the light source (figure 3.5).[26] In this system only one color is assigned to each polygon, and as such flat shading produces blocky and unrealistic images when used to represent smooth or curved surfaces. Thus researchers interested in the realistic simulation of curved surfaces began developing interpolative shading algorithms that could produce images that would more closely approximate the smooth curve of an object defined by the tessellated blocks of a polygon mesh. The University of Utah was the principal site for research into object shading during this period, and in the first half of the 1970s, graduate students Henri Gouraud and Bui Tuong Phong each produced distinct techniques for shaded surfaces still widely in use today. Both Gouraud and Phong moved to Salt Lake City from Paris as part of a wide-ranging effort made by Sutherland

Figure 3.5
Rudimentary flat shading of three-dimensional block letters spelling the word "GRAPHICS," where each surface is assigned a single shade based on the position and intensity of simulated light in the scene. University of Utah, 1968. Courtesy of the Special Collections Department, J. Willard Marriott Library, University of Utah.

to recruit key talent to the university from academic institutions in France, where he believed the most significant mathematical research was being done.[27] Gouraud had graduated from the École Centrale Paris in 1967, and on the advice of an adviser at the Institut supérieur de l'aéronautique et de l'espace, moved to Utah in September 1968 to work with Evans and Sutherland. On arriving Gouraud had no experience with computer graphics, and had only worked in Fortran and numerical computation as part of his training at the École Centrale. Nonetheless, he quickly took to the culture of problem solving that defined the Utah program, and began developing tools for the shading and display of complex objects. As discussed in chapter 2, Gouraud's colleague John Warnock had recently produced a functional solution for hidden surface removal, though it required long render times and the mediation of long-exposure photography in order to produce a visible image. Another colleague, PhD student Gary Watkins, was attempting to solve these issues by designing a technique to display solid objects in real time on a television CRT. His technique was based on comparing vector lines and the facets between them in order to determine their points of intersection, thereby eliminating hidden facets and speeding up render time significantly.[28] Both Warnock's and Watkins's algorithms were in wide use at Utah, and would be crucial for Gouraud's work, but in order to take advantage of them, he could not use the curvature techniques that had been established by Bézier and Coons as they did not utilize polygonal surfaces, relying instead on interpolated curves. If Gouraud were to break down each Bézier surface into a collection of faceted polygons, it would create an angular appearance to what were meant to be smooth curved surfaces. In order to quickly render smooth and irregular object shapes, Gouraud needed to develop a technique to produce the appearance of a smooth surface even when the geometry of an object was composed of angular polygons.

The idea came to him in a signal processing course taught by Utah professor Thomas Stockham: if he created the appearance of a smooth surface with proper shading, the eye would simply ignore the angular form.[29] In other words, if he privileged the appearance of the image over any underlying geometry, he could calculate shaded images in real time. A quick Polaroid test image of a spherical dome confirmed the results, as despite the polygonal construction of the object, it appeared smooth and seamless to the human eye. Initially this work was met with resistance by Gouraud's advisers. Sutherland did not see smooth shading as a fundamental problem for the design and construction of objects, as it operated only at the level of rendered output as an image, and hence did not affect the underlying construction of the object itself. A subsequent test image of a three-dimensional airplane model convinced Sutherland of the algorithm's validity, and he encouraged Gouraud to take up the shading algorithm as the topic of his thesis (figure 3.6).[30] Ultimately Gouraud developed a technique for smooth shading that estimates the surface normal of each vertex in a polygonal 3D object and makes lighting calculations based on a reflection model.[31] In effect, Gouraud's shading algorithm applies the interpolation seen previously in the simulation of curves to the polygon mesh of modeled surfaces, using the vertices of these surface polygons as the data points from which to build its interpolation.

In the same year Gouraud defended his dissertation, the department at Utah took on a new graduate student from the Institut national de recherche en informatique et en automatique in Paris—a young Vietnamese man named Bui Tuong Phong whose family had fled to France during the Vietnam War.[32] While at Utah, Phong extended Gouraud's work on shading and reflection algorithms for 3D rendered models, producing a shading model that improved on some of the difficulties in Gouraud's algorithm by making a separate color computation for each individual pixel.[33] This "Phong shading" is much more computationally expensive than "Gouraud shading,"

a)   b)

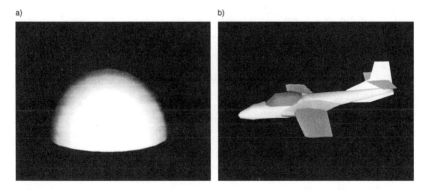

Figure 3.6
The first Polaroid image made to test Henri Gouraud's smooth shading algorithm (left), and the shaded image of a plane that convinced Ivan Sutherland (right), ca. 1970. Courtesy of Henri Gouraud.

FLAT SHADING   GOURAUD SHADING   PHONG SHADING

Figure 3.7
Modern implementations of flat, Gouraud, and Phong shading algorithms made in
Blender 2.79. Davi.trip, 2017 CC-BY-SA-4.0.

and as such, it was considered highly experimental at the time of its development (figure 3.7). Arguably more influential was Phong's simultaneous
development of a model for the reflection of light on curved surfaces, which
allowed for the rendering of highlights before it was possible to create rendered reflections through ray tracing, the technique widely used by contemporary software to simulate the movement of light between objects.[34]

Significantly, neither of these methods transforms the geometry of an
object itself; they simply alter the appearance of a given surface. A dome
rendered using Gouraud or Phong shading will still have visible flat edges
along its outer surface, though this effect is minimized by the shading illusion. Here the split between computer-aided geometric design and rendering techniques falls into sharp relief. While computer-aided models for
engineering and design are built to precise material specification, such
that the model and object are mathematically identical, shading and other
rendering techniques are developed to produce the illusion of a material
effect (smooth surfaces, light, color, etc.), but do not necessarily reflect any
underlying mathematical or material form. While one might presume that
these illusionistic algorithms are simply small steps on the road to a more
accurate model for material effects such as curvature or smooth surfaces, in
fact they have remained largely unchanged for the past forty years. Both
Gouraud and Phong shading are still industry standards, and can be found
in all contemporary 3D computer graphics suites such as Autodesk Maya,
Blender, or Cinema 4D.

In the work of Gouraud and Phong, we can see the break of image from object—a decoupling of geometry from visualization that has come to define the contemporary field of graphical research. This is likewise the moment that the illusory quality of graphical images becomes formalized at the algorithmic level such that the images produced by these systems no longer reflect the underlying architecture of the objects they represent. In contrast with the dream of perfect simulation articulated by Sutherland's "Ultimate Display," Gouraud's display—one that we have inherited and shapes all manner of contemporary images—is a negotiation between image and object, in which each serves as a contextual interface with distinct applications. It is a display that sacrifices accuracy for efficiency, privileging appearance. In spite of the popular narratives of technological development associated with graphical techniques for visual simulation, the realism of computer graphics remains highly conscripted, and is limited to the visual appearance of an object largely divorced from its physical or geometric structure. This split persists well into the present, and has been complicated by subsequent splits with real-time graphics for digital games, raster graphics for interface design, and countless other subfields that remain structured by research first developed in the 1960s, even as they become differentiated into unique fields of practice.

Model Experimentation

Gouraud and Phong's work coincides with a period of intensive research at the University of Utah, in which graduates and faculty were looking for a new set of objects to be used in the testing of various algorithms for material simulation. As Utah graduate Frank Crow recalls in an article for *IEEE Computer Graphics and Animation*,

> There was a constant shortage of data for interesting shapes to be displayed with these algorithms. Tiring quickly of spheres, cubes, tubes, and other easily generated shapes, interesting efforts were often mounted to capture more elaborate data. One set of efforts took the form of developing automated methods for capturing physical measurements. 3D digitizers using mechanical means, photogrammetry, and even lasers were developed. However, much of the interesting data was completely handcrafted.[35]

The data were pulled, most often, from that which was near—either sketched on the fly or traced and mapped directly from the surface of

Figure 3.8
Model plane marked for digitization, ca. 1970. Courtesy of the Special Collections
Department, J. Willard Marriott Library, University of Utah.

existing physical objects (figure 3.8). Here the field enters a period of experimentation where objects derived from the physical world were altered to
conform to the parameters of graphical simulation—a period marked by
speculative methods for production and design, prior to the standardization of the digital object form as a discrete set of techniques on which
subsequent research could be performed. Many of the resulting object simulations were the first of their kind, but their primacy is less significant
than the ways they assisted in the formalization of the tools, methods, and
conceptual framework that allowed for a standard object to emerge.

One of the earliest attempts at digitizing a physical object for computer
simulation was Marsha Sutherland's Volkswagen Beetle—the object with
which this book begins. In many ways the Beetle was an ideal object. Its
iconic design predates computational methods for automobile manufacturing, but is made digital at precisely the moment that Bézier and others were

radically transforming techniques for the design and production of automobiles. Likewise, its distinctive curved shape—made famous by a series of minimalist ad campaigns by New York's Doyle Dane Bernbach ad agency (figure 3.9)—was irregular enough to present a set of unique challenges for full-scale digitization. In order to digitize the car, students divided it into individual parts such as the hood, roof, and trunk, which were then measured in a somewhat-rudimentary fashion by drawing lines directly onto the surface of the vehicle. As Utah graduate Robert McDermott recalls,

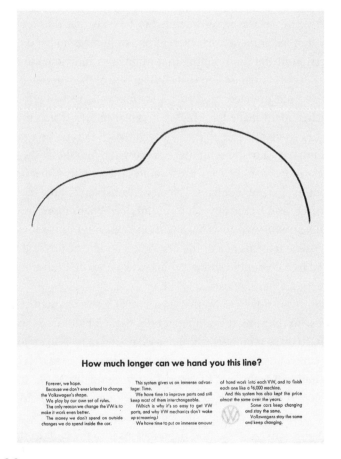

How much longer can we hand you this line?

Forever, we hope. Because we don't ever intend to change the Volkswagen's shape.
We play by our own set of rules. The only reason we change the VW is to make it work even better.
The money we don't spend on outside changes we do spend inside the car.

This system gives us an immense advantage: Time.
We have time to improve parts and still keep most of them interchangeable.
(Which is why it's so easy to get VW parts, and why VW mechanics don't wake up screaming.)
We have time to put an immense amount

of hand work into each VW, and to finish each one like a $16,000 machine.
And this system has also kept the price almost the same over the years.
Some cars keep changing and stay the same.
Volkswagens stay the same and keep changing.

Figure 3.9
1960s' Volkswagen advertisement by Doyle Dane Bernbach showcasing the Beetle's distinctive curved shape.

Jim Clark (PhD '72) and I were taller so we arranged to have the higher points of the car. Bui Tuong Phong (PhD '73) and Raphael Rom (PhD '75) were shorter so they measured the lower sections. . . . A volleyball stanchion and joints in the pavement formed a three-dimensional reference system. We used yardsticks to measure the x, y, and z coordinates of the painted points on the car surface.[36]

As the car was a symmetrical object, the students measured only one of its halves, which could be flipped and mirrored to create a complete simulation. Once each element had been extracted, the final data set was entered as a list of point coordinates into text data files and rendered using a system developed by Watkins to imprint shaded images onto a direct film recorder.[37] Significantly, the car was never intended to be constructed as a whole. As this was a class assignment, each student had only measured and produced a small section of the car, resulting in a number of individual images and geometric data of car panels and parts. When one of the computer lab staffers decided to put the pieces together, they found that small errors on the part of each student made for a highly irregular model, which took weeks to adjust into an identifiable object. The technician, Dennis Ting, compared the human time cost to the computer time cost and found that the image of the VW cost more than the car's street value, and even this final image was not without its share of problems. The model consisted of little more than a skin or surface, and lacked any depth or interior. What's more, it was missing several key features such as headlights and wheels. Despite these limitations, the Beetle remains one of the first objects from the physical world to be rendered by a computer, and was quickly taken up by Utah students as a test object for graphical research.

That same year, Edwin Catmull used a similar system to digitize his own hand for use in the earliest example of fully shaded halftone 3D computer animation. To make his model, Catmull used plaster of paris to mold a cast of his hand, which was then covered with a thin layer of latex so that polygons could be drawn directly onto the model's surface (figure 3.10). As Catmull recalled, "it was necessary to extract the three-dimensional coordinates of some 270 corner points defining the surface of the hand, organize them into about 350 polygons, and organize the polygons into the parts of the hand" in order to produce an accurate model.[38] Once the hand had been mapped, it was digitized using a coordinate measuring machine consisting of a table on which a large gantry-style rig was constructed with an articulated arm. The arm was fitted with a grasping device that, with the push of a foot pedal,

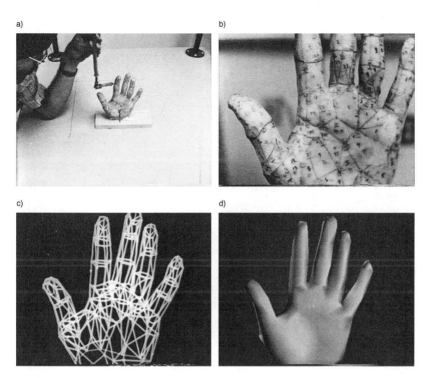

Figure 3.10
Constructing the plaster model of Edwin Catmull's hand (top) and its computer-generated equivalent in wireframe and smooth shading (bottom). Edwin Catmull and Fred Parke, *Halftone Animation* (1972), 16 mm, http://vimeo.com/16292363.

captured the precise location of the object it was touching in threespace. By capturing each of the vertices of the plaster model, Catmull was able to digitally reconstruct the hand from its polygons.[39]

The subsequent short film—produced with researcher Fred Parke, and featuring his work on the computer animation of faces—is one of the first films produced using modern graphical techniques—that is, as a collection of shaded polygons that simulate a moving object (figure 3.11).[40] This distinction is subtle but significant. Earlier animated films, like those made at Bell Labs in the late 1960s using Ken Knowlton's BEFLIX program language, produced the visual animation of shapes through a manipulation of the pixels of a screen image, creating the illusion of three dimensions.[41] Catmull's system takes three-dimensionally modeled objects and simulates them in accordance with an internal logic. Indeed, this was the principal

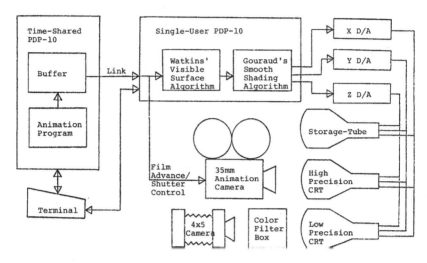

Figure 3.11

System diagram for Edwin Catmull and Fred Parke's animated film. Fred Parke, *Computer Generated Animation of Faces*, Technical Report UTEC-CSs-72–120 (Salt Lake City: University of Utah, 1972), 456. Courtesy of Fred Parke.

contribution of Catmull's research. While the model produced by Catmull is quite striking in its accuracy, it was developed largely to test a programming language called MOtion Picture (MOP), which Catmull developed that same year as part of his dissertation research. As discussed in chapter 4, MOP uses object-oriented principles to manipulate graphical models as objects within a relational system. Here again, as with the hidden surface algorithm, we see a move from image space to object space. While early systems manipulated image output to create the illusion of movement, Catmull's system programs the simulation of movement into the object itself. The resulting images in turn become the progenitor for an entire practice of image making, as both Catmull's hand and one of Parke's faces were subsequently used in Richard Heffron's 1976 film *Futureworld*, making them the earliest examples of 3D computer animation in a feature film (figure 3.12).[42]

Object qua Object

Having established the basic forms and methods for digital modeling, an entire world of simulation opened up to the field. Researchers began modeling, scanning, and capturing all manner of objects, transforming them

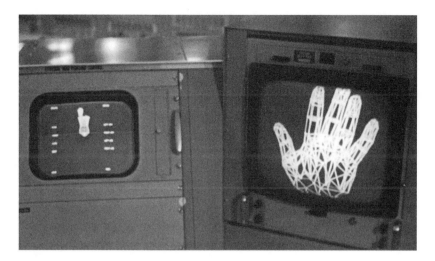

Figure 3.12
Frame capture from Richard Heffron's *Futureworld* (1976), showing a wireframe model of Edwin Catmull's hand.

into subjects of research. These objects in turn formed the basis for subsequent research into optical and environmental phenomena, such as shading, color, reflectance, and light. In this sense, the graphical object becomes a medium in its own right, serving as the ground onto which these algorithmic processes could be applied and tested. In this early moment, the labor of producing one's own object for testing was substantial. To model, scan, digitize, and render an object simply to test an algorithm for light reflectance on its surface would have been be an enormous task, and so researchers started to trade and circulate a limited set of object forms that would become icons among graphics researchers for decades. These objects could be quickly and easily rendered so that the work of testing could be performed.

It was in this context that Martin Newell was conducting his doctoral research at the University of Utah, having emigrated in 1972 from England, where he worked for a government-funded research institute for CAD techniques known as the CADCentre.[43] Newell's research at Utah dealt with techniques for what he called the "procedure modeling" of graphical object forms.[44] To visualize his work, Newell needed objects that exemplified the then challenges of the field, drawing first on Sutherland's VW Bug model to demonstrate polygonal rendering procedures.[45] Newell also wanted to test objects constructed using Bézier curves, which would require an accessible and recognizable object that could clearly demonstrate object curvature in the final render. Describing this challenge to his wife, Sandra, while at home one day for afternoon tea, she suggested he model their teapot—a simple, white, ceramic, German-made Melitta she had recently purchased at the Zion's Cooperative Mercantile Institution in downtown Salt Lake City, just across from Temple Square (figure 3.13).[46] Newell quickly took a rough sketch of the teapot's profile on graph paper, capturing the essence of its shape but not its precise dimensions (plate 10).[47] From here he guessed at the location of suitable control points for the cubic Bézier splines that would form the teapot's curved surface, and then measured these points using the graph paper grid.[48] To turn this sketch into a three-dimensional model, Newell treated the lid, rim, and body of the profile sketch as a surface of revolution that could be carried around 360 degrees to form a closed surface. He then estimated the control points for the handle and spout, and constructed them using three-dimensional tubes. Once the data set had been generated, it was processed into a series of patch parameters that

Figure 3.13
The original Utah teapot, housed in the Computer History Museum in Mountain View, California. © Mark Richards. Courtesy of the Computer History Museum.

could be input into a line drawing program using a Tektronix storage tube connected to a DEC PDP-10 minicomputer in order to display the teapot as a wireframe (figure 3.14). The final patch array consisted of 144 numbers, but infamously lacks any bottom geometry.[49]

In its initial context, the teapot was not singled out as unique or significant, and was modeled and rendered alongside a full tea set complete with cups, saucers, spoons, and a creamer.[50] It was not until a year later that the teapot began to gain recognition, when it was used in a paper coauthored by Newell and his colleague Jim Blinn to demonstrate and expand on the texture mapping technique that had been developed by Catmull the previous year.[51] Titled "Texture and Reflection in Computer Generated Images," the paper was a massive leap forward in terms of visual realism, with over a half-dozen permutations on the teapot with various examples of texture, lighting, and reflection (figure 3.15). The decision to use the teapot as the

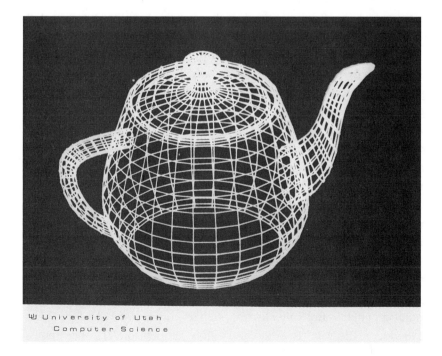

Figure 3.14
Early wireframe render of the Utah teapot, ca. 1974. Note the model lacks any bottom geometry. Courtesy of the Computer History Museum and University of Utah's School of Computing.

principal object of the study was made by Blinn, who saw it as an ideal object for testing as its surface textures could be made to resemble ceramic glazes with varying degrees of reflectance, producing a diverse set of highly realistic images.[52] The pot's simple, modern shape was also an ideal fit for the then-current challenges to the field: it was a convex object, contained saddle points, had a concave element (the hole in the handle), self-shadowed, had hidden surface issues, and looked reasonable when displayed without a complex surface texture. In other words, it was complex enough to test the problems that challenged the field, but was also an elegant, simple, and recognizable design.

Significantly, Blinn's version of the teapot is squatter than Newell's original model. On a 2006 SIGGRAPH special panel commemorating the history of the teapot as icon and object, Blinn recalled that the model was initially scaled in the vertical axis during a lab demo for ARPA shortly after its initial render.[53] Art historian Ann-Sophie Lehmann has suggested this was an attempt by Blinn at an unsuccessful joke, implying that the Department of Defense would be particularly interested in simulations of squashing things.[54] This anecdote was given as a corrective to the often-misquoted story that Blinn initially rendered the teapot on a frame buffer developed by E&S, whose pixels were not square but instead rectangular, such that in order to make the model conform to the pixel raster, Blinn squashed it into its now-iconic shape. Yet in what is likely the earliest historical account of the teapot, written by Crow in 1987, Blinn refuses the anecdotal narrative form altogether, noting that the teapot was scaled and transformed a number of times in its early life, and the teapot's final shape was simply an aesthetic choice, stating, "We thought it looked good."[55] These conflicting efforts to mythologize the origins of this object speak to the challenge of historicizing the quotidian work of research along with the arbitrary nature of the teapot as a singular, specific, and unique object whose very value is its function as multiple, generic, and universal.

It was this secondary model that Blinn would further popularize in a number of publications after leaving Utah to work at NASA's Jet Propulsion Laboratory. The data set would also follow Catmull to NYIT, then Industrial Light & Magic, and ultimately Pixar, where it would be used in a wide range of test images throughout the 1970s and early 1980s. Indeed, one effect of the large network of influence that the Utah program had on the subsequent development of the field of computer graphics was the wide

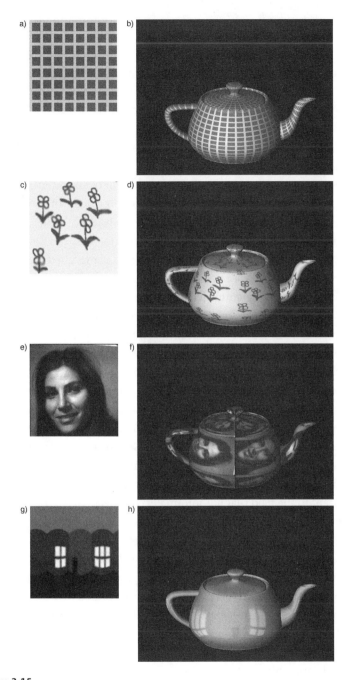

Figure 3.15
Early texture mapping tests by Martin Newell and Jim Blinn, including textures for simulating reflectance (bottom). Jim Blinn and Martin Newell, "Texture and Reflection in Computer Generated Images," *Communications of the ACM* 19, no. 10 (October 1976): 542–547. Courtesy of Jim Blinn and Martin Newell.

distribution of Newell's teapot through informal networks to a variety of research institutions. Many of these research sites were themselves networked via the ARPANET, which had expanded by the mid-1970s, giving Utah students and faculty access to dozens of research sites across the country. Utah was one of four hubs on the initial deployment of the ARPANET in 1969, such that some of the first pieces of information to be transferred via the distributed network that is the progenitor of our modern internet were in fact graphical data, and would have eventually included the simple sets of numerical patch strings that make up the Utah teapot. Later, in 1986, Crow posted the original teapot Bézier patch control points to the internet, where it was copied and replicated by researchers across the United States and Europe.[56] As the data set was free to use, anyone working on a new texture, lighting, or effects algorithm could quickly drop in the teapot as a test object, rather than go through the process of designing and entering their own geometric data. Due to this broad accessibility, along with the model's relative simplicity and effective geometry, it was readily taken up by computer graphics researchers at various institutions.

Over time, the teapot has become an icon. While it would be impossible to accurately substantiate the claim, the Utah teapot is likely the most rendered object in the history of the medium.[57] Over the past forty years it has appeared in thousands of research papers, SIGGRAPH panels, and graphics demos. If we were to count every instance and frame in which the teapot has been rendered, they would surely number in the billions. The teapot is so important to the field that it is informally considered one of the base geometric primitives from which all other objects are constructed. In a famous ray-traced image by James Arvo and David Kirk from 1987, the teapot sits atop a stone column next to the five platonic solids—those regular, convex polyhedrons with congruent faces of regular polygons and the same number of faces meeting at each vertex.[58] The image is titled "The Six Platonic Solids," and has given the teapot the playful nickname "teapotahedron" (figure 3.16). In most contemporary rendering and geometry programs such as AutoCAD, Lightwave 3D, and 3ds Max, the teapot is included as a default object and can easily be dropped into any simulation. Some RenderMan-compliant renderers even support the teapot as a built-in geometric primitive accessible by calling `RiGeometry("teapot", RI_NULL)`.

That said, the teapot is not simply some technical tool, known only to researchers and graphics professionals. As computer graphics have become

Figure 3.16
James Arvo and David Kirk, *The Six Platonic Solids*, 1987. Featured on the cover of the February 1988 issue of the *Communications of the Association for Computing Machinery*. The "teapotahedron" can be seen in the center back row. Courtesy of the Association for Computing Machinery.

more visible and accessible to everyday users, so too has the teapot. It appears as an Easter egg in a number of places, perhaps first as an object in the Windows operating system's "3D Pipes" screen saver, released in 1994 alongside Windows NT 3.5.[59] In 1995, the teapot was featured prominently in Pixar's first feature-length film, *Toy Story*, during a tea party scene, and it also appears in an October 1995 episode of *The Simpsons*, which featured a brief scene rendered in 3D (plate 11).[60] Since 2003, the teapot has been the unofficial mascot for Pixar's RenderMan software, with the company producing custom windup teapot toys to be distributed from its booth each year at the annual SIGGRAPH conference.[61] The teapot in this context functions as both a nod to the history of the medium and knowing wink to those who understand its broader significance. Its appearance as an everyday object allows it to hide in plain sight—a graphical analog to Erwin Panofsky's "disguised symbolism," there for knowing eyes to see and interpret.[62] Indeed the teapot has become a kind of shorthand for computer graphics itself—a metonymy that stands in for an industry, art form, and field of practice.

Yet this is more than simply figurative, as the teapot can in a very material sense stand in for any and every graphical object. In standardizing the object world and the means by which it is simulated, computer graphics creates this broad equivalence in which one object can serve as the functional equivalent of any object and the part embodies the whole. Media standards are by no means exclusive to computer graphics, as almost all media formats have a set of standard objects that are used to gauge the proper function of the technologies required for their reproduction.[63] Such standards are a byproduct of mass production, allowing each iteration or reproduction to be tested against a given standard that conforms to the technical specificity of the medium. Unlike other media standards, however, the teapot does not test for any one particular function, but instead serves as a placeholder or proxy for the simulation at hand—a generic signaling of any object whatsoever. As such, the teapot transforms to suit the needs of research. In a given simulation it might be made of glass, metal, or even water; if dropped, it could shatter, float, or bounce; we could cover it in hair, fill it with liquid, or make it squash, stretch, and dance, as suits our need.

That this particular object has become an icon within the field of computer graphics is due largely to chance and to the influential culture of research that thrived at the University of Utah in this period. Nonetheless, in the teapot's role as standard-bearer for an entire field of practice, we can see a much broader historical transformation taking place. Looking back to Newell's original research, it is clear the teapot was never meant to become a universal object. Rather, the goal of his work was to model a new way of thinking about graphical objects themselves. Prior to this period graphical objects were modeled from a set of base primitives, such as polygons, which were stored in a fixed database. For each object in a scene, the computer would need to construct a geometric model from these primitives, which took a great deal of time and processing power, and limited the forms of objects that a given program could render. For his dissertation, Newell proposed a highly flexible system that would store complete objects that could be rendered as individual instances and modified using a set of transformations. As he notes, "In many modeling situations the items to be processed bear a strong resemblance to one another. Significant savings can be realized in such cases if the items can be represented by a single model defined in terms of a set of parameters. Each item can then be considered a parameterized instance of this single representation."[64] In effect, each object in a given scene is an instance of a generic master object, or what we would today consider an object-oriented design. This system allowed for images of greater complexity to be rendered much more easily, since each object did not need to be modeled from scratch but could instead be executed as an instance of an existing master object. Perhaps a more fitting object to represent Newell's research would have been the massive grid of chess pawns visible in the third and final image set included in his dissertation (figure 3.17). While chess pawns are some of the earliest test objects to be rendered in computer graphics due to their simple symmetrical shape, Newell's contribution was to make every pawn an instance of a single object, allowing for an exponential growth in the complexity of a rendered scene.

This structuring paradigm may seem obvious now given that nearly all computational systems we interact with are shaped by this same logic, but in examining Newell's system we can see the true historical transformation that the teapot exemplifies. Just as the teapot is both a physical object shaped by a distinct history and a generic form extracted from it, it marks the moment in which computer graphics adopts this broad ontology whereby all objects are functionally equivalent, mere instances of any

a)

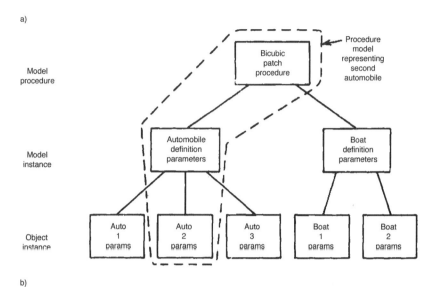

b)

Figure 3.17
A visualization of the procedure modeling structure of Martin Newell's program (top), in which its object-oriented structure of inheritance is clearly visible, and a grid of chess pawns rendered using this technique (bottom). Martin Newell, "The Utilization of Procedure Models in Digital Image Synthesis" (PhD diss., University of Utah, 1975), 45, 87. Courtesy of Martin Newell.

object whatsoever. Every render of the teapot is an instance of Newell's model, just as every graphical object is, in some sense, an instance of that original Melitta.

World Building

Despite this historical flattening of all objects into a single teapot, it is telling what specific objects we find at the origin of this expanding field—those things that first became legible as objects for simulation to begin with. As with early research by Coons and Bézier into modeling irregular curves and surfaces, at Utah we find a proliferation of ships, planes, and other vehicles that are readily modeled and measured. Unsurprisingly, one of the first applications for this research—and a principal motivation for its funding by the Department of Defense—was its use in flight and vehicle simulation for military and commercial training. As with the history of computing broadly, it is the potential for future military application that drives research into early computer graphics, such that it is no surprise that these are some of the first objects made legible to computation. Soon, however, we find a proliferation of everyday objects that speak to the culture of the individuals that reproduced them through simulation. These were the objects that were ready to hand as researchers began their work, and in that moment of recognition became transformed into objects of study to be graphed and modeled mathematically. The significance of this nearness is precisely the way it exemplifies the kind of world building that computational simulation enacts: only that which is knowable as present may become an object of study for simulation.[65]

This contextual shift in spheres of practice between the site of research and that of everyday life is woven throughout these histories, though the historical significance of such objects can be difficult to capture as their origins are distilled over time into anecdotes that often elide the material, affective, and embodied practices that made legible a particular set of objects. What does it mean, for instance, that in this space of research, in which almost no female scientists are historically remembered, a teapot appears, purchased by the wife of a young computer scientist at a Mormon department store in Salt Lake City? What does it mean that what few women we find in this history are wives and partners offering teapots, and in more than one instance, their faces or bodies to be modeled and measured? While the earliest objects

Gouraud used to test his algorithm were spheres and airplanes, the most striking and widely remembered is the model of a face, which Gouraud digitized manually from a photograph of his wife, Sylvie. First drawing polygonal sections directly onto her skin, he then photographed the results to build a digital model in the Utah graphics laboratory (figure 3.18).[66] The resulting life mask is among the earliest examples of a complete and shaded human face, though Parke would create a similar model soon after using his own wife's face as the basis for his experiments in computer animation (figure 3.19). Our proximity to particular objects in the world both limits and defines that which is made knowable and therefore available for simulation. This is true not only for the category of objects themselves—be they teapots or airplanes—but for how we understand and in turn describe them.

If one inspects the photographic collection of E&S, it appears that the entire staff responsible for the assembly of computer hardware in the early 1970s were women (figure 3.20). Their presence here recalls the hidden labor of women at a time when women *were* computers, responsible for entering punched card data and running the machines that made computation work.[67] Theirs was the labor of the material objects of computing, of the hardware itself. It is telling that the presupposed immateriality of computer graphics elides the same labor of circuits and soldering that these women made possible, that it is women who are traced but leave few traces of their own work and influence on the production of a new form of technical practice. This labor of modeling and simulation points to the central contradiction of computer graphics as a technology shaped by a deeply material history that insists on its own virtuality.[68] Indeed, countless objects in use today hold a material connection to these generic object forms first shaped nearly half a century ago: the bow of a ship, the curve of a face, the handle of a teapot. Yet this connection is too often abstracted out and occluded by a culture of use that insists on its own immateriality as something that emerges without labor and without history.

Standard Worlds

In 1989, the SIGGRAPH convention for research into computer graphics was held in Boston, home to the Computer Museum, which has since been shuttered. On display were a number of artifacts from the museum's collection, including the original Melitta teapot that inspired Newell to create

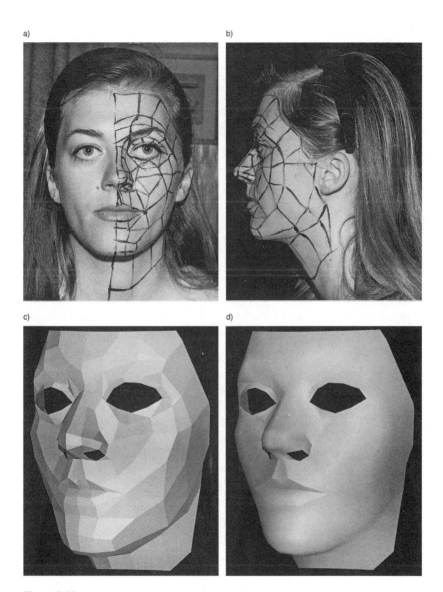

Figure 3.18
Photographs of Sylvie Gouraud marked with polygons for digitization (top), and subsequent models of her face in flat and Gouraud shading (bottom), 1971. Courtesy of the Computer History Museum and Henri Gouraud.

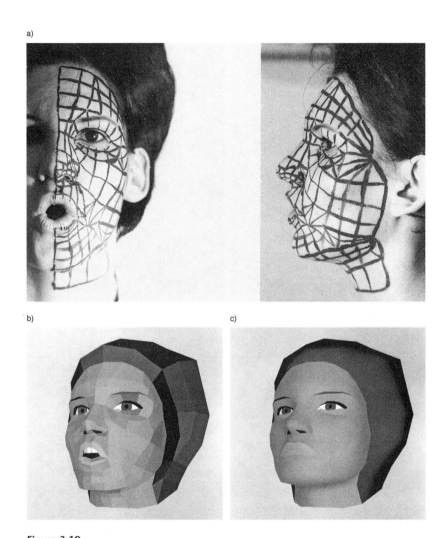

Figure 3.19
Photographs of Vicky Parke marked with polygons (top), and subsequent digital models used in computer animation (bottom), 1972. Frederic Parke, *Computer Generated Animation of Faces*, Technical Report UTEC-CSs-72–120 (Salt Lake City: University of Utah, 1972), 2, 27. Courtesy of Fred Parke.

a)

b)

Figure 3.20
Women working on circuits and other computer hardware in the clean room of the Evans and Sutherland Computer Corporation (top), and a woman soldering a circuit board at the Evans and Sutherland Computer Corporation (bottom), early 1970s. Courtesy of the Special Collections Department, J. Willard Marriott Library, University of Utah.

his computer graphics icon, donated by Sandra Newell five years prior in 1984. Surrounded by photos of the teapot from its fifteen-year history, the exhibit functioned as both a deliberation on the place of the teapot in the field and a vivid reflection of the field's most enduring concerns—geometry, light, texture, and surface. The teapot itself was housed in a small display box under which a number of switches were rigged. Next to the box was a CRT monitor of the same size displaying an image of the Utah teapot (plate 12). Visitors were prompted to flip the switches under the physical teapot, which triggered a set of colored lights to shine on its surface. In response to these switches, the CRT image would change to match the light of the physical model, offering its simulated pair. Through this playful presentation, the exhibit restages the primal scene of computer graphics, prompting viewers to ask themselves: in what ways does one approximate the other?

Of course, the teapot that can be summoned by any RenderMan-compliant software with a simple string of code is not the same as that teapot purchased by Sandra Newell in 1974, which now sits behind glass at the Computer History Museum in Mountain View, California. Nonetheless, their relationship is not simply one of source and simulation. From the anecdotes of its origins, the Utah teapot sought to approximate of the materiality of its original—the irregular curve of its iconic midcentury design, the legibility of its shape and form. Yet unlike the vessel purchased half a century ago, the Utah teapot has no bottom and can hold no liquid, save perhaps for a liquid simulation. Stranger still, our ceramic teapot could just as easily be rendered *as* liquid: a translucent pot held impossibly together, reflecting simulated light not off its surface but through its bright clear body. The Utah teapot can be any number of things the Melitta cannot, in that it may simulate any form of object that has been made legible to the material structure of graphical simulation. While it is tempting to dismiss such simulations as mere representation lacking any material basis in the world, this chimeric quality points to computer graphics' long-standing investment in the simulation of material form—how an object looks, changes over time, interacts with other objects, or transforms when it is bent and broken. This is an investment that begins in this precise historical moment, when objects from the physical world were first digitized and transformed such that their material qualities could become disarticulated onto a flattened plane of object simulation. In examining the history of the teapot, we illuminate the materiality of the medium of computer graphics in the cultural and technical context of its production—a materiality that, while often highly encoded and effaced, persists. It is the product of decades of research into geometric modeling and visualization, such that objects we see now as graphical simulations are shaped by the long and negotiated process through which computer science first developed a theory and model of the object. In time, this theory will become disarticulated from these rendered geometries, abstracted into a broad structuring logic that escapes the frame of the visible image.

4 Object Paradigms: On the Origins of Object Orientation

Daughter: Daddy, why do things have outlines?

Father: Do they? I don't know. What sort of things do you mean?

D: I mean when I draw things, why do they have outlines?

F: Well, what about other sorts of things—a flock of sheep? or a conversation? Do they have outlines?

D: Don't be silly. I can't draw a conversation. I mean *things*.

—Gregory Bateson, *Steps to an Ecology of Mind*

In creating the possibility for computational mediality, object orientation opens the rigid, linear logic of serial computation onto the brute messiness of the world, inviting the entire breadth of lived experiences to be incorporated into a self-fulfilling, self-reinforcing feedback loop. The more our culture is reordered as object oriented, the more the belief of systems theory and its ideological offspring . . . become empirically reified. After all, object orientation was never about computing a solution to a problem; rather, it is about creating a believable simulation.

—Casey Alt, "Objects of Our Affection"

In his early history of the Smalltalk programming language, Alan Kay describes his first meeting with David Evans on beginning his graduate work at the University of Utah in 1966: "On Dave's desk was a foot-high stack of brown covered documents, one of which he handed to me: 'Take this and read it.' Every newcomer got one. The title was 'Sketchpad: A man-machine graphical communication system.'"[1] Produced between 1961 and 1963 by a young Ivan Sutherland as part of his dissertation research at MIT, Sketchpad is one of the most influential pieces of software ever written. Using an x-y point plotter and light pen as its interface, Sketchpad allowed researchers to create and manipulate lines and shapes directly on the screen of a computer, organizing them into "objects" that could later be recalled and "instances" that could be manipulated en masse. Sketchpad was the first program to experiment with computer animation, use a rudimentary form of inheritance between objects, develop a gestural interface for manipulating screen objects, and much more. The program is widely regarded as the first modern interactive graphical system, and served as inspiration for thousands of early researchers in the nascent field of computer graphics. Kay would later describe Sketchpad as the first object-oriented software system and nonprocedural programming language ever written for its treatment of graphics as expressive, interactive objects.

After meeting with Evans, Kay sat down at his desk and discovered his first assignment: "On [my desk] was a pile of tapes and listings, and a note: 'This is the Algol for the 1108. It doesn't work. Please make it work.' The latest graduate student gets the latest dirty task."[2] In fact it was much more than the Algol for the UNIVAC 1108; it was a rough English transliteration of Ole-Johan Dahl and Kristen Nygaard's Simula programming language, developed from 1962 to 1967 at the Norwegian Computing Center in Oslo, and arguably the first object-oriented language ever written.[3] After several days examining the program listing, Kay had a revelation:

> What Simula was allocating were structures very much like the instances of Sketchpad. There were descriptions that acted like masters and they could create instances, each of which was an independent entity. What Sketchpad called masters and instances, Simula called activities and processes. Moreover, Simula was a procedural language for controlling Sketchpad-like objects. . . . This was the big hit, and I have not been the same since.[4]

Graphical objects in Sutherland's Sketchpad behaved like linguistic objects in Dahl and Nygaard's Simula. They both share a theory of what an object is and how it relates to the world around it—that is, they both posit a new kind of computational ontology derived from objects as they are understood and engaged in the world. This revelation marked the beginning of a transformation in the structure and function of computational systems, and we now live in a world shaped by this ontological claim.

Kay was one of the first students recruited by Evans on founding the Utah program in 1965. A highly unconventional student, in the five years prior to joining the graduate program at Utah he had failed out of an undergraduate degree in biology, worked as a guitar instructor, and served in the

United States Air Force working on several early computers, including the IBM 1401 and Burroughs B500.[5] While Kay ultimately returned to complete a BS in mathematics and molecular biology at the University of Colorado at Boulder, he arrived at Utah with almost no knowledge of computer graphics and a wildly inconsistent transcript. Nonetheless he was quickly recruited by Evans, who made a policy of admitting students based on background and experience rather than academic performance.[6] Students were then put to a trial by fire that encouraged independent research driven toward solving key problems. As discussed in each of the previous chapters, most students completed dissertations focusing narrowly on a single issue, developing an improvement in techniques for hidden surface removal or a more efficient shading algorithm. By contrast, Kay looked to reimagine the computer as a whole—what it was for, and how it would be used.[7] Starting with his doctoral thesis, Kay developed a series of speculative machines designed for personal, graphical computing that would radically transform computation as a technical and cultural practice.[8] This work began with the realization that computation could be structured by a theory of objects, and that this theory would allow us to engage computing as part of our lived environment. His revelation would ultimately lead Kay and a team of researchers to develop the Smalltalk programming language at Xerox PARC in the early 1970s, designed with the groundbreaking Xerox Alto computer as the first fully object-oriented programming language.

Kay was not alone in this realization. Beginning in the early 1960s, the concept of object-oriented design emerged across the field of computer science, though it would not be named or formalized until well into the 1970s. Its appearance marked a sea change in how researchers imagined computing to function, driven in large part by the development of new uses for computational systems—principal among them the growth of interactive computer graphics. Prior to this moment, computers functioned largely as machines for the procedural calculation of data. Programs needed to be planned in great detail and were then executed along a designated trajectory, running to completion in order to produce a given result. We might visualize these early programming methodologies as a flow chart or diagram, in which the path from initiation to completion is set out in advance, and the program moves, loops, and transforms following a pregiven set of conditions. Object-oriented systems, by contrast, are a topology of objects structured by a set of communicative relations (figure 4.1). These objects relate to one another in

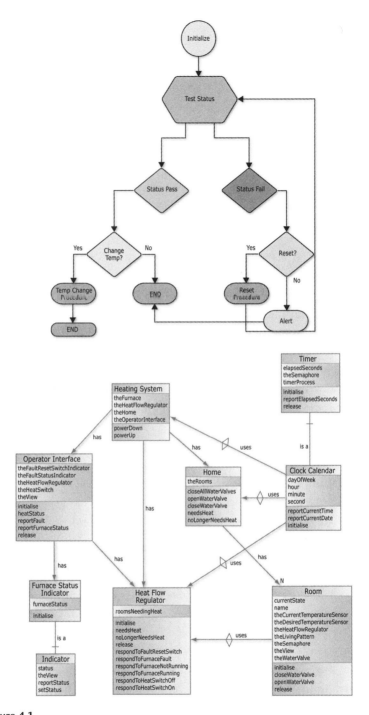

Figure 4.1

The treelike structure of a procedurally executed program architecture (top), contrasted with the network-like architecture of an object-oriented programming architecture (bottom). Courtesy of Joline Zepcevski.

complex ways, inheriting qualities from other objects, passing information between one another, and performing unique functions depending on the context and form of that information. While both methods are capable of modeling systems through simulation, object orientation shifts away from the simulation of *processes* and toward the simulation of *objects* capable of discrete forms of interaction.

This shift starts in the 1960s, but comes to define the vast majority of contemporary computational practices. All modern mobile applications, much of the web, most computer operating systems, media players, and graphical interfaces, the structure of video games and interactive software, compilers, database management, and much, much more are structured by the object logic revealed to Kay in this moment of serendipity.[9] Yet the influence of this reorientation toward the object world reaches far beyond the specific application of object-oriented programming for contemporary computing. Likewise, the influence of the graphical paradigms developed at the University of Utah reach beyond the time and place of their development, and beyond computer graphics as a discipline or practice. To begin the work of tracing these influences and afterlives we must look to the emergence, formalization, and application of object orientation. Doing so reveals a logic abstracted out from the world and transformed into a process whereby all manner of material objects are made newly legible to computation. Peering through this lens of object orientation, we can see how computer graphics transformed not only the way programs were designed but also the way computer science imagined the world to be structured and in turn came to structure the world.

Orientation

The phrase "object-oriented" suggests a number of things. The term broadly refers to a programming paradigm structured around modular, reusable objects. Objects in an object-oriented system are relational in that they are structured and defined as classes with instances, and interact with one another through discrete forms of communication or message passing. In this sense they model themselves on our understanding of objects in the material world, clustered into broad categories of function and use. The phrase comes from Kay's work in the mid-1970s at Xerox PARC, where he developed Smalltalk—the first fully object-oriented programming language—along with Adele Goldberg, Dan Ingalls, and the other members of the Learning Research

Group.[10] As such, most formal definitions of object-oriented programming include the four general properties found in the Smalltalk language that distinguish object orientation from other programming paradigms: abstraction, encapsulation, polymorphism, and inheritance.[11] "Abstraction" is the process of separating ideas from specific instances of those ideas at work; in an object-oriented system, only specific instances of an object model or class exist, which are abstractions of a more generalized object. "Encapsulation" is the process of hiding or black boxing a software object's internal function from other parts of the system, as well as a means of bundling both data and methods within a particular object. "Polymorphism" means that different instances of a given class can have different behaviors depending on the objects they are addressed to, much in the same way that the word "cut" would mean different things to a barber, surgeon, and actor, and therefore would produce a different action. Finally, "inheritance" means that classes may be used to create other classes that adopt or inherit the structure, attributes, or behavior of their parent class, such that the class "car" might inherit much of its function from a broader class "vehicle," but with modifications particular to its use or function. While not exclusive to object-oriented systems and thus not included in most formal definitions, "recursion"—in which a method or function is defined in terms of itself—is also central to the object-oriented paradigm in that each object can be understood as a recursion on the notion of the computer itself—that is, each object can be understood as its own discrete computer designed for a particular purpose. The goal of object-oriented systems is precisely this modularity—objects are independent and discrete entities within a broad topology, but are constructed from existing elements or classes of objects with which they share properties. While objects are dependent on one another to function, they need not be aware of the particular functionality of another object in order to communicate with it; all that matters are the input and output signals generated by objects as they interface with one another.

While this turn toward objects is most often associated with the appearance of object-oriented programming languages like Simula and Smalltalk, the design paradigm both emerged from and transformed a wide range of fields. As early as 1961, the United States Air Force was beginning to think about files as modules that contained data, procedures, and an array of pointers or instructions for interaction not unlike programmable objects.[12]

By the early 1970s, object-oriented structures could be seen in the design of computer architecture, with the PDP-11 family of minicomputers using one of the first orthogonal instruction sets that could be understood as polymorphic, a fundamental feature of object-oriented programming.[13] Perhaps the most expansive system that shares concepts found in object-oriented programming is the network structure of early time-sharing architectures such as the ARPANET, which functions based on a system of message passing and encapsulation shared by object-oriented methods. Frequently overlooked in discussions of this shift, however, is the role that computer graphics played in reorienting the field toward the object world. During this early period, computer graphics shared a concern for modeling the world based on object interaction, and I have argued that research into computer graphics marks the beginning of a concern in computer science for the nature of objects. In attempting to display and instrumentalize objects as they appear and function in the material world, computer graphics is one of the first fields to create computational models that mimic the structure of objects in relation to one another, independent of their engagement with a particular action or process. As Kay's anecdote shows, the graphical paradigms in circulation at Utah had a profound influence on how computational objects were first imagined and understood, and can be linked directly with later developments in object-oriented design at research centers formed in the afterlives of the University of Utah program.

To see this shift, it is important we do not focus too narrowly on object-oriented programming as it has been defined by Kay and others, but instead look to the broader discourse of objectness that emerges in this period to distinguish new ways of thinking through computation as a method for parsing complexity. In doing so, we will find that while the origin of object orientation's formalization as a programming paradigm is clearly evidenced in Kay's work on Smalltalk, the principals behind object orientation can be traced back much further to a number of software, hardware, and linguistic paradigms that emerge in the 1960s. Looking back further still, the intellectual progenitors of this transformation can be found in the emergence of systems theory, information theory, and cybernetics in the first half of the twentieth century, and their sweeping influence on a wide swath of academic disciplines starting in the late 1940s. These postwar disciplines each offer new ways to parse complexity through scientific and mathematical structures, modeling the world in such a way that it might be made action-able. Object orientation takes up this charge by reimagining computation as a communicative system of objects, though one that reflects the interests and needs of the growing field of computer science in this early period. Tracing the origins of object-oriented thinking in early computer graphics will allow us to inquire into the ontological assumptions that undergird this now-ubiquitous structuring form. Pulling this thread through to the pres-ent, I will explore the influence of object-oriented thinking on the material history of our contemporary object world, such that it will become possible to argue that the shape and form of the object you now hold in your hands is derived from this very history.

Monad Science

In 1963, a twenty-four-year-old Sutherland defended his doctoral disserta-tion in electrical engineering at MIT. Three years prior, while working on other projects, Sutherland had become familiar with the TX-2 computer in use at Lincoln Laboratory—a transistor-based machine built in 1958 as the successor to the TX-0, itself the successor of the earlier Whirlwind computers used in the SAGE air defense system. While working with the TX-2, Suther-land noted that its design had many of the core components of a graphical system: it had both a light pen for input and CRT screen for display, which, coupled with its then-massive core memory capable of holding up to 280,000 bytes, seemed an ideal system for graphical experimentation.[14] The machine could also be modified with little difficulty, and Sutherland requested the addition of a bank of push buttons that could be used as an additional input device. Work on Sketchpad began in earnest in fall 1961, eked out in the early hours of the morning when the TX-2 wasn't being used for research into national security and defense. The program developed quickly, and by mid-1962 Sketchpad could draw lines and circles, including objects that extended beyond the computer's narrow seven-inch screen (figure 4.2).[15]

Later that year, Sutherland produced a short film demonstrating the basic capabilities of the Sketchpad system.[16] At just under seven minutes, the film runs through the software's basic graphical operation using a composite image of the computer's screen, light pen, and push-button interface. Voice-over narration describes the process of constructing and manipulating drawings in real time, while Sutherland's hand shapes and transforms the

Figure 4.2
Ivan Sutherland operating Sketchpad at the TX-2 terminal, featuring the light pen and push-button interface, ca. 1962. Courtesy of the MIT Museum.

on-screen image. The software appears quick and seamless, with little flicker or lag in response to the light pen's movement. Even more impressive are the moments when Sutherland's hand disappears entirely, and the computer automatically calculates various transformations in shape and scale. A rough, irregular sketch of a bracket morphs on command into clean parallel lines and right angles. Objects are copied and pasted. Classes of objects are modified, and those modifications transform all derivative instances. The film ends with a dramatic zoom out, revealing the scale of the virtual paper on which Sutherland has been drawing—a quarter of a mile on each side.[17] Even today the film feels decades ahead of its time, presaging the tactile interaction that now defines the vast majority of computational media. On completing the film, Sutherland showed it to students and teachers around the MIT campus to solicit advice, and copies quickly made their way to other campuses, where it was shared among researchers and engineers. Working at the University of California at Berkeley in 1963, Evans recalled multiple copies of the film circulating "like an underground movie. It was immediately obvious that this was beyond what anyone else had done. It was elegant."[18] The film made its official debut at the Spring Joint Computer Conference in Detroit in 1963, setting the scope and agenda of graphical computing for the subsequent two decades.

Of course, almost no one ever used the software itself.[19] Despite the highly abstracted framing of Sutherland's film, in which the program seems to function as nothing more than a tactile interface divorced from any particular machine, Sketchpad could only be run on the one-of-a-kind TX-2 computer at MIT's Lincoln Laboratory—a massive, room-sized, multimillion-dollar machine whose design and function were entirely unique.[20] Built by MIT physicist Wes Clark from 1956 to 1958, the explicit purpose of the TX-2 was to test and develop applications in human-computer interaction.[21] Decades before widespread personal computing was even thinkable, the TX-2 functioned much as contemporary machines do today, with a console at which a single user could sit and interact directly with the computer.[22] Yet despite the familiarity of its operation, translating Sketchpad into a software object that could be implemented at scale would take decades. In this sense, Sketchpad functions as both a software object with a distinct set of material restrictions and a conceptual representation divorced from the historical context of any practical computational machine in this period. In other words, Sketchpad functions to both *compute pictures* in a way never before possible and *picture computing* as a tactile, interactive, and explicitly visual practice.

Sutherland's film made it clear that a system for interactive graphics was possible on a machine as powerful as the TX-2, but these early innovations in display and interaction were perhaps not the most significant and lasting contribution of the Sketchpad system. Beneath Sketchpad's interface lay an entirely new structure for the design of computational systems— one informed by the logic of objects as modular, relational structures. The graphics in Sketchpad were constructed through the application of rules or constraints that could be placed on collections of lines and curves to form addressable objects. For example,

> a square might begin as a rough, four-sided figure, but the operator could then instruct the program always to keep the lines joined in a closed shape, to make them equal in length and to keep all four angles locked at 90 degrees. Thereafter, if one side of the square was moved on the screen, the other sides would be forced to come along in order to obey the constraints associated with that shape.[23]

With these simple tools, a wide variety of complex shapes could be made (figure 4.3). Once constructed, a shape comprised of points, lines, and curves could be linked together to form an object that could be enlarged, reduced, and rotated on the screen. If desired, an object could be stored in memory and recalled later as one or multiple instances of this master drawing. Changes to the structure of the original object would subsequently inherit

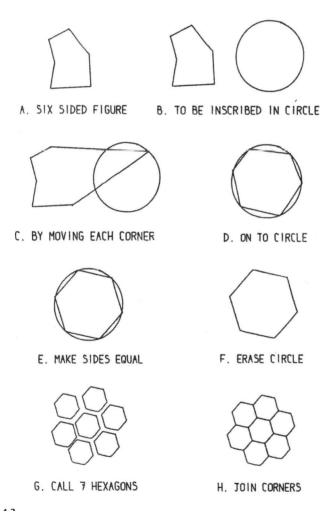

Figure 4.3
The construction of a complex shape using constraints. Ivan Sutherland, "Sketchpad: A Man-Machine Graphical Communication System" (PhD diss., Massachusetts Institute of Technology, 1963), 15. Courtesy of Ivan Sutherland.

to each of its instances. In this way, a complex drawing could be produced as a hierarchy of simpler components, each of which could be moved and modified separately, or collapsed into an object whole and stored.[24] In Sutherland's Sketchpad, we can see the most basic conditions of an object-oriented system: a structured topology in which objects are understood as relational, nested things comprised of like substances capable of discrete interaction.

This partitioning of objects into classes with instances that inherit from the general to the specific forms the ontological basis for Sutherland's system. It is an explicitly relational system, and this relationality is built into the hardware of the program itself in the form of a storage system Sutherland describes as a recursive "ring structure." In Sketchpad, all objects in storage point to those that they are dependent on, and in turn, those that are dependent on them, in a causal relationship Sutherland analogizes with the terms "hens" and "chickens":

> Certain picture elements depend in a vital way for their existence, display, and properties on other elements. For example, a line segment must reference two end points between which it is drawn; a set of digits must reference a scalar which indicates the value to be shown. In three dimensions it might be that a surface is represented as connecting four lines which in turn depend on end points. If a particular thing depends on something else there will be in the dependent thing a reference by pointer to the thing depended upon. In the ring structure used in Sketchpad, there will be a ring with a "hen" pair in the thing depended on and at least one "chicken" pair in a dependent thing. For example, a ring will connect a point with all lines which use it as an end point; the chicken pairs of this ring, being in the blocks for the lines in question, point to the point as an end point of the lines.[25]

Certain elements form the basis of other elements, which then form the basis for yet other elements—chickens all the way down.

In this way, Sketchpad parses complexity through the imposition of an emergent object logic. All objects in this system are comprised of clusters of simple primitives, such that all matter is abstracted from a single, essential substance that may be arranged to form objects of greater and greater complexity. In this the software evokes Gottfried Wilhelm Leibniz's *Monadology*—a connection not lost on Kay, who recalled in the initial moment of discovery that opens this chapter "the monads of Leibniz, the 'dividing nature at its joints' discourse of Plato, and other attempts to parse complexity." Unlike Leibniz's ontology, though, whereby the world is constructed and regulated through a preestablished harmony, Sutherland's system adopts a relationality in which objects interact and communicate with one another to form complex systems—a structure that more closely resembles the ontological argument in Baruch Spinoza's *Ethics*, taken up by Gilles Deleuze in his work on Spinoza as a "laying out of a common plane (*plan*) of immanence on which all bodies, all minds, and all individuals are situated."[26] This same logic forms the basis for all modern graphical software, even as the complexity of individual objects has grown to encapsulate an ever-larger number of attributes. Thus while it is the appearance of the Sketchpad program as an explicitly graphical interactive system that most inspired researchers, this appearance was entirely dependent on an internal object logic that would be formalized in the coming decade by researchers such as Kay.

That this paradigm has such longevity is due in part to the way it is derived from the formal structure and design of graphical systems, and the ability to abstract that logic out into an ever-wider number of applications. For anyone who has designed, edited, or produced media with a computer, the logic of Sutherland's Sketchpad may seem intuitive and even obvious. Nearly all contemporary digital media consist of nested structures of modular objects compiled into a legible whole.[27] To make it clear how radical Sutherland's historical contribution was, it is useful to examine a contemporaneous system developed in isolation from Sutherland's work at the Lincoln Laboratory, but with much the same goals and motivations.

NOMAD Science

Almost three years prior to Sutherland's initial work on the Sketchpad system, researchers at GM were developing their own system to assist in the design and manufacture of motor vehicles.[28] GM was one of the first companies to adopt computing technology across a wide range of applications, and as early as 1952, its General Motors Research Laboratories was using a card-programmed digital computer for engineering and scientific analyses. That said, these early systems had no applications for graphical design and display—processes that were essential to the conceptualization and manufacture of motor vehicles. To gauge the value of a graphical design system, GM began an internal study of its own designers and engineers in the late 1950s. The study's principal question was simple: "How could computational techniques significantly impact the design process?"[29] Unsurprisingly, the team found that drawings, pictures, and models were the principal media for the communication and documentation of ideas, and a system that was capable of handling graphical data would have a massive impact on the process of designing motor vehicles.

Based on this feedback, the research team recommended a system with the ability to work with existing drawings that could be digitized for computation, manipulate data once they had been entered into the computer, compare graphical data and multiple designs, and support and display textual information on the display screen. It was felt that if a computer could read sketches and drawings, then it could be programmed to produce further drawings, engineering data, and control tapes for numerically controlled machine tools. To test the feasibility of such a system, prototype hardware and software components were developed toward the end of 1959, beginning with an IBM 704 computer equipped with a 740 CRT recorder to plot the results of engineering computations.[30] For the purposes of this early demonstration, IBM also provided a display unit that operated alongside the film recorder so that the plotting could be seen by the machine operator. This film recorder and display unit became the basis for GM's earliest experiments in interactive computer graphics.[31] In 1959, following the success of this early prototype system, a five-person project team was formed and set to work on what would become the DAC-1, or Design Augmented by Computer, although the final system would not be completed until 1964 (plate 13).[32]

The DAC-1 is significant for several reasons. Since the computer is one of the earliest examples of an interactive graphical system, many of the solutions it developed for graphical problems—like those discussed in previous chapters—are unique, and serve as important predecessors to later research into computer graphics at sites like Bell Labs and the University of Utah. Yet the most interesting dimension of the DAC-1 is probably its input-output function, which is unlike any subsequent system for CAD. The DAC-1 was produced with a particular function in mind, and was specially built to suit the workflow requirements of GM researchers. As such, the machine needed to incorporate existing media forms used in the design of automobiles, principally paper line drawings. Unlike contemporary CAD software, the DAC-1 was built not to construct simulated objects within the computer itself but rather to accept and manipulate digitized models from paper drawings.[33] Thus the DAC-1 was built with a surprisingly old media interface, in which physical sketches were photographed and produced as transparencies that the computer could scan using a CRT.

A digital circuit was designed to use the signal from a photomultiplier tube mounted in a hood covering the display unit to detect the presence or absence of light and set one of the sense lights on the IBM 704 computer accordingly. Drawings and sketches were traced onto a clear plastic overlay mounted on the face of the IBM 780 display unit. The lines on the overlay were then digitized by finding those points where the light, from a spot of light plotted on the display unit, was occluded by the line on the overlay.[34]

The process of digitizing drawings was largely automatic, and the computer could translate abstract drawings into functional data sets using its customized line-scanning system.[35] If any errors appeared once an image was digitized, its points and lines could be debugged using an interactive light pen, and incorporated into or compared against an existing model. The final stage was a return to the material, in which models were "printed out" using the same photographic mechanism so that they could be compared with other models, or shared among designers and researchers.

To anyone familiar with contemporary CAD software, this may seem a bizarre and surprisingly analog process, but this gesture of digitizing the physical to facilitate the traditional practices of the GM engineer is significant. The computer in this instance is a machine for data processing, a calculator of drawings and graphics, and a tool for procedural problem solving. Its role was to automatically process images in a way that was analogous to procedural programming, with the ability to trigger queries for its human operator at decision points embedded within the program.[36] This form of human-machine communication was extremely innovative in the late 1950s, but it models the computer as little more than a calculating machine, and its operator as a heuristic interlocutor—quite unlike the object-oriented methods developed by Sutherland in this same period.

Ultimately the scanning interface that GM developed proved more cumbersome than useful, and was scrapped in the mid-1960s in favor of a system that more closely resembles contemporary CAD design and interaction. Even its designers acknowledged the photo scanner as the least significant contribution of the DAC-1 project, a fascinating but failed form of graphical human-machine communication.[37] Instead they viewed the most remarkable and lasting features of the system as its innovative early use of time-sharing in the form of a multiprogramming and source program storage allocation control system, and its development of a disk library of programs available during program execution. This disk library allows a control subroutine to view other subroutines as black boxes which required certain inputs and produce outputs. The size and name of the black box does not need to be known at programming time and, in fact, are data at execution time, for the control subroutine. This feature allows continued growth of the design support programs with no change to control programs.[38]

In effect, the DAC-1 included a system for the encapsulation of design support programs that could be called on to function as expressive objects using a custom language called NOMAD. The NOMAD language was derived from the Michigan Algorithm Decoder (MAD) language, an Algol-58 derivative widely used at the nearby University of Michigan. NOMAD modified the MAD language to include new operator and data types that were designed to allow systems programs or graphics programming to be expressed in a high-level language.[39] The name NOMAD was also chosen to reflect the language's itinerant functionality, which produced location-independent code—"that is, code that could execute at any load address or wander from place to place. Compiled object modules were stored on disk in libraries in a nonlinkage edited format and loaded into memory for execution upon demand."[40]

Despite the procedural nature of its interface and input-output hardware, at the linguistic level the DAC-1 was designed to reflect the modular nature of graphical objects, encasing them in nomadic black boxes that could be called on and executed as necessary. Like the Utah teapot of chapter 3, researchers acknowledged the utility of objects outside the initial context of their digitization, and so a system was developed for encapsulating them so that they could be stored, moved, manipulated, and executed at will. It is here a distinction begins to emerge, a new formal structure tied to the graphical logic of this early system. Despite its rather linear analog-to-digital interface for graphical interaction, the DAC-1 already points to the future potential for treating graphics as object-oriented systems that model the world based on material interactions. In this sense, it marks a moment of transition in which the procedural logic of calculation is inflected by the object logic of computer graphics.

Trajectories

This early period is marked by a shift in the conception of computational technologies from the linear to the spatial, from the branching tree of the flow diagram to the topology of the distributed network. This reorientation crystallizes with the development of object orientation, understood less as a programming paradigm than a theory of complexity derived from our phenomenal experience of objects in the world. For media theorist Casey Alt, the development of object orientation marks the emergence of the computer as an interactive medium, given that object orientation brings with it a sense of spatial relation and communication.[41] This theory is convincing in part because the rise of object orientation coincides with—and indeed stems from—the development of graphical computing, and with it a transformation of the computer into what Kay and Goldberg would come to call a "metamedium" in which all media could be simulated through computation.[42] This connection is nowhere more clear than in the Smalltalk programming language itself, which cannot be disentangled from its interactive graphical system for interfacing human and machine.

Smalltalk modeled both its linguistic architecture and graphical interface on the same object principal, such that the development environment of Smalltalk was also the user interface that Smalltalk programs ran in.[43] This object-oriented interface—first developed for the Xerox Alto in the early 1970s—introduced many of the concepts that would later be adapted for contemporary graphical user interfaces. The windows that now populate the screens of nearly all personal computers function as objects in Kay's sense of the term, each a member of the class "window," and each functioning as a black boxed instance of a computational object, distinct and polymorphic.[44] In fact, a direct thread can be pulled from Kay's Dynabook concept first developed the University of Utah in the late 1960s through the Xerox Alto at PARC to the Apple Macintosh (figure 4.4). Arguably the most direct successor to the Smalltalk language is NeXTSTEP, the operating system developed for Steve Jobs's computer and software company NeXT, Inc., founded after he was pushed out of Apple in 1985. On returning to Apple in the late 1990s, Jobs adapted NeXTSTEP into OS X, the user environment for all contemporary Apple computers.[45] Key here is how those parts of a system we often consider representational and therefore secondary to its deeper function—in this case, the graphical interface—are in fact central to and cannot be disentangled from the design of the system as a whole. This claim can be made of Smalltalk and NeXTSTEP, but it can also be made of Sketchpad and, to a lesser degree, the GM DAC-1, structured as they are as systems for the description and display of graphical objects.

a)

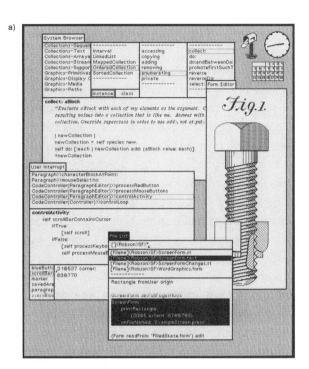

b)

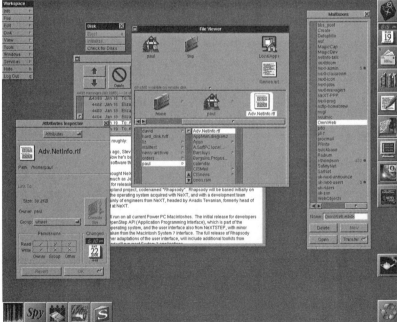

Figure 4.4

Screenshot of the object-oriented Smalltalk graphical user interface for the Xerox Alto (top), 1980, and screenshot of the graphical interface of the NeXTSTEP operating system (bottom), 1989, structured by an object-oriented architecture.

In this chapter I have focused primarily on Smalltalk and the legacy of Kay's vision for the future of personal computing, as it draws the clearest connection between the history of computer graphics and development of object orientation.[46] However, my goal is not simply to suggest that it is object-oriented programming that transforms the computer from a calculating machine into an interactive medium, but rather to suggest that computer graphics is a catalyst for the introduction of a spatialized theory of computing into computer science, which played a principal role in the reorientation of the field toward the multimedia machine we know today. This is made clear if we return to Utah and a more explicitly graphical object: Edwin Catmull's digitized hand. In chapter 3, I discussed the importance of Catmull's hand as marking the moment when graphics researchers began to digitize objects from the physical world, creating models from their lived environment. Yet the film Catmull produced with Fred Parke was primarily designed to test research into object movement and animation, in addition to basic modeling and shading. In the film's most dynamic sequence, the hand rotates, closes into a fist, and opens before extending a single index finger and pointing directly at the viewer (figure 4.5). To accomplish this movement, Catmull had to rig the hand as a system of interrelated parts that could be programmed to move synchronously. Catmull describes these parts as "objects" that he defines as a set of polygons that would transform together and could be organized into a group known as a "body."

> For example, the body of a hand is made up of several smaller objects: the palm, the bottom of the thumb, the middle of the thumb, the top of the thumb, etc. The objects are organized in a tree structure. By using a tree structure, any transformation applied to an object at a node also applies to its children. If one rotates the bottom of the thumb, the other two parts of the thumb follow automatically.[47]

Adopting the genealogical language of Sutherland's Sketchpad—in this case, "parents" and "children" in place of "hens" and "chickens"—Catmull's system allows for simple inheritance between objects, not of abstract data structures as in object-oriented programming, but of the physical structure of simulated objects such as the modeled hand.[48] In order to accomplish this synchronicity of movement within an object, Catmull developed his own programming language called MOP, which he used to generate instructions for the object manipulation routine, or MOTION. As Catmull notes,

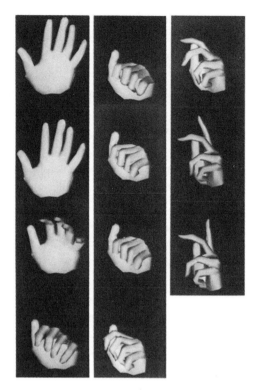

Figure 4.5
Frame captures of Edwin Catmull's hand closing and opening via object instructions using the MOP language. Edwin Catmull, "A System for Computer Generated Movies," in *ACM '72 Proceedings of the ACM Annual Conference* (New York: Association for Computer Machinery, 1972), 425–426.

> Typical programming languages are much too sequential in nature for specifying easily the kinds of simultaneous and overlapping action we expect in a movie. . . . The language MOP is designed to allow concurrency from the point of view of the user. It generates instructions for MOTION which changes and displays the objects.[49]

To be sure this is a minor example, and it would be a stretch to describe Catmull's MOP language as object-oriented in Kay's sense of the term, but if we view Catmull's film as the predecessor to later graphical systems for object rigging and animation, its implications become clear.[50] This general structure of object inheritance remains true for almost all contemporary animation programs, game engines, and 3D modeling software, which are designed around a node architecture in which objects inherit qualities such as color and shading, and are set in motion using a relational system like the one Catmull first developed in 1972. Much as we might draw a through line from Smalltalk to OS X, we could likewise draw a line from MOP to RenderMan, developed by Catmull and a team of researchers at Pixar some twenty years later, used in the production of all the studio's animated films, and sold as an off-the-shelf software solution to rendering, animation, and visualization for both scientific research and entertainment.

The further we push into the 1970s, the more explicit this connection between graphics and objects becomes, and the more widely this logic disperses out from the University of Utah to those research sites and institutions at which its graduates continued their work. While the accomplishments of the Utah program during its first fifteen years are significant, it is in the afterlife of the program as it moves from the university into industry that the broad influence of these graphical paradigms can be seen most clearly. For nearly all students and researchers at Utah, that transition began with E&S.

Simulations

In 1972, three years after graduating from the University of Utah, John Warnock began working for the California regional branch of E&S. Warnock was initially hired as part of a group contracted by Ames Research to help develop weather forecasting applications for the ILLIAC IV supercomputer, but in 1974 he was approached by Evans to build a small team for a unique project of unprecedented scale: constructing a fully interactive model of New York Harbor for the Maritime Academy's Computer Aided Operations Research Facility (CAORF).[51] At the time, it was the largest and most complex digital simulation ever built; so big, in fact, that it had to be housed in its own massive stand-alone building at the United States Merchant Marine Academy in Kings Point, New York (figure 4.6 and plate 14).[52]

> The trainees were to sit on the mockup of a ship's bridge, surrounded by five 12-foot-high, 30-ft-long (3.6-by-9-meter) screens displaying a computer-generated representation of New York Harbor, complete with buildings, piers, movable buoys, changing weather conditions, and other ships to be avoided. The system had to produce images in full color for five projectors at 30 frames a second.[53]

This is arguably the end result of the millions of dollars that the Department of Defense pumped into the Utah program in the decade from 1965

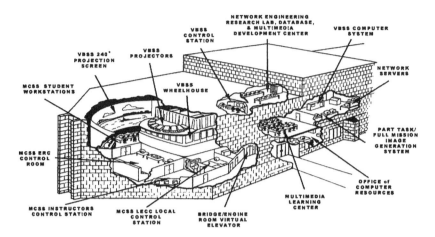

Figure 4.6

Cutaway of the CAORF building. Joseph J. Puglisi, Jack Case, and George Webster, "CAORF Ship Operation Center (SOC)—Recent Advances in Maritime Engine and Deck Simulation at the Computer Aided Operations Research Facility (CAORF)" (paper presented at the International Conference on Marine Simulation and Ship Maneuvering MARSIM 2000, Orlando, FL, May 8–12, 2000).

to 1975—the military application for computer graphics that justifies ten years of experimental research. It is a common narrative in the history of computing that computers are essentially technologies of war, and it is only after decades of military use that swords become plowshares, and computing is transformed into a commercial enterprise and everyday practice. But if we trace the trajectories that radiate out from these early objects we find a broad field of influence that touches all manner of objects that at first glance do not appear computational in the slightest.

Take a moment to reflect on the shape and form of the book you now hold in your hands. No doubt it seems a familiar object, made of paper and ink, not unlike the billions of books printed over the past five hundred years. Or perhaps it is electronic paper and E Ink simulating the materiality of the printed page, or even a bootleg PDF ripped from the web and loaded into software to be underlined and marked with digital marginalia. Regardless of its form, each of these objects are the product of research that can be traced to this simulation of New York Harbor constructed nearly fifty years ago in the afterlife of the Utah program. The book you now hold is an image object, a product of this transformation in the materiality of the physical world as it has been made to interface with computation. In fact, for over thirty years all printed documents have been as much graphical objects as any screen interface or teapot simulation, even as they often appear identical to those paper objects that precede them.

This shift becomes visible if we look to the period in which the field of computer graphics begins to commercialize into a wide-reaching industry—a transformation that arguably starts with E&S. Until the 1970s, most computer graphics were produced on custom-rigged, general-purpose computers using oscilloscope displays, but as the field developed it required standardized tools to suit its unique needs—frame buffers, graphics terminals, clipping dividers, and more. E&S was founded to fill that need, drawing on its ARPA connections and the resources of the University of Utah.[54] The earliest hardware the company developed was a graphical workstation for CAD, as discussed in chapter 5, but it quickly expanded to large-scale simulation technology for the military and commercial aerospace industries, which were looking for machines to train pilots for challenging flight scenarios without endangering the pilot's life or risking expensive equipment.[55] The earliest simulators the company developed were basic software applications for use with its graphics terminals, resembling advanced arcade games complete with joystick controls and primitive "game over" screens that would display if a pilot crashed the plane—a row of fish for a water landing or a bright white cross if one crashed on land (figure 4.7).[56] Then in 1972, the company partnered with the British firm Redifon to produce fully interactive simulators housed in specialized capsules on hydraulics that would rise and fall to correspond with the movement of a virtual cockpit (figure 4.8).[57] While these early simulators were the culmination of over a decade of research and military funding, they were also the beginning of a new kind of media practice and a new way of producing technical things.

A simulator on the scale of the CAORF was truly unprecedented, with no existing models for how to design, program, or execute a real-time simulation such as this. Due to this complexity, and the fact that the project had been repeatedly delayed and was well behind schedule, E&S decided that the hardware and software would be developed simultaneously and in parallel, the first by a team in Utah and the second by a team led by Warnock in California. This double-blind restriction was key, as Warnock later recalled in a 1986 interview:

a)

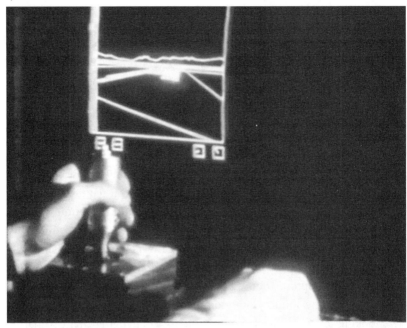

b)

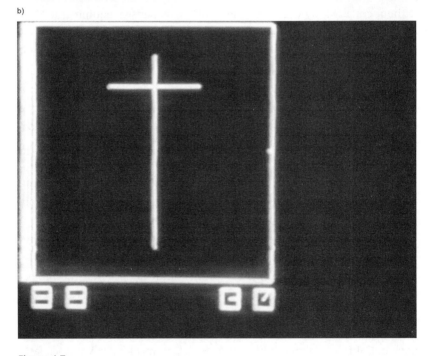

Figure 4.7
Frame captures from a demonstration of early flight simulation applications using the Line Drawing System graphics terminal, complete with "game over" screen for crash landings, 1969. Courtesy of the Special Collections Department, J. Willard Marriott Library, University of Utah.

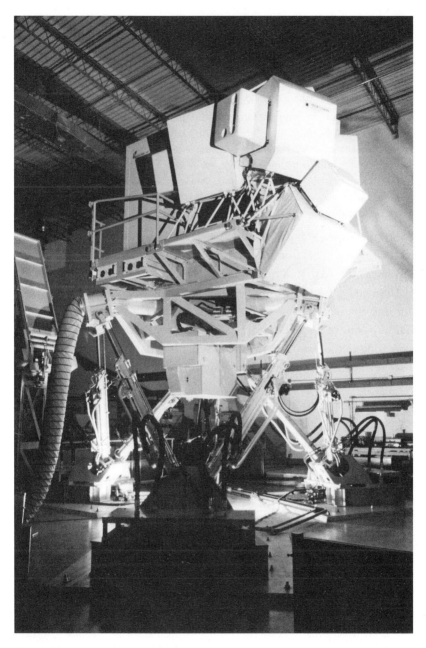

Figure 4.8
Flight simulator rig designed by Redifon for the Evans and Sutherland Computer Corporation, 1970s. Courtesy of the Special Collections Department, J. Willard Marriott Library, University of Utah.

We needed to write a huge, three-dimensional database and a lot of real-time software to make the simulator work the way they wanted it to. We had a year to complete this massive undertaking. It was a full-color model with all three dimensions. We decided the most stupid thing we could do was to design this database in a form that would be used directly by the simulator. In other words, to bind it up too tightly. We decided to create a text file and then write a compiler to compile the text file into the form that the simulator would need (whenever we decided what that would be). We still didn't know what the simulator was going to look like. So we started building this huge database in text form. In digitizing the database and in building this big three-dimensional model, it became very obvious that rather than having a static data structure in the text file, it was much more reasonable to have a language. It needed to be a very simple, easily parsed, and extensible language.[58]

By abstracting the simulation from the particular hardware it needed to run on, Warnock and his team began to abstract graphics out from the realm of the descriptive to that of the linguistic.

Ultimately the team found that feeding information about the harbor into the database was an arduous task.[59] To make things easier, John Gaffney—one of Warnock's team members—spent a weekend writing a software routine that would generate information about the simulation from a set of menus. Objects were constructed from databases that contained properties that could be called on by other objects in a given simulation—a system of nested objects not unlike Sketchpad or other object-oriented graphical systems.[60] Rather than program each object in the environment individually, the routine categorized the simulation into classes of objects with shared properties and behaviors. For example, the simulation anticipated four types of ships that could be in the harbor, each of which would have different models with unique properties that could be scaled in size or transformed in position, but would share a set of common properties to all ships, such as movement and collision. As they discovered different types of objects, they would write a program to collect basic information about the object and output the appropriate text files.[61] In effect they applied an object-oriented solution to a graphical problem, transforming a catalog of individual things into a relational system of interactive objects (plate 15).

This was a transformative moment in which researchers stopped thinking about graphics in isolation and started to structure them as large-scale interactive systems. By the time the harbor simulator was completed, Warnock had discovered how powerful an object-oriented language could be.

"Unlike Basic or Fortran, say, which require the user to spell out every last instruction, [an object-oriented language] packs all those details into modules, or objects, which the user controls with just a few directives."[62] Making software independent of the device in this way gave researchers the leverage and flexibility to scale the system to meet the massive CAORF project. Those lessons learned, Warnock's group turned to expanding Gaffney's interpreter into a full programming system for CAD. In 1977, that project was released by E&S as the Design System, though only one copy of the system was ever released, as a test bed for later development.[63] The language behind the system was eventually repackaged by E&S as JOY and would be integrated into subsequent graphics terminals such as the E&S Picture System, described in chapter 5.[64]

Here again we find object orientation at work. While earlier E&S simulators superficially resemble contemporary digital games in their arcade-like interface and interaction, they were necessarily limited in their complexity. Less than a half a decade later in the CAORF, we find an exponential growth in object number and complexity, due largely to the implementation of Warnock and Gaffney's system. While the images produced by the simulator may appear simple by contemporary standards, they were created nearly five years before the black and white pixel graphics of Atari Asteroids, and more closely resemble the graphical complexity of early 3D systems like the Nintendo 64 (1996). This complexity was made possible by the object system developed by Warnock and his team, whose formal logic has since been integrated into the tools used to design and play nearly all contemporary interactive games.

PostScript Prints Anything

Based on the success of the CAORF project, E&S tried to promote Warnock to a position in Salt Lake City, but he was not interested in leaving California and left the company in 1978 for a position at Xerox PARC, joining Kay, Newell, Robert Taylor, and several other Utah alumni and former faculty. While at PARC, Warnock worked in the Computer Sciences Lab under Taylor, and quickly realized he needed an interactive interpretative tool bench for his experiments. To this end, he decided to reimplement the E&S Design System with PARC colleague and Utah teapot developer Newell.[65] "We added all the graphic operators so we could do graphics and test out ideas on screens and different medium," Warnock recalled. "We called it JaM for 'John and Martin.'"[66] Like the harbor simulator, JaM was device independent, had the same postfix execution semantics as Gaffney's Design System, and was based on the E&S imaging model, but it augmented the E&S system by providing a much more extensive set of graphical primitives.[67] Newell and Warnock implemented JaM on various Xerox workstations, and by 1981 JaM was in use at Stanford on its Xerox Alto machines. At this same time, Xerox had been working on a series of experimental raster printers and had developed a relatively device-independent page image description scheme called "Press format," which was used to instruct raster printers what to print. The format was extremely successful, but not without its limitations, and by the early 1980s the team had decided to modify Press to introduce many of the graphical elements developed for JaM, naming the resulting hybrid protocol Interpress (figure 4.9).[68] The Interpress language was hugely successful within the Xerox Corporation. Nonetheless, the company hesitated to distribute it as an industry standard. Frustrated by Xerox's unwillingness to enter the commercial market, Warnock met with colleague Charles Geschke about starting their own company. "Why don't I get on an airplane, go talk to Dave Evans, my old thesis adviser, and get some advice from him," Warnock recalled. "[Evans] introduced us to [investment banker] Bill Hambrecht who said, 'Sure, let's go for it.' We founded Adobe on December 2, [1982]."[69]

Adobe Systems was founded largely to take advantage of the systems Warnock had developed, first at Utah, then at E&S, and finally at Xerox PARC. At Adobe, Warnock and Geschke took the ideas behind Interpress and transformed them into the PostScript language, which has become the global standard for desktop publishing. PostScript marked the first time a full programming language had been used to control a printer. By setting a common language that all printers could be made to understand, PostScript allowed software and graphics to interface efficiently with devices for printed output, standardizing the way printed graphics are understood and manipulated. While PostScript is not object oriented by Kay's narrow definition, it treats text as graphical objects, allowing written text to be scaled to any size and rotated to any angle, making possible complex and artistic textual graphics unlike any previous computational printing method. While many of these early effects now seem dated and cliché, such as the WordArt-style spiral proof-of-concept image in figure 4.10, in the 1980s and 1990s, they had a transformative effect on the publishing industry. Experiments with typeface

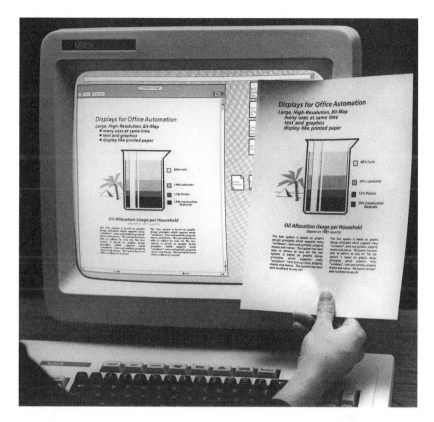

Figure 4.9
The Xerox Star computer, which used Interpress for WYSIWYG printable graphics, 1981. Courtesy of the Digibarn Computer Museum and Xerox Corporation.

and layout in magazines like *Emigre* and *Ray Gun* paved the way for new textual aesthetics in print and graphic design—all of which was made possible by the technologies behind PostScript (figure 4.11).[70] Today almost all text produced using computational methods is touched in some way by systems based on research done by Warnock and others at Xerox PARC and Adobe Systems, from pamphlets and magazines to this very book.

How then did we get from New York Harbor to something like Adobe PageMaker?[71] While at first these objects may appear quite distant from the graphical simulations that are the principal objects of this book, it is precisely this difference that makes them significant. From graphics come other technical forms, informed by the logic of object simulation cultivated

Figure 4.10
Early PostScript test using text layout that was not possible with previous printing methods. David C. Evans Papers, Box 145, Fld 12. Courtesy of John Warnock.

Figure 4.11
Text layout of *Emigre* magazine, made possible through newly available desktop publishing software. "Ambition/Fear," special issue, *Emigre* 11 (1989): 2–3. Courtesy of Emigre Magazine.

at Utah, and transformed by the dozens of research and commercial institutions that form its afterlives and shape and structure our contemporary
media landscape. As with Kay's revelation on his first day in Salt Lake City, it
is the simulation of objects as structures built for the purpose of interactive
graphical display that inspired this new design paradigm. What began with
the graphical description and simulation of objects in the physical world
came to transform the design of built systems, from architecture to programming languages and typography. In this way, graphics may be understood
as more than the image output of computational systems; they are material
structures that shape the conditions of possibility for the ways we have
come to design our world. If the goal of object orientation was to bring
computing closer to human experience, the result is arguably a reciprocal
reshaping of that experience to conform to the structure of object orientation. While object orientation begins as a shift in the way we imagine and
design technical systems, it comes to transform the way we understand the
world to function as a system.

5 Procedure Crystallized: The Graphics Processing Unit and the Rise of Computer Graphics

Developing a new theoretical basis for computer science will not be easy; indeed, the task has been put off in part because it is very difficult to combine notions of logic with notions of topology, time, space and distance, as a new theory will require.
—Ivan Sutherland and Carver Mead, "Microelectronics and Computer Science"

Hardware is really just software crystallized early.
—Alan Kay, "The Early History of Smalltalk"

Let the hardware do the hard work.
—Evans & Sutherland Computer Corporation, "LDS-1 Manual"

Inside every modern computer sits an object in which the entire history of computer graphics is embedded. It is minuscule and nondescript: a simple square chip of silicon. Yet it is largely responsible for the explosive emergence of computer graphics in popular visual culture at the end of the twentieth century. This chip, developed first by a Utah graduate in the late 1970s to accelerate graphical calculation, would ultimately come to transform our very notion of what computation is and is for, marking a dramatic shift away from universal architectures and toward the highly specialized parallel computation seen today in countless applications. This chip likewise marks our final image object, not because it heralds the end of this history or the culmination of the object logic brought about by the development of computer graphics, but because it marks the moment in which computer graphics first became tangible as both spectacular illusion and everyday practice—when digital images began to proliferate in film, video games, and on personal computers. This is also the period in which most popular histories of computer graphics begin, and it is for this reason that I have largely avoided engaging with those familiar visual texts that mark the technology's transformation into a popular medium. To be sure this is a significant historical moment in the development of computer graphics, but as I have stressed in the preceding chapters, it is a moment built on a foundation of over thirty years of research, the development of new methods, solving of key problems, and construction of a set of objects for the calculation and display of digital images. Thus rather than turn toward the cultural and historical discourses that emerge at this moment around the newness of this decades-old technology, we might instead ask what shifts in the field of computing made possible this sudden rise in visibility. What changed to allow for the integration of graphics across an unprecedented range of visual media?

The two decades leading up to this moment were marked by academic and commercial research directed at solving key problems for the display of graphical objects: hidden surfaces, smooth shading, perspective projection, and much more. While multiple and competing solutions were developed for each, over time these solutions were largely standardized into a series of operations tasked with the complex work of transforming a set of objects described in memory into a fully rendered image on the display of a computer screen. Despite this standardization, each step in this process was highly specialized, such that producing computer graphics required expensive terminals devoted exclusively to graphical calculation and display. Therefore while the tools and technologies to produce 3D graphics had been available since the late 1960s, they remained largely inaccessible outside large-scale research and industry contexts. To bring about a transformation whereby graphics could find new and expanded uses outside this narrow field required an archetypal shift in the material form that enabled graphical calculation. This was a shift in the very nature of computational hardware at the level of scale, function, and formal logic, a move away from software and toward the development of a hardware object that would come to redefine the contemporary field of computing for the next forty years: the GPU.[1]

The GPU is an object designed exclusively for the calculation of graphical data, functioning in effect as a separate computer that has been hardwired to perform graphical tasks in tandem with or alongside the more general-purpose CPU (figure 5.1). While graphics processors have existed

Figure 5.1
NVIDIA GeForce GTX 780m graphics processor, found in contemporary high-end graphics cards. Courtesy of NVIDIA.

in some form since the first graphical systems, it was the development of very large-scale integration (VLSI) for integrated circuit design in the early 1980s that hardwired each of the disparate and highly specialized objects that were required for graphical calculation into a single silicon chip, formally fixing them for the purpose of acceleration. This transformation of graphical processing in both price and scale pushed 3D computer graphics out of the laboratories and corporate research centers that defined the first two decades of their development, and into new industries and contexts. More than any other object, it is the GPU that made possible the explosion in graphical computing in this period, leading to the rise of digital visual effects in film and television alongside the domestication of graphical technologies in video games and personal computing. Today GPUs can be found in smartphones, personal computers, workstations, and game consoles. They are essential to the form and function of modern computer graphics, and it is through the GPU that we might come to understand the unique role computer graphics play within our contemporary culture of computing.

While the GPU's architecture emerged from the historical development of graphical computing as a unique computational problem, in designing for the particular, computer graphics researchers offered up a universalizing view of the world as a gigantic data task to be solved through massively parallel computation. Over the last twenty years, the GPU has shifted and transformed; modified for nongraphical tasks, it now dominates emerging fields of research in large-scale data processing, neural networks, cryptocurrency, artificial intelligence, and machine learning. More than any other computational technology, the GPU has enabled a modern revisioning of what computation is for while simultaneously reimagining what the future of computation might look like. Yet despite this orientation toward computation's possible *futures*, it is in the GPU that we might ultimately identify the historical claim of the field of computer graphics more broadly. In the GPU, each of the objects that have occupied the previous chapters of this book are transfigured into a single metaobject to be embedded within a computational system. Through this mise en abyme technique, the computer as an ontologically discrete object is transformed into a nested structure of objects within objects, machines within machines, scaling out and down to form a highly parallel and recursive structure that formally fixes as well as generalizes its own cultural and historical formation. This crystallization of procedural calculation flattens and normalizes some sixty years of graphical research, such that the historical field of computer graphics itself becomes an embeddable image object—one that erases the complex and messy work of its own history by fixing it within the logic of a silicon chip.

Specialization

Graphics have always required specialized equipment to translate the fundamentally nonvisual nature of geometric data into images that can be viewed via the interface of a screen. This is due to the highly repetitive nature of graphical computing, in which a limited set of calculations must be made for each object in a scene and each pixel on a screen for each frame to be displayed, over and over again. In most modern computers there are three operations that every graphics system performs to transform graphical objects stored in memory into fully rendered images on the screen of a computer: a move from object space to world space to screen space. Together these operations make up what is commonly referred to as the "graphics pipeline," comprised of a series of tasks that must be computed sequentially, but that operate in parallel to transform a 3D scene to a 2D screen (figure 5.2).[2]

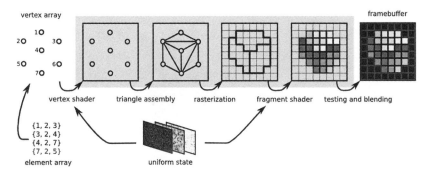

Figure 5.2
Simplified view of the OpenGL graphics pipeline. Courtesy of Enlightenment.org.

Prior to a given render, each geometric object in a scene is defined in a system's memory as a vertex array.[3] These objects are usually stored in their own local coordinate system, or object space, making their definition more general and easier to transform. Therefore the first thing that happens to graphical objects on their way from object memory to display is a transformation of their vertex coordinates from this object space into world space—that is, from an abstract coordinate system into the contextual space of the scene to be rendered. This is done using a 4x4 matrix, which allows transformations such as translation, rotation, and scale to be done with a single entity.[4] In this stage, the computer also calculates lighting and other global effects that apply to the scene as a whole.

Once this transformation is complete, the scene must be projected into a particular view or perspective. In this step, the virtual camera or observer is defined so that an image can be calculated with respect to the appropriate viewing position, understood as a frame or window onto the scene. While the final render will appear to us as a flat, two-dimensional image, in three dimensions this viewing window is understood as a set of planes that extend outward from the rectangle that defines the two-dimensional boundaries of the screen, forming what is known as a viewing frustum, which marks the limit of what is visible to the viewing position of the observer (figure 5.3). Objects are then clipped to these planes or window boundaries, such that any object that lies outside the planes is either deleted or redrawn so that only its visible lines are calculated.[5] This clipping enacts a logic similar to hidden surface removal, discussed in chapter 2, where that which is known

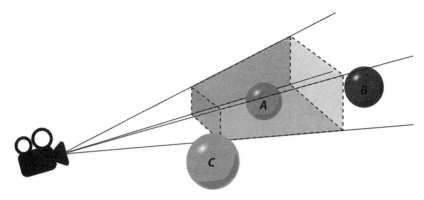

Figure 5.3
The view space of a 3D-rendered scene, showing the frustum in dotted lines with clip planes on all six sides. Only the sphere labeled A would be viewable in this scene, as sphere B lies beyond the far clip plane, and sphere C is outside the near clip plane. Altered. Tetromino, CC BY 3.0.

but invisible to the viewer must be determined so as to preemptively erase these objects before they are rendered.

The final step in the pipeline is the translation of this world space into the screen space of a particular output device. In this stage, the entire render is scaled to the proportions of the screen or window it is to be displayed in, and rasterized such that for each pixel in the render area, a color value is derived from the corresponding object in the scene. This pixel data may then be passed through to the frame buffer that holds it until it is ready to be pushed to the screen of the display. This work of translating graphical data into simulated images is a complex and computationally intensive procedure, and in contemporary real-time applications such as 3D gaming, these operations must take place thirty to sixty times every second. To express the sheer magnitude of this process numerically, in order to maintain seamless real-time moving images, a computer must perform trillions of calculations per second.[6]

It would be wildly inefficient to occupy the CPU of a computer with these highly repetitive calculations. Not only is the CPU already tasked with the various nongraphical calculations of a given system, but it is structured around the sequential operations of program execution, in which only a single operation is given the full processing power of the CPU at a given time.[7] Theoretically a CPU can perform any computable task—it is a general-purpose processor, universal in its design and application. Nonetheless there exists a practical limit to universal computation, whereby theoretically computable operations would take so long to calculate that they become functionally incomputable. Computer graphics is precisely this kind of procedure. While graphical calculations are readily computable by any computational device, processing graphical tasks on a sequential CPU would slow render time to the point of making real-time interaction impossible. In this strange exception to the universality of computational systems, we can see the surprising paradox of computer graphics as a historical practice. While the scale and repetition of computer graphics made it one of the most computationally demanding tasks that could be executed by a computer, it had to appear immediately responsive, perfectly seamless, and functionally invisible. This remains true today, as evidenced by the sudden, noisy whir of a cooling fan kicking into high speed at the launch of a graphically intensive game or the sudden drop in frame rate during a particularly intense moment of play.[8] It is due to this surprising exception to the universality of general-purpose computing that computer graphics was one of the first fields to develop processing hardware designed narrowly for a single purpose, marking the emergence of a new paradigm that would radically transform our very notion of what a computer is and is for.

The narrowest example of this specialization comes from graphical machines designed for a single use, such as the system boards used in stand-alone arcade machines in the early 1970s.[9] Arcade machines are, in essence, specialized computers designed for the display of interactive graphics—quite literally GPUs. Early arcade system boards were designed as codeless state machines built around discrete logic circuits that hard coded each element of the game. Unlike home consoles such as the Atari VCS, arcade boards were custom built for one game and one game only.[10] An exemplary case of this kind of formal specialization is the Atari game *Space Race* from 1973. Visually, *Space Race* closely resembles its immediate predecessor, *Pong*, with its mirrored layout and single play screen, but in lieu of a ball bouncing back and forth, the game is a sea of asteroid-like obstacles that the player must avoid as they launch a rocket ship. The game is widely acknowledged as the first *Frogger*-style game where the player moves along the y-axis while avoiding obstacles along the x-axis. Significantly, the game's rocket ship is the only real game object that is more than a single moving pixel. While later game software such as the cartridges used with the Nintendo Entertainment System used

ROMs to store game data, in this early period ROMs were too expensive for commercial products like an arcade cabinet. If a company wanted a bitmap for graphics it would have to lay it out as a set of diodes on the board itself. Examining the *Space Race* board, one can clearly see the bitmap of a half ship, soldered into the hardware of the board and mirrored to produce the game's most iconic object (figure 5.4).

Arcade system boards are the most extreme and vivid example of this logic, as they are one of few computers in this period designed for a single fixed use. Most graphical systems still needed to adapt to a wide range of graphical objects and outputs, such that prior to the development of graphics processors all computer graphics applications relied on general-purpose architectures for calculation. Procedures such as hidden surface removal were executed "in software" using a range of unstandardized algorithmic methods, with render times that could range from several seconds to several minutes for a single image or frame. Acknowledging the limitations of this system, researchers in the late 1960s began to develop terminals with specialized hardware for graphical calculation and display.[11] These early systems functioned using display lists that defined a series of graphical commands in memory to be interpreted by a "display processor" for output onto a screen.[12] It was the display processor that made information legibly visible given the material restrictions of the hardware architecture being used. It was also extremely expensive, accounting for more than half the cost of most display systems, and largely unstandardized such that the design of a given display processor would greatly affect the programming techniques that could be used with the system—most of which had to be programmed directly by the end user themselves.[13] Early display processors functioned largely to convert digital information from a display list into signals that could be processed through analog function generators and shown on the calligraphic display of a CRT.[14] Unlike contemporary systems, graphical terminals in this period were primarily technologies of interpretation and conversion rather than stand-alone calculation, and as such, the graphics they produced were restricted to simple shapes and lines that could be derived from analog functions. In order to render complex geometric objects, new hardware needed to be developed that could take on the task of calculation itself, albeit a calculation catered specifically to graphical data.

a)

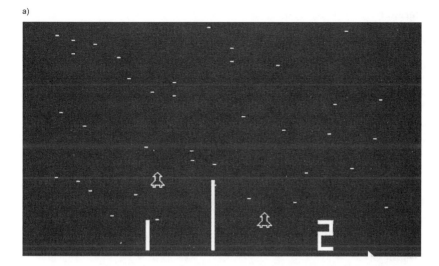

b)

Figure 5.4
Screenshot from Atari's *Space Race* (1973) showing its graphical rocket ship design
(top), and the game's system board with the soldered bitmap of that ship (bottom).
Courtesy of Ed Fries.

Iteration

With this transformation from interpretation to calculation the display processor emerges as the first stand-alone object that we might identify as a progenitor to the modern GPU, though at this early stage it is unclear precisely what form such an object might take. It was this question that motivated Ivan Sutherland and Theodore Myer to begin research into the design of display processors in the late 1960s, thus leading them to a realization that presages one of the principal structuring logics of contemporary graphical systems. In specializing for a specific kind of computing, graphics falls into a recursive cycle in which each part of the system tends toward selfsame discreteness—a transformation whereby the site of the computer as a distinct and singular object is lost through an iterative process of ever increasing complexity:

> We approached the task [of designing a display processor] by starting with a simple scheme and adding commands and features that we felt would enhance the power of the machine. Gradually the processor became more complex. We were not disturbed by this because computer graphics, after all, are complex. Finally the display processor came to resemble a full-fledged computer with some special graphics features. And then a strange thing happened. We felt compelled to add to the processor a second, subsidiary processor, which, itself, began to grow in complexity. It was then that we discovered a disturbing truth. Designing a display processor can become a never-ending cyclical process. In fact, we found the process so frustrating that we have come to call it the "wheel of reincarnation."[15]

This trend has only accelerated over time, with modern GPUs comprised of dozens of cores capable of parallel computation. From its very origins, graphical hardware tends toward this mise en abyme logic, whereby a computer becomes a nested structure of machines within machines within machines.[16]

In graphical systems, unlike the singular focus of the general-purpose CPU, computational hardware functions as a series of nested instances of the same iterative object, such that complexity can be understood as the internal repetition of a single structure or logic. For Sutherland and Myer, this recursion is not simply a logical or linguistic property but instead an emergent quality of the material structure of computational hardware itself, at least as it is applied to graphical calculation. This "wheel," as they describe it, points to the unique challenge of computer graphics as a computationally intensive and demanding procedure whose simulation can be endlessly supplemented by smaller and more specialized computers—a structure or topology that will appear again and again as the field evolves over the next fifty years.[17] An exemplary contemporary instance of this process can be seen in what is commonly known as Blinn's law, named after graphics researcher Jim Blinn and his observation that "as technology advances, rendering time remains constant."[18] Put simply, as computer hardware improves over time it is tasked with performing increasingly complex graphical procedures, such that the render time of a given image is restricted by cultural and economic mandates over how much time a human operator is willing or able to wait. Even as individual processors grow faster and more efficient, the number of processors in a given system continues to grow to keep up with the demands of Blinn's law.

From this moment graphical systems continue to grow in scale and complexity, supplemented by custom hardware designed to rapidly perform the operations of the graphics pipeline. This process was well underway by the early 1970s, with display processors gradually supplemented by specialized hardware to form complete graphical systems for the commercial market. Once again, E&S was at the forefront of this transformation, releasing its Line Drawing System (LDS-1) in 1969 with a playful appropriation of the formal name of the Church of Jesus Christ of Latter-day Saints—a nod to the regional context in which the machine was developed and the religion, current or former, of many of its developers.[19] The LDS-1 was specifically built to outperform the IBM 2250, the machine that was the outgrowth of IBM's working partnership with GM on the DAC-1 and arguably the first commercial graphics terminal.[20] While the 2250 was well suited to most basic graphical applications, it had major limitations. Most critically, the system was designed to operate as a terminal relying solely on a graphics program loaded into a mainframe computer, making it extremely slow. As discussed above, speed is a crucial component of any graphics system, particularly for any interactive system that requires a high refresh rate. These limitations restricted the kinds of graphical work that could be done on the 2250, and did not suit the real-time needs of large-scale simulation.

E&S decided to tackle this issue directly with the LDS-1, which functioned as an independent stored program processor devoted exclusively to graphical calculation. The terminal was designed to supplement and share memory with a general-purpose central processing computer, and could be further broken up into a number of dedicated component parts to be purchased separately depending on the needs of a customer or facility. The goal of the system was acceleration through specialization—that is, transforming those graphical operations that were previously done by the central processor into dedicated hardware objects operating alongside the general-purpose computer.[21] Unlike earlier display processor systems, the LDS-1 offered custom hardware units for each stage in the graphics pipeline, with a twelve-inch vector display or "scope," clipping divider, and matrix multiplier to supplement the stand-alone display processor.[22] This complete implementation in hardware made the LDS-1 the first computational device that we might now identify as a complete GPU—albeit in a physical form radically different from contemporary systems. In its initial release, the LDS-1 sold for $150,000—over $1,000,000 today—and consisted of three cabinets weighing a total of 475 pounds with an installed footprint the size of approximately two refrigerators (figure 5.5).[23]

The LDS-1 achieved its flexibility and efficiency not only by deploying specialized hardware but also by implementing what E&S termed "cascaded asynchronous processing," in which graphical tasks were calculated simultaneously and in parallel with one another. As noted in the machine's manual, in one of the earliest uses of the term "graphic processing unit," "The result is a 'pipeline' effect wherein each graphics processing unit operates simultaneously on a different picture line. As the Scope paints one line, the Clipping Divider computes the next line, the Matrix Multiplier processes the following line, and the Display Processor fetches still another line."[24] Unlike the PDP-10 minicomputer that it was designed to augment, the LDS-1 was able to synchronize these highly repetitive graphical tasks to enable rapid calculation for real-time display. While this may appear a minor change, it is a fundamental transformation in the temporality of computation—a move away from the linear fetch, decode, and execute instruction cycle of general-purpose computing, and toward synchronous, highly parallel calculation.[25] This transformation allowed, for the first time, a true range of programmable 3D graphical applications for the commercial market, from aircraft simulation to glacier and iceberg flow studies. As the manual suggests, "For the first time, the user can develop true motion pictures, zoom in to review detailed material in a massive drawing without losing orientation, and easily rotate complex three-dimensional objects to study their shape and characteristics. Utilization possibilities are limitless" (figure 5.6).[26]

In the LDS-1, computation was reimagined as an explicitly graphical process—one tied to the logic of graphical systems in which each image is

Figure 5.5
Ivan Sutherland (right) tests an early implementation of the Line Drawing System (LDS-1) at Evans and Sutherland Computer Corporation, 1969. Courtesy of the Special Collections Department, J. Willard Marriott Library, University of Utah.

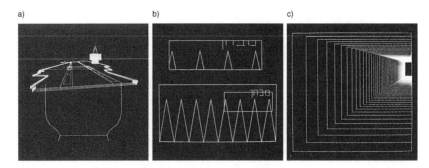

Figure 5.6
Screenshots taken from the LDS-1 system showing various applications, including flight simulation and CAD, 1969.

understood as an assemblage of discrete computational objects to be processed and passed along the graphics pipeline. This object orientation is likewise reflected in the software produced for the LDS-1 at the University of Utah, where researchers developed a system for parsing object complexity to accelerate render time. This picture-oriented technique (POT) deployed generalized graphical procedures to simplify storage and calculation. Rather than treat each instance of an object as separate and unique, the software was designed such that for any instance of an object, the system need only point to a single set of data, an abstract "symbol" that could be transformed as necessary in the graphics pipeline for each rendered instance. "For example, there may be a procedure which draws any arbitrary rectangle given its left-bottom and right-top points. Then in POT there exists only one copy of this pure procedure which may be referenced several times; each time associated with a different set of coordinate values."[27] All instances of an object are in effect the same object. The only changes that must be stored are those transformations that change its appearance in a given render.[28] Defining geometrically similar objects in this way, as symbols, "allows the display program to operate on the same basic coordinate data, producing the same object in different sizes and in various locations throughout the picture. Programming is simplified considerably."[29]

This language of orientation is telling, concurrent with Alan Kay's research at Utah on the Dynabook system that would form the basis for his work on the Smalltalk programming language at Xerox PARC. Indeed, "symbols" here function almost identically to classes in object-oriented systems, such that all graphical objects may be considered instances of a given symbol. As chapter 4 made clear, Kay's object-oriented design has its origins in a range of technological developments throughout the 1960s, but the widespread use of object-oriented models in early graphics research from Sketchpad to the LDS-1 suggests the primacy of the image form in the construction and conceptualization of computational objects. This picture orientation—as a technique for parsing complexity through the instancing of simple object forms or primitives—points to a structuring logic whose diffusion into contemporary systems through the lineage of the GPU begins here.

Miniaturization

While the theoretical and conceptual framework of the GPU has its origins in some of the first graphical systems ever developed, these terminals were massive, expensive, and highly specialized. Machines like the LDS-1 sold relatively few units commercially, and saw little use outside industries already invested in graphical design and simulation.[30] These machines are best understood as the progenitors to the rapid growth in graphical simulation that begins in the 1980s, but the catalyst for this transformation would require a dramatic shift in scale. The 1970s had seen the speedy development of the microprocessor, a technique for incorporating the functions of a computer's CPU into a single integrated circuit, thereby greatly reducing the cost of processing power and increasing the efficiency of computational systems generally. Over the course of the 1970s, the number of transistors that could be fit on a single chip increased exponentially, leading to the so-called revolution in VLSI toward the end of the decade.[31] At the time, VLSI functioned as the historical test case for what has come to be known as Moore's law, or the theory that the number of transistors that could fit on an integrated circuit would double every two years—a theory that has since been extrapolated into any number of growth metrics in computer science.[32]

The origins of the transistor itself as a discrete technical object can be traced to the late 1940s, and the integrated circuit to as early as 1959, but it was not until 1971 that Intel developed and commercialized the first single-chip microprocessor, dramatically reducing the size and cost of computational hardware over the subsequent decade (figure 5.7).[33] Along with this

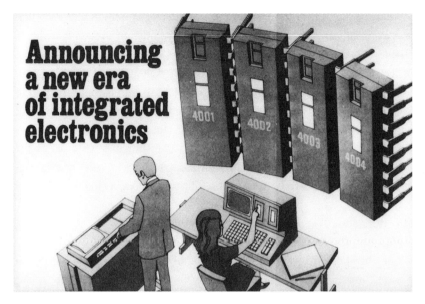

Figure 5.7
Intel's first microprocessor advertisement, *Electronic News*, November 1971. Courtesy of the Intel Corporation and the Computer History Museum.

drop in price came a rapid growth in the use of computers across a wide range of industries. As Intel's first annual report following its initial public offering in October 1971 notes,

> Innovative design work by our engineers in 1970 and 1971 culminated with the introduction of MCS-4 and MCS-8, which are microcomputers built around one-chip Central Processor Units (CPUs) selling for less than $100 each. The low cost of the CPUs will allow them to move into hundreds of product areas which never before could justify the use of a general purpose computer.[34]

Motivated by the possibilities of this scaling, an engineering professor named Carver Mead began teaching integrated circuit design courses at Caltech in the early 1970s, recruiting key researchers in hopes of spearheading the industry that would quite literally come to define what is now known as Silicon Valley.[35] Among them was Sutherland, who had left Utah for Los Angeles in 1974 with the aspiration of capitalizing on his graphical research by founding a computer animation firm called the Electric Picture Company.[36] This goal proved premature—Sutherland later described the project as a spectacular failure—and within six months he sold his interest in the business and took a job at the RAND Corporation. It was at RAND that Sutherland met and was recruited by Mead to become the founding chair of the new computer science department at Caltech.[37] Within a year Sutherland had conducted a major ARPA study of the limitations of then-current techniques for microelectronics fabrication, recommending new research into the system design implications of "very-large-scale integrated circuits" to tackle the needs of the field of computer science in the coming decade.[38]

This work culminated in January 1976 when Sutherland wrote a letter to his brother Bert, who had joined the research team at Xerox PARC one year prior, suggesting that PARC and Caltech work together to attack the system complexity problem.[39] While not explicit until this moment, the careers of the two brothers had overlapped and intersected throughout the 1960s and 1970s. Like Ivan, Bert received his PhD in electrical engineering from MIT under the advising of Claude Shannon. His thesis built on Ivan's work on computer graphics with specific applications in graphical programming language design, after which he managed the computer science division of Bolt, Beranek and Newman (BBN), where he helped to develop the ARPANET and became one of the earliest E&S customers.[40] Bert joined PARC in 1975 as lead of the Systems Science Laboratory, where he helped in the development of the Smalltalk programing language with Kay, Goldberg, and Ingalls. While never explicitly tied to the Utah graphics program, Bert played an instrumental role in the success of its network of researchers and engineers as they moved from the academy to industry.

By the end of 1976 the Sutherland brothers had established a research collaboration between PARC and Caltech that brought together Mead and engineer Lynn Conway with a small group of researchers "to explore and develop design methods and tools that would enable complex digital system architectures to be more readily implemented in silicon than in the past."[41] This work would eventually lead to the so-called Mead and Conway revolution in VLSI, responsible for the exponential growth in speed and processing power that has marked the field of computing for the last fifty years. As Michael Hiltzik suggests in his popular history of PARC, "VLSI [turned] every telephone, washing machine, and car—and thousands of other workaday appliances as well—into tiny computers."[42] Often overlooked in this language of inevitability is the labor of research and design, facilitated by cultural networks working across institutions and developed over decades. It is telling that some six years after joining the Utah program and founding

E&S, Ivan joined a network of Utah colleagues and students in California to work on a new set of problems facing the field of computer science.[43] This extension of an existing network into new research fields supported and enabled this transformation, even as its focus shifts from explicitly graphical problems onto more generalizable hardware applications.

While at first glance this shift from graphics to circuits may seem a dramatic departure, it mirrors the dissemination of graphical concepts into the field of computing more broadly.[44] Indeed, the "revolution" that Sutherland and others catalyzed in this period was arguably only possible by virtue of the graphical technologies that had been developed in the decade prior. While the earliest transistors were designed as physical blueprints with ink and paper, as microprocessors shrunk in size and grew in complexity they demanded an increasing degree of computational mediation. Sutherland's now-infamous letter bringing together research teams at Caltech and PARC states explicitly that a collaboration was necessary due to the graphical capabilities of the systems Xerox was developing at that time. The goal of the collaboration would be to learn how to "program" an integrated circuit from conception to manufacture, such that a researcher could simply "describe [a] design to a computer in terms corresponding to his conception, have the design simulated to see if its performance is what he expects, obtain computer help in executing the layout, and have the masks prepared automatically."[45] Central to this process was the use of computer graphics to design the circuits and simulate their function prior to manufacture.[46] Xerox was in fact an ideal partner specifically because it was one of only a few research facilities with access to the Alto minicomputer and its object-oriented graphical user interface (figure 5.8). Using the Alto workstations, the team at PARC could design and prototype new methods for the manufacture of those hardware objects that would make possible the growth of computational systems in the subsequent decade.

In this moment we can see an epistemic break, in which the design and function of the computer itself becomes a recursive process—one that is always already computational, operating at a scale and speed that demands the mediation of graphical simulation. As Friedrich Kittler once famously suggested, this is a grammatological shift in which "the bulk of written texts—including this text—do not exist anymore in perceivable time and space but in a computer memory's transistor cells." For Kittler, "the last

Figure 5.8
Lynn Conway in her office at Xerox PARC with an Alto computer behind her, 1983.
Courtesy of Margaret Moulton.

historical act of writing may well have been the moment when, in the early seventies, Intel engineers laid out some dozen square meters of blueprint paper (64 square meters, in the case of the later 8086) in order to design the hardware architecture of their first integrated microprocessor."[47] In off-loading the design of hardware from the hand of the engineer into graphical software, the computer ceases to cohere under the *dispositif* of writing or inscription, transformed by the logic of simulation. Indeed, the manufacturing process for microprocessor technology may be viewed as an extension of this image logic as integrated circuits were, and still are, manufactured through a photolithographic process in which layers of circuits and components are etched directly onto a wafer of photosensitive silicon, such that the object of this hardware is quite literally the tracing of an image in light.[48] What marks this epistemic shift is not simply a transformation in size, speed, or complexity but rather the graphical mediation that these transformations necessitate. For Kittler this is the abstraction of *software*, yet I would argue that the interface and its graphical simulation are the principal features of this abstraction. It is here that we start to see a recursive transformation in the material form of computation itself, the moment when the computer becomes an object that can only be designed and produced by another computer, *digital* not only in its function but also its material structure, a self-replicating system, an image object.

Recursion

At PARC this transformation begins in 1976 with the development of the ICARUS integrated circuit layout program—a graphical CAD system for the Xerox Alto built specifically for the design of integrated circuits.[49] Using a windowed interface that engineers could draw and layer circuit elements onto, ICARUS allowed researchers to scale from the lowest level of circuit layout up, producing dense and complex systems that would be near impossible to model in a physical medium (figure 5.9). This was accomplished through a design logic structured around "symbols," which allowed designers to define commonly used circuit architectures as objects to be stored in memory and recalled repeatedly as needed. In this sense, ICARUS adopts the object logic seen in earlier CAD systems—such as Sutherland's Sketchpad or the LDS-1—as a technique for modeling complexity in a nested hierarchy. In fact, the physical limitations of the Alto necessitated this methodology, as

Figure 5.9
Alan Bell, architect of the prototype MPC software system, overseeing the final merge and die layout planning of MPC79 projects in ICARUS, Xerox PARC, December 4, 1979. Courtesy of Lynn Conway.

the computer had only 128 KB of RAM and each unique layout form needed to be stored separately in memory. By storing each symbol only once and recalling that same object repeatedly throughout the drawing, much less memory was used. These symbols could be clustered to form larger symbols in turn, working their way up to complete chips laid out by the hundreds or even thousands on a single silicon wafer.[50]

The research team's goal was to create a robust and scalable system for microchip development, and to this end, it developed a number of technologies to help catalyze this change. While ICARUS was essential for design and layout, it was supplemented by a custom programming language, graphical file format, and set of rules developed by Conway to standardize circuit design methodologies so that hardware could be manufactured on a wide range of systems, in a variety of facilities, and at scale.[51] Conway's rules were arguably the most important contribution to this process. In the mid-1970s, the development environment for circuit design was highly balkanized, with complex and evolving production standards that varied by manufacturer. Conway's contribution was to designate a scalable standard unit that could be adjusted to suit any given production system and, more important, scale as the density of semiconductors increased over time following Moore's law. As Conway observes, "[Semiconductor] design rules should not be framed as sets of lengths but as sets of ratios of lengths. Such dimensionless rules could then be scaled to any process as multiples of a basic length unit in microns, a unit I called Lambda (λ)" (plate 16).[52] The size of Lambda was derived from the smallest functional resolution of the photolithographic printing process, tying the scale of VLSI and its growth to the physical limitations of the optical technology that enabled it. This was a complete reimagining of the way hardware had been designed to date. Conway's team at PARC was, in effect, rewriting the rulebook on computer hardware in anticipation of the promise of exponential growth, not only in transistor density, but in the potential future uses for microchip technology. What was once a highly specialized and unstandardized process was now something that could be taught to any undergraduate computer science student. This work led Conway to propose the production of a textbook that would concretize and legitimize the methods the team had developed. PARC was an ideal test bed for the project as the team had access to its experimental printers and Interpress page description language, as described in chapter 4. This meant they could prototype a full-color textbook on a small scale, and then "debug" their methodology by deploying the book in select computer science programs across the country.

Early drafts of what would become Conway and Mead's *Introduction to VLSI Systems* were developed in 1978, and deployed in classes at the University of California at Berkeley and Caltech.[53] Later that year, Bert Sutherland urged the team to expand its scope, pushing Conway to launch the first full course on VLSI design at MIT that fall.[54] The class was an opportunity for Conway to develop a clear pedagogy on VLSI design and proved hugely successful, pushing the Mead and Conway approach to the forefront of academic and industry conversations on hardware design and manufacturing. Encouraged by this success, Conway sought to test the system at scale, leading her to develop an updated VLSI course in 1979 that would be offered simultaneously at twelve universities around the country.

To accomplish this significant task, the course was coordinated across each institution using the ARPANET, networking the team's efforts through the standard formats and protocols developed by Conway and her research team at PARC. "With such a system, we could send messages to the chip 'authors,' coordinate all activity, . . . and then at the design cut-off time, reel in the final projects' design files."[55] Unlike in commercial chip manufacturing where a single chip is printed in large quantities, Conway's VLSI system allowed for the production of multiproject chips (MPCs) in which a range of experimental designs could be printed on a single silicon wafer, allowing students and researchers to test a variety of highly specialized integrated circuit architectures (figure 5.10). While this style of large-scale collaboration via the internet is now commonplace, it was unheard of at the time and a huge risk for PARC researchers looking to prove the validity of their design methodology.[56] They called the experimental demonstration trial MPC79, and it would ultimately lay the groundwork for an industry-wide transformation in the design of computer hardware, propagating VLSI methods into over a hundred universities and scores of start-up companies within only a few years.

Parallelization

That same summer, James Clark attended a three-day workshop led by Mead and Conway for a handful of faculty and staff at Stanford University.[57] Five years prior at Utah, Clark had worked under Sutherland to develop an experimental program for designing curved b-spline surfaces using a head-mounted display system—one of the earliest applications for virtual reality.[58] On graduating, Clark took a faculty position at the University of California at Santa Cruz before leaving to join Utah colleague Edwin Catmull at NYIT. Less than a year later, Clark was fired from NYIT for expressing concern over the unconventional leadership of its director, Alexander Schure, and in 1979 returned to California as an untenured associate professor at Stanford University. There Clark took up an interest in VLSI, seeing in it the potential to address the demanding computational and financial costs of graphical systems.[59] Given the proximity of PARC and its close relationship with the university, Clark asked Conway if he could sit in at the research center to learn the basics of chip design and produce a product for MPC79. She agreed, and that fall Clark produced a proof-of-concept microchip for what he would come to call the "Geometry Engine," a VLSI processor designed exclusively for the calculation of graphical data: the first

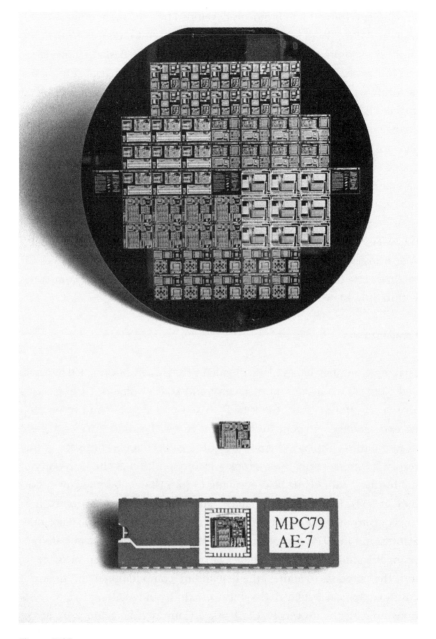

Figure 5.10
MPC79 wafer type A along with packaged and wired-bonded project chip AE-7, January 2, 1980. Courtesy of Lynn Conway.

modern GPU (plate 17).[60] In this watershed moment, the field of computer graphics turns in on itself once again, as a graphical system developed for CAD is used to produce microchips whose complexity necessitates graphical simulation, and that in turn forms the basis for the production of specialized hardware built explicitly for the display and acceleration of computer graphics. The threshold for what constitutes a graphical object here begins to blur between algorithm, software, hardware, and image, with each of the previous logics described above collapsing into a single form.

The Geometry Engine deployed VLSI to accomplish a range of repetitive and generalizable tasks for computer graphics visualization, coalescing each part of the graphics pipeline into a single object—a massing of its historical articulation into a unified whole.

> A single chip type is used in 12 slightly different configurations to accomplish 4x4 matrix multiplications; line, character, and polygon clipping; and scaling of the clipped results to display device coordinates. The system will do these functions in a highly parallel organization having an effective operation rate of about four million floating-point operations per second; 48 identical units, four per chip, each will do a floating-point operation in about 12 microseconds. Thus, the system will transform, clip, and scale incoming floating-point 2D or 3D coordinates representing endpoints of lines or vertices of polygons at a rate of about 3500 lines, or 900 polygons, every 1/30 second.[61]

This was an exponential shift of the scale, speed, size, and relative cost of graphical calculation. Not only did Clark's system create a chip customized for floating point calculation in graphical systems, but each chip could be slightly modified and deployed in multiples to accomplish full renders in parallel, allowing for the true real-time calculation of complex three-dimensional scenes. Clark's inspiration came from an early clipping divider by Sutherland and Sproull, designed in 1968 and later produced in hardware for use in the E&S LDS-1. Sutherland and Sproull's machine achieved its high performance by programming four clipping units to operate in parallel, one for each bounding edge of the screen or window.[62] Modeling his Geometry Engine on the clipping divider archetype, Clark built parallel calculation throughout the design of his Geometry Engine, such that coordinate transformation along the x, y, and z axes, as well as the four-sided clipping calculations, were all made using a highly parallel pipeline configuration.[63] This logic of parallel calculation persists as a principal feature of the GPU today, even as it has become increasingly disarticulated from strictly graphical procedures. Indeed, it is the primary logic that distinguishes graphical computing from general-purpose calculation.

By 1982 Clark had left Stanford to found Silicon Graphics, Inc. (SGI), taking with him a group of seven graduate students and research staff from the university (figure 5.11).[64] The team spent the following two years developing the Integrated Raster Imaging System (IRIS) line of workstations, powered by the final iteration of Clark's VLSI design known as the Geometry System and an accompanying software interface known as the IRIS Graphics Library (IRIS GL).[65] Clark had initially planned to use SGI to market both personal computer systems and CAD turnkey workstations for the high-end market, but the company ultimately abandoned personal computing in favor of large corporate contracts and high-end workstations for design, entertainment, and engineering.[66] The IRIS 1000 line of machines, released by SGI in 1984, marked a new generation of graphical hardware.

Figure 5.11
The founding team at Silicon Graphics, Inc. in 1986 (from left to right): James Clark, Marcia Allen, Diane Wilford, Kurt Akeley, Marc Hannah, Tom Davis, Rocky Rhodes, and Mark Grossman. Courtesy of the Computer History Museum.

It was smaller and more immediately interactive than earlier technologies, and even at $37,500 significantly cheaper than systems produced by E&S a decade prior.[67] Logically the IRIS was structured around all the same technologies that had been developed over the past twenty years, but in formalizing and miniaturizing these objects into a discrete and highly parallel metaobject, the entire process was accelerated. What was once a calculation to be executed over minutes, hours, or days had become a real-time, interactive process.

With the GPU began a radical reshaping of the field of computer graphics and visual culture more broadly. As Hiltzik notes, "After the appearance of Clark's chip, the art and science of computer graphics would never be the same: The computer-aided design of cars and aircraft, the 'virtual reality' toys and games of the modern midway, the lumbering dinosaurs of the movie *Jurassic Park*—they all sprang from [this] tiny chip."[68] Early applications for SGI machines were largely limited to mechanical engineering and chemistry, where researchers needed relatively inexpensive machines for 3D modeling and simulations. With little interest in 3D graphics from workstation manufacturers such as Hewlett-Packard, Apollo Computer, and Sun Microsystems, SGI had little competition and was able to establish a stronghold in these niche industries. By the mid-1980s, the company had expanded into applications in special effects and motion graphics, including collaborations with Industrial Light & Magic, the famed special effects division of Lucasfilm, beginning in 1987. Many of the early graphics associated with the rise of digital special effects are the product of SGI machines, from the liquid metal cyborg featured in the film *Terminator 2* (1992) to the special effects in *The Hunt for Red October* (1990) and *The Abyss* (1989); even the 3D scenes in *Beauty and the Beast* (1991) were all created on SGI computers.

One of the company's most prominent successes was the film *Jurassic Park* (1993), whose spectacular special effects were developed using SGI machines. In keeping with the futuristic vision of computer graphics at the time, SGI workstations were also featured prominently in the film's narrative and set direction as part of the high-tech genomics lab used to engineer the film's dinosaurs—a conceit not far from the truth given that the machines were largely responsible for the existence of the dinosaurs on screen (figure 5.12).[69] This period culminated in a collaboration between SGI and Industrial Light & Magic to produce a high-tech entertainment

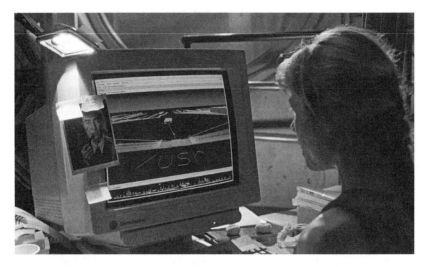

Figure 5.12
"It's a UNIX system, I know this!" A Silicon Graphics, Inc. workstation featured in Steven Spielberg's *Jurassic Park* (1993). The interface seen here is the 3D File System Navigator for the IRIX operating system, which as its name implies, is based on UNIX.

special effects laboratory called the Joint Environment for Digital Imaging, marking a shift toward entertainment applications for SGI and the field of computer graphics generally. From 1995 to 2002, all films nominated for an Academy Award for Distinguished Achievement in Visual Effects were created on SGI computer systems, but the company's influence was not limited to special effects in popular cinema.[70] From 1994 to 1996, the company worked with the Nintendo corporation to develop the Reality Co-Processor microchip that made possible the 3D graphics of its Nintendo 64 game console, bringing 3D graphics into the home as an accessible domestic technology years before such images were commonplace on most commercially accessible personal computers.[71] In many ways, SGI defined the visual aesthetic of computer graphics in the period in which the technology was most visibly new.[72]

Crystallization

By the late 1990s, stand-alone workstations began to converge with graphics card technologies to produce the modern GPU as it is widely understood today. Products like the NVIDIA GeForce 256—released in 1999 and marketed as the "world's first GPU"—mark this convergence of high-end graphics with stand-alone hardware that can be embedded within a personal computer.[73] 3D graphics had finally become a widely accessible technology, even as SGI fell into rapid decline, filing for bankruptcy in 2006 after struggling for years to adapt to a changing market.

Today, SGI's original Mountain View headquarters is home to the Computer History Museum. After the building's sale in 2002, it was heavily renovated as part of a two-year, $19 million makeover from 2009 to 2011, yet despite this transformation, it retains much of the original structure: the faceted curve of the building's facade still resembles the pixelated grid of a computer screen, and the conference rooms inside are still lined with custom canvas blinds that evoke the sails of a ship—one of Clark's favorite pastimes (figure 5.13). On visiting the museum's archives in 2012 to view materials related to the history of SGI, I was placed in an empty cubicle in the upstairs offices, as there was no designated space at that time for researchers to view the museum's collections.[74] Watching a VHS tape of promotional material from 1996, in which a man demonstrated the graphical capabilities of an SGI workstation, I was struck by the strange familiarity of the scene: the low, angular desk at which he sat, and the bright purple cubicle dividers that surrounded him.[75] Pushing back from the television, I realized I was sitting at that same desk, surrounded by those same dividers, custom designed for SGI in 1994 to mirror the bold colors of its IRIS workstation towers, on display one floor below me as part of the museum's permanent collection (plates 18–19). On selling the building in 2002, SGI had simply abandoned what remained—objects that were then taken up and repurposed by the museum in a palimpsest that mirrors the work of history itself.

It is no exaggeration to suggest that the silicon microchip is one of the principal catalysts in the rapid growth of the computing industry over the past forty years—a transformation that necessitated the mediation of graphical systems, and for which a graphical object, the GPU, was arguably its most radical and innovative test case.[76] Yet even while the GPU marked the beginning of a graphical transformation that would grow to touch almost every aspect of our visual culture, it was also the culmination of a decades-long restructuring of the very concept of computation from linear, procedural calculation to a highly parallel and recursive process oriented toward the simulation of the world as discrete computational objects. Far

Figure 5.13
Facade of the Silicon Graphics, Inc., headquarters in Mountain View, California (Paul Warchol, 1994). Courtesy of Paul Warchol.

from marking a revolutionary moment in which a single technology is developed that allowed for the rapid transformation of an obscure field of research, the GPU is an object displaced throughout the history of graphics, coming to cohere under a discrete historical function at the start of the 1980s. Through its fixing of the logic of software into a discrete hardware object, the GPU distills each of the material objects that make up the history of computer graphics—and indeed this book—into a single metaobject, collapsing their complex material and historical specificity into an embeddable chip. In this way the GPU articulates the historical claim of computation itself, whose future-oriented teleology flattens and operationalizes the messy work of history. Unlike those media that defined the episteme of the twentieth century, in which history is preserved through the act of recording the passage of time, graphical hardware does not preserve history; it hardens into a singular logic that executes the act of representation.[77] Yet the historical thing it crystallizes is not change or transformation but rather the logic of procedural flows, of repetition and acceleration, a *procedure crystallized*. While the GPU is perhaps the clearest example of this logic, we might extrapolate this historical claim onto the culture of computer graphics more broadly, whose investment is in the formalization and acceleration of the graphics pipeline.

By understanding and tracing this ethos, we can begin to identify the logic that the GPU enacts beyond the screen and mark its influence more broadly as one of the principal technologies of our contemporary media landscape. While the radical innovation of the GPU was its narrow specialization that fixed and delimited what kinds of computation its processor could do, the GPU goes through one final transformation in the early 2000s that turns graphics in on itself once again. Starting with the release of the NVIDIA GeForce 3 in March 2001, graphics processors become programmable, such that each pixel and geometric vertex can now be processed by a short program called a "shader" before being output on a screen.[78] These shaders are sometimes called the "Gutenberg press for graphics"—a cliché in the history of technology, but surprisingly accurate in this case, as a shader materially resembles the function and scale of this earlier transformation. Rather than render a book letter by letter—or in this case, a movie pixel by pixel—shaders render entire pages at once, stamping out complete images in rapid succession. In effect, each pixel on a screen is transformed into a custom computer, capable of highly parallel programmable computation. Shaders are so powerful that they have subsequently been adapted for nongraphical calculation.[79] These general-purpose GPUs have grown to become nearly as flexible as CPUs, but can calculate at orders of magnitude faster due to the highly parallel nature of their architecture, derived from the unique needs of the graphics pipeline. GPU-enabled systems now form the infrastructural backbone of almost all high-end computational research into machine learning, big data, computer vision, neural networks, and much more (figure 5.14). GPUs and other derivative processors are likewise used in the mining of cryptocurrency and other blockchain applications, linked together in dozens and sometimes hundreds of processors to perform brute-force calculations. Looking forward, highly customized and

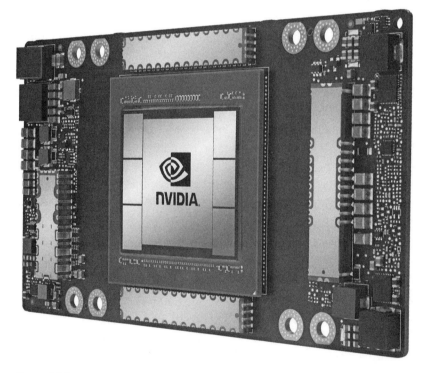

Figure 5.14
Rendering of an NVIDIA A100 Tensor Core GPU, used for artificial intelligence, data analytics, machine learning, cloud computing, and countless other high-performance applications. Courtesy of NVIDIA.

application-specific processor chips are being developed for future applications in artificial intelligence and related fields. Through the GPU, we have effectively reimagined the world as a massive computational task that can be solved through parallel processing—a compelling vision that is not without costs or consequences.[80]

Graphical calculation began as an exception to the universal quality of general-purpose computing. The scale and speed it required pushed researchers to develop entirely new hardware objects customized to the unique needs of computer graphics. The discrete and highly parallel quality of the graphics pipeline offered a vision of the world as a gigantic data task to be solved, with each pixel of its window onto the world a discrete computer capable of independent calculation. In a surprising transformation, this picture has come to supplant the universalizing vision of general-purpose computing, and has in turned transformed our very notion of what computing is and can be. It would be a simplification to suggest the future of computing is derived from the history of computer graphics, but we likewise cannot ignore the origins of the highly specialized parallel computation that defines that future. In this sense, the history and attendant logics of computer graphics have come to radically transform the field of computing at almost every level, even as this connection is effaced through the crystallization of its procedural logic.

Coda: After Objects

To "transcode" something is to translate it into another format. The computerization of culture gradually accomplishes similar transcoding in relation to all cultural categories and concepts. That is, cultural categories and concepts are substituted, on the level of meaning and/or language, by new ones that derive from the computer's ontology, epistemology, and pragmatics. New media thus acts as a forerunner of this more general process of cultural reconceptualization.

—Lev Manovich, *The Language of New Media*

Because a line has been crossed, technology/software/code is in and of the world and there's no getting out of it. Some architects can look at a building and tell you which version of Autodesk was used to create it. The world is defined by our visualizations of it.

—James Bridle, "#sxaesthetic"

In 2018, Volkswagen announced it was discontinuing production of the VW Beetle—the last in a series of ends for the now-iconic object. The original Type 1 that so inspired Ivan Sutherland's students had been decommissioned years before, following the release of the redesigned "New Beetle" at the end of the 1990s.[1] In 2012, the car was reimagined once more—this time as a sleek coupé—in hopes of appealing to younger drivers, but ultimately the company could never reproduce the success of the original icon. Promotional images released to announce the 2019 "Final Edition" show the Beetle posed in a variety of hip, urban environments (figure 6.1). As is common in nearly all marketing material today, these images are entirely digital. Pieced together as composites of digital photographs and computer-generated models, the cars are seamlessly integrated into the scene. Each has been shaped by the smooth spline curves that define the aesthetic of all modern vehicles and

a)

b)

Figure 6.1
Promotional materials for the 2019 Volkswagen Beetle A5, showing alternate models and colors.

rendered to reflect the virtual environment that surrounds them—casting shadows across the pavement below, skinned in the texture of plastic, rubber, and metal, reflecting light off every possible surface. They are ideal image objects. Taken in isolation, each car is largely indistinguishable as computer generated; only in the aggregate is their artifice revealed. In different images rendered for different markets a near-identical scene unfolds, swapping out models, colors, and trims to present objects customized to the tastes of a given demographic.

These are not pictures of objects in the world. They are pictures of a way of making the world, an articulation of a particular relation toward objects as computational systems. At first glance they may resemble that afternoon in 1972 when Utah students took yardsticks and yellow paint to the surface of Marsha Sutherland's car, transforming it into the first rendered image derived from a material object in the physical world, but in the intervening half century that world has undergone a radical transformation, such that a vast number of the objects we see, use, and touch every day are derived from this same logic, products of the history of computer graphics.[2]

Today over 75 percent of product images in IKEA's annual catalog are fully computer generated (figure 6.2). This includes at least 35 percent of IKEA's nonproduct images—domestic scenes of offices, kitchens, and bedrooms, all fully computer generated.[3] Far removed from the uncanny spectacle of digital monsters and special effects, these everyday spaces exemplify a mundane intimacy that elides their digital construction.[4] These are the background objects with which we surround ourselves—objects that shape

Figure 6.2
A digital catalog render of the VIMLE love seat currently sitting in the author's office.

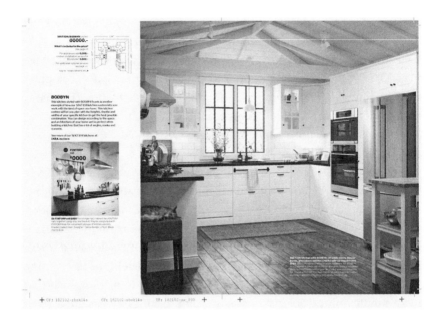

Figure 6.3
3D scene from the 2016 IKEA catalog. Rendered with 3DS Max and V-Ray. Martin Enthed, *IKEA, VR, AR, and Meatballs*, November 14, 2017, https://vimeo.com/243860738.

the environments in which we live and work, and in turn, shape our very notion of how these spaces appear, our very notion of what looks like home (figure 6.3). This work began in 2005 with a single wooden chair, but has grown to encapsulate the vast majority of the images the company produces. Rendering images in this way is not only simpler given the scale of production and the number of objects IKEA makes but also allows for object variability in color and material, and for highly localized images that translate this sense of domesticity into different cultural contexts and for different markets.[5]

In a strange sense, the IKEA catalog functions as the perfect articulation of Ivan Sutherland's "ultimate display," that futurist fantasy of a room in which a computer can control the existence of matter. If the challenge of graphical realism is the highly uneven quality of its simulation, IKEA solves for realism by controlling the limits of what can be simulated. Each room is filled with objects designed and produced by IKEA—objects whose dimension and texture is known in profound detail. "A chair displayed in such a room would be good enough to sit in."[6] Indeed, these rooms are filled with chairs that you may purchase and assemble, and in which you might ultimately sit.[7] That these rooms are ideal sandboxes for graphical simulation is due largely to the fact that the objects staged within them begin their lives within a computer. Nearly every IKEA product is created first as a Solid-Works CAD file—an image object well before it is ever physically assembled out of particleboard and laminate. These same files form the basis for both the computer-aided manufacturing process that renders each object into flat-packed cardboard boxes, and the digital rendering of perfectly staged bedrooms and kitchens with 3DS Max and V-Ray, creating photo-realistic scenes to be laid out in InDesign and printed with a PostScript-compatible device.[8] These are objects uniquely suited to this environment, as much rendered as they are designed.

While it is tempting to view these images as a new kind of spectacle, what these images demonstrate is the surprising proximity of the image object, and the banality of its use and appearance. Computer graphics saturate our lived environment in the most unremarkable ways, and this everydayness transforms our orientation to the world through those very categories with which we make sense of that world as phenomenally knowable. It is this unremarkable quality that makes most computer graphics invisible to our everyday experience, yet these are the objects that exemplify the collapsing of the space between the digital and physical, that embody the and/both quality of our world: image and object.

Rather than page through the most recent IKEA catalog and marvel at the surprising realism of the images it contains, we might turn to the BILLY bookcase next to us in an effort to make it present as a digital object. To reenvision the world in this way requires a suspension of the visible as our primary mode of analysis. Nearly all images we encounter today are structured by computational objects whose function has been naturalized by the historical claim of computation. In surfacing these histories, we find complex and competing techniques for the production of mimetic simulation—complexities that are effaced in the standardization of hardware and software that black box the social and cultural contexts of their production. The chapters that make up this book mark only a fraction of these objects, but point toward a broad technique for the investigation and description of our digital culture—one we might deploy in the analysis of any number of technical practices that exceed the frame of the digital image.

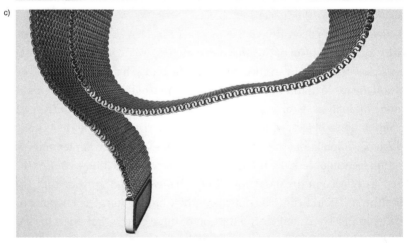

Figure 6.4
Frame captures from the 2014 Apple Watch "Reveal," featuring detailed views of a computer-generated model that appears to animate itself, with dials turning and wristbands clasping on their own.

In 2014, at the company's annual "September Event" in Cupertino, California, Apple surprised audiences by announcing the Apple Watch, the company's first original product following the death of cofounder Steve Jobs in 2011.[9] The announcement was made via a video that played at the end of CEO Tim Cook's presentation.[10] Opening with a dramatic image of the earth from low orbit, we watch the sun rise as the planet rotates into view as if to signal the dawn of new era. As the camera pans right, we see that this image is in fact the high-resolution screen of a device at great magnification. Gliding along the object's surface, the camera pores over the device in meticulous detail from the grooves in its metal to the polish of its glass, fixated on its material form while refusing a total picture of the thing itself. Suddenly, as if in response to our gaze, the device is animated. Its mechanical knob turns independent of any hand; its magnetic strap curls midair to snap closed on its own (figure 6.4). Slowly more of the object is revealed in an increasing number of colors and finishes, until dozens of watches can be seen floating toward the camera, each rotating to display a different image or application on its screen until a watch displaying a picture of the whole earth wipes away the scene, zooming down toward Cupertino and back to the shot with which we began.

For most viewers this would have been their first encounter with this particular object form: a wearable computer at once altogether new, and yet superficially familiar in form and appearance. It is therefore unsurprising that the video dwells in such detail on the minutia of the device, revealing it slowly and at great magnification. Yet as this spectral performance of twisting and floating should make clear, there is nothing physical about the object we see: it is entirely computer generated. Its curved surface is little more than a bevel and extrude operation in Autodesk Maya; its ray-traced screen reflects virtual light, filmed by a virtual camera. Despite the video's fascination with the material intricacies of this highly fetishized technical object, its materiality is more teapot than timepiece.

Like nearly all Apple devices produced today, the Apple Watch exemplifies a contemporary collapsing of computer and screen, such that the computer as a discrete object has become indistinguishable from its pixelated surface. Such objects clearly exemplify the crisis that digital media scholars have spent over twenty years cautioning against, insisting that computation and visualization are mutually inessential, and warning that the conflation of one with the other is detrimental to our understanding of an increasingly computational world. Looking past the simulated images described above, they might insist we open up the beautifully rendered black box and examine what is inside. In doing so, we would find that inside every first-generation Apple Watch is an S1-integrated computer. At 2.5-square centimeters, it includes nearly all technical components of the watch computer itself, including RAM, Wi-FI, gyroscope, and microcontrollers for power management, touch interaction, and more (figure 6.5). Embedded within this computer sits an integrated

Figure 6.5
Illustration of the S1-integrated computer used in the first-generation Apple Watch, which includes an integrated PowerVR SGX543 GPU. Even this official image is a digital composite of the S1, which likewise hides the internal board and microelectronics.

PowerVR SGX543 GPU, no more than half a centimeter across. Within this minuscule object sits the entire history of computer graphics, a crystallization of some sixty years of research. Thousands of times per second the Apple Watch executes that history as it processes and pushes graphical output to its screen. While this screen cannot be taken as synecdoche for the computer itself, the computer is nonetheless a graphical object in its representation, form, and material function. In its flattened instrumentalization we can see a manifestation of the historical claim of computation, along with the twinned fantasies of exponential growth and perfect simulation that drive nearly all research into contemporary computer graphics.

At the 2019 annual SIGGRAPH conference for computer graphics research, Intel announced the development of a new "law" to supplement—or perhaps replace—the now-famous Moore's law, first proposed by Intel CEO Gordon Moore in 1965 to describe the exponential growth over time in the number of transistors that can be fit on an integrated circuit.[11] Raja's law, named after Intel computer scientist Raja Koduri, suggests that the major macroarchitecture used for computing changes roughly every twenty years, with each transition increasing total computing power by a factor of ten (figure 6.6). Beginning with single-core CPUs at the start of the 1980s, the law asserts we have transitioned through the multicore CPUs of the early 2000s to arrive at the age of the GPU, a macroarchitecture that will define the next ten years of computational research.[12] While the meaning and motivation behind this new law is debatable, its observation about our historical present is undeniable. Nearly all contemporary cloud computing applications take advantage of the massively parallel architecture of GPU computing, and GPUs are central to the promises of machine learning and artificial intelligence, from self-driving cars and virtual assistants to computer vision and the Internet of Things. While most domestic applications for GPUs are still tied to high-end computer graphics for personal computer and console gaming, on a commercial and industrial scale, all manner of computational tasks are increasingly outsourced to cloud services and computing centers running GPU-enabled machines. These render farms and data centers may seem quite distant from the everyday cultures of contemporary digital media, but they are the machines that undergird the platforms that drive computational culture, such that every interaction one has with a computer is processed by or output through graphical systems.[13] The information these machines process may have nothing to do with the visual, geometric, or

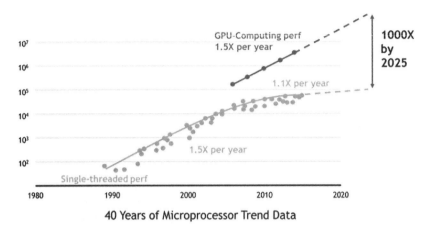

40 Years of Microprocessor Trend Data

Figure C.C
An NVIDIA graphic suggesting that the limits of semiconductor physics have caused CPU performance to diverge from Moore's law. The company suggests that GPU computing offers a path forward, restoring Moore's law and providing a one thousand times speedup by 2025. Courtesy of NVIDIA.

graphical applications that the GPU was originally designed for, but they are still materially shaped by this history and the formal logic that adheres to graphical systems. They function, in effect, as an array of image objects, and are used to reproduce the world as a data set made legible to the parallel logic of graphical computing.

The computer is not a visual medium. And yet computation as we know it today has been fundamentally shaped by computer graphics. It was the desire to make computation legible and accessible to human users that drove researchers to develop systems for graphical human-machine communication. While visual representation is in no way essential to the theory of computing or the practice of procedural calculation, computer graphics were largely responsible for the development of the computer as a technical *medium*, and for shaping our modern understanding of what computers are for and can do. In this sense computer graphics are not simply images appended to the textual, mathematical, or logical practice of computation; they are the process by which computation was made legible to us—a process that in turn reshaped computation to better reflect our understanding of the sensible world. Computer graphics mark a transformation in the very notion of what computing is through the imposition of a formal logic tied to our phenomenal understanding of the world as a structure of visible, interactive objects. As such, we must understand computer graphics not only as simulated images but also as computational objects set into relation with a simulated environment.

Over the past sixty years this ontological claim has, in turn, become an object itself—abstracted, embedded, and disarticulated to escape visual regimes altogether, transforming the way the material world is built, how systems are designed, and our very understanding of computation as a highly parallel system of discrete calculation.[14] Put simply, graphical systems have come to reshape the world, such that our lived environment is now saturated with objects transformed by this history of images. The phone in your pocket is a CAD file, as is the toothbrush sitting on your bathroom counter. The same file can be output as a visual image or physical object; it is at once both together. The shoes on your feet, the car you drove to work, the computer on which I write this, and the book you now read, each are indelibly tied to the history of computer graphics.

In 2010, artist Artie Vierkant published a PDF essay on the surf club website JstChillin.org. Titled "The Image Object Post-Internet," it serves as an artist statement and manifesto for a series of works Vierkant has continued to produce and adapt since 2011, collectively titled *Image Objects* (plate 20).[15] These works exist in a deliberate space of indeterminacy as sculptural objects that seem ripped from the screen of a software program bearing the trace of digital paint strokes and clone stamp tools—an inverted trompe l'oeil. The object's uncertainty is compounded by its documentation, which uses these same digital tools to subtly alter their appearance in postproduction, creating a unique digital watermark that becomes, in effect, an additional iteration of the work. The project responds to the ongoing crisis of digital art in which there is pressure to produce work that cannot be copied or reproduced, and at the same time, work that will circulate widely online as a digital image. It is difficult to sell a digital file as you would a painting, but the more an object is digitally circulated, the more valuable it becomes. In attempting to bridge the gap between the physical and the digital, Vierkant's *Image Objects* make a radical proposition. "First, nothing is in a fixed state: i.e., *everything is anything else*, whether because any object is capable of becoming another type of object or because an object already exists in flux between multiple instantiations."[16] These works are neither images nor objects, but exist in a lenticular state that shifts with our perception of them. In aestheticizing indeterminacy, they make visible this imperceptible quality of the world we now occupy. If we hope to understand our lived environment, shaped as it has been by the seventy-year history of computer graphics, we must learn to perceive this coexistent quality of that world.

Notes

Introduction

1. It is standard in all modern graphical systems to use triangles as the basis for a polygon mesh, but this moment is prior to this broad standardization, such that students measured and digitized Sutherland's Volkswagen as a mesh of square polygons.

2. In 1847, Young assigned Orson Pratt to design the future city of Salt Lake by drawing on Smith's plan for the city of Zion. Smith's original plan for a city of God was meant to be built near Independence, Missouri, but following his death at the hands of an anti-Mormon mob in Carthage, Illinois, in 1844, Smith's followers moved West, occupying the tribal lands of the Northwest Shoshone people to establish Salt Lake City in 1847. The gridded structure was intended as a spiritual utopia oriented around twenty-four temples built at its center, and while the plat of Salt Lake ultimately diverged from Smith's original ambitions, it maintains the structured grid and totalizing vision that draws an important parallel between the kinds of ideal forms that structure the utopian project of Mormonism and the Platonic idealism of graphical objects.

3. There are many earlier 3D models created entirely in software and not derived from real-world data. There are also many other models created around this time from physical objects, such as the hand used by Edwin Catmull in his 1972 film, *Halftone Animation*, discussed in chapter 4. The VW Bug is often considered the first model, but is primarily the most memorable, though it marks—along with these others—a historical shift in graphical modeling toward complex, real-world objects.

4. In advertisements throughout the 1960s, Volkswagen emphasized how little the Beetle's model had changed, noting that replacement parts could be used from most any year, and suggesting that the only thing that had changed in the design of the car from the 1950s to the 1960s was the available colors. These advertisements likewise stress the iconic shape or curve of the Beetle's design.

5. Robert Joseph McDermott, "Robert Remembers: The VW Bug," *Utah Teapot: Quarterly Newspaper for the Alumni and Friends of the University of Utah School of Computing* (Fall 2003): 7.

6. There exists a great deal of work on early artistic applications of computer graphics, but comparatively little on the history of computer graphics in computer science and engineering. See Tom Sito, *Moving Innovation: A History of Computer Animation* (Cambridge, MA: MIT Press, 2013); Wayne E. Carlson, *Computer Graphics and Computer Animation: A Retrospective Overview* (Montreal: Pressbooks, 2017), https://ohiostate .pressbooks.pub/graphicshistory/; Daniel Cardoso Llach, *Builders of the Vision: Software and the Imagination of Design* (New York: Routledge, 2015); Inge Hinterwaldner, *The Systemic Image: A New Theory of Interactive Real-Time Simulations* (Cambridge, MA: MIT Press, 2017).

7. This is principally true for commercial computer graphics in film and video games. There are a number of contemporary artists working to shift, break, or transform the way we use and see computer graphics, and in doing so, opening up a space for a critical engagement with the way graphics construct the illusion of photorealism. See Alan Warburton, *Goodbye Uncanny Valley*, October 2017, 14:38, https:// alanwarburton.co.uk/goodbye-uncanny-valley.

8. This is particularly true in film studies, where computer graphics are synonymous with special effects and visual simulation, slotting into discourses of realism, spectacle, indexicality, and attraction. See Kristen Whissel, *Spectacular Digital Effects: CGI and Contemporary Cinema* (Durham, NC: Duke University Press, 2014); Michele Pierson, *Special Effects: Still in Search of Wonder* (New York: Columbia University Press, 2002); Stephen Prince, *Digital Visual Effects in Cinema: The Seduction of Reality* (New Brunswick, NJ: Rutgers University Press, 2011); Richard Rickitt, *Special Effects: The History and Technique* (New York: Billboard Books, 2000); Dan North, *Performing Illusions: Cinema, Special Effects, and the Virtual Actor* (New York: Wallflower Press, 2008); Andrew Darley, *Visual Digital Culture: Surface Play and Spectacle in New Media Genres* (New York: Routledge, 2000); Dan North, Bob Rehak, and Michael S. Duffy, eds., *Special Effects: New Histories, Theories, Contexts* (London: British Film Institute, 2015).

9. Vivian Sobchack, "Afterword: Media Archaeology and Re-Presencing the Past," in *Media Archaeology: Approaches, Applications, and Implications*, ed. Erkki Huhtamo and Jussi Parikka (Berkeley: University of California Press, 2011), 325.

10. This focus on objects rather than the culture of the people that produced them runs the risk of erasing the agency of human subjects and the deeply political context in which these objects were produced, used, and circulated. As media historian Laine Nooney suggests, "Media archaeology so often ignores: human specificity, the way enactments of power fall upon certain types of bodies more than others." My hope is that this book creates a space for precisely this work by attending to the material conditions for the emergence of early computer graphics while opening a space for research that expands on the historical articulation of computer graphics within cultures and communities of practice. Laine Nooney, "A Pedestal, a Table, a Love Letter: Archaeologies of Gender in Videogame History," *Game Studies* 13, no.

2 (2013), http://gamestudies.org/1302/articles/nooney. See also Siegfried Zielinski, "Media Archaeology," special issue, *CTheory*, ed. Arthur Kroker and Marilouise Kroker (July 11, 1996), http://www.ctheory.net/articles.aspx?id=42; Jussi Parikka, *What Is Media Archaeology?* (Cambridge, UK: Polity Press, 2012); Erkki Huhtamo and Jussi Parikka, eds., *Media Archaeology: Approaches, Applications, and Implications* (Berkeley: University of California Press, 2011); David Parisi, *Archaeologies of Touch: Interfacing with Haptics from Electricity to Computing* (Minneapolis: University of Minnesota Press, 2018).

11. The reasons behind this concentration of research are explored in AnnaLee Saxenian's *Regional Advantage*. While the concentration of talent at the University of Utah has a great deal to do with a regional culture of research and mentorship, Utah cannot be said to benefit from regional advantage in Saxenian's expanded sense. Nonetheless, it was connected to these regions of influence via funding, social networks, and later, the technological network of the early ARPANET. See AnnaLee Saxenian, *Regional Advantage: Culture and Competition in Silicon Valley and Route 128* (Cambridge, MA: Harvard University Press, 1996).

12. David C. Evans, *Graphical Man/Machine Communications* (Salt Lake City: University of Utah National Technical Information Service, 1966), https://collections.lib .utah.edu/ark:/87278/s61n8j92.

13. For a detailed discussion of the University of Utah program, see Jacob Gaboury, "Other Places of Invention: Computer Graphics at the University of Utah," in *Communities of Computing: Computer Science and Society in the ACM*, ed. Thomas J. Misa (San Rafael, CA: Morgan and Claypool, 2016), 259–285; James Lehning, "Technological Innovation, Commercialization, and Regional Development: Computer Graphics in Utah, 1965–1978," *Information and Culture* 51, no. 4 (2016): 479–499.

14. This extended period in which Marsha had to use the car for her daily errands as it was slowly transformed into a digital object was described to me in an interview with Al Davis, one of the graduate students in Ivan Sutherland's class and subsequent chair of the computer science department at the University of Utah. Interview with Al Davis, University of Utah, March 20, 2012.

15. *Toy Story* (1995) is considered the first feature-length computer-animated film. Though the history of computer graphics in the cinema is significantly longer, many industry professionals and researchers see *Jurassic Park* (1993) as a watershed moment for computer-generated special effects in this period. The earliest console game to use 3D graphics was *Starfox* (1993), which included a coprocessor called the Super FX chip that enabled the acceleration of the Super Nintendo's existing graphics hardware. The first fully 3D console was the Nintendo 64, made possible by the use of a specially designed graphics chip called the Reality Co-Processor, developed by Utah graduate James Clark's company Silicon Graphics, Inc., and described in chapter 5. See John Lasseter, dir., *Toy Story* (1995; Emeryville, CA: Pixar Animation

Studios, 2016), Blu-ray Disc; Steven Spielberg, dir., *Jurassic Park* (1993; Los Angeles: Universal Pictures, 2018), Blu-ray Disc; Katsuya Eguchi, dir., *Star Fox* (Kyoto: Nintendo Entertainment, 1993), ROM cartridge.

16. Bruce Sterling, "War Is Virtual Hell," *Wired*, January 1, 1993, http://www.wired.com/1993/01/virthell/.

17. See Lisa Gitelman, *Always Already New: Media, History, and the Data of Culture* (Cambridge, MA: MIT Press, 2008); 6); Lisa Gitelman and Geoffrey B. Pingree, eds., *New Media, 1740–1915* (Cambridge, MA: MIT Press, 2004); Wendy Hui Kyong Chun, "Introduction: Did Somebody Say New Media?," in *New Media, Old Media: A History and Theory Reader*, ed. Wendy Hui Kyong Chun and Thomas Keenan (New York: Routledge, 2006), 1–10.

18. Literary and digital media scholar Nick Montfort has named this tendency to misinterpret the site of computational critique "screen essentialism," a concept further elaborated by Matthew Kirschenbaum in *Mechanisms*. See Nick Montfort, "Continuous Paper: Print Interfaces and Early Computer Writing" (paper presented at ISEA 2004, Helsinki, August 20, 2004), http://nickm.com/writing/essays/continuous_paper_isea.html; Matthew G. Kirschenbaum, *Mechanisms: New Media and the Forensic Imagination* (Cambridge, MA: MIT Press, 2008), 27–35.

19. This shift is most clearly reflected in the fields of software studies, critical code studies, and platform studies, which premise themselves on a refusal of the immaterial, textual, and cultural in favor of an engagement with those technical objects that structure computational media. We might also include under this rubric scholarship that looks to the material infrastructures that shape and support the digital as a way of refusing the presupposition that computing is somehow untethered from the material restrictions of the physical world, as well as scholars who seek to undo theories of immateriality by situating technology within a broader historical or political field. See Matthew Fuller, *Software Studies: A Lexicon* (Cambridge, MA: MIT Press, 2008); Nick Montfort and Ian Bogost, *Racing the Beam: The Atari Video Computer System* (Cambridge, MA: MIT Press, 2009).

20. The double nature of this surface-depth schema is perhaps most clearly articulated by the early computer artist Frieder Nake, who suggests that everything that comes out of the computer exists as both a sensibly perceptible surface (*Oberfläche*) and symbolically manipulable subface (*Unterfläche*). "The surface is there for us, for the human. The subface is there for them, for the computers. For us, it all begins with the senses. For the machine it begins with the code" (translation mine). Frieder Nake, "Oberfläche & Unterfläche / Vom Zeichnen aus großer Ferne" (paper presented at Node 10 Forum for Digital Arts, Frankfurt, November 15–20, 2010), http://node10.vvvv.org/events/lecture-day.

21. See Nicole Starosielski, *The Undersea Network* (Durham, NC: Duke University Press, 2015); Sarah T. Roberts, *Behind the Screen: Content Moderation in the Shadows of*

Social Media (New Haven, CT: Yale University Press, 2019); Nathan Ensmenger, "The Environmental History of Computing," *Technology and Culture* 59, no. 4 (2018): S7-S33.

22. Tara McPherson, "US Operating Systems at Mid-Century: The Intertwining of Race and UNIX," in *Race after the Internet*, ed. Lisa Nakamura and Peter A. Chow-White (New York: Routledge, 2013), 35.

23. I am influenced here by Tung-Hui Hu's work on the cloud as a simultaneously material and virtual infrastructure, an "emptiness" we must learn how to view. Yet unlike Hu's proposition that the cloud is a fundamentally cultural phenomenon, and therefore should be analyzed discursively and obliquely, the heuristic quality of the image object proposes that we need not only learn how to perceive computer graphics differently but rather that perception alone is insufficient if we hope to understand the function of the image object. See Tung-Hui Hu, *A Prehistory of the Cloud* (Cambridge, MA: MIT Press, 2015), xx.

24. In this I follow the work of Alexander Galloway when he suggests that,

> The computer however, is not of an ontological condition, it is on that condition. It does not facilitate or make reference to an arrangement of being, it remediates the very conditions of being itself. If I may be so crude: the medium of the computer is being. But one must take this in an entirely unglamorous way. It is not to say that the computer is the ontological actor par excellence, that it marks the way of doing for some cyborg *Dasein* of the future. No, the point is that the computer has so degraded the ontological plane, that it may reduce and simulate it using the same principles of logical relation. Being is its object, not its experience.

While Galloway suggests that the computer is not an ontology but rather an ethic, I hope to demonstrate that computer science is nonetheless marked by an ontological claim that is necessarily impoverished by this ethical formation. Alexander Galloway, *The Interface Effect* (Cambridge, UK: Polity Press, 2012), 21–22.

25. William Fetter is often attributed with coining the term "computer graphics," though he notes in an article from 1982 that it was likely Hudson. Hudson was Fetter's boss, and was responsible for proposing and authorizing the initial First Man project in 1959. See William Fetter, "A Progression of Human Figures Simulated by Computer Graphics," *IEEE Computer Graphics and Applications* 2, no. 9 (1982): 10; William Fetter, "Computer Graphics," *Design Quarterly* 66–67 (1966): 15.

26. Fetter also notes that the first human figure rendered by a computer was the "landing signal officer" that stood on the deck edge of a simulated aircraft carrier developed in 1960. This figure, however, served no interactive purpose, was extremely primitive, and was used primarily for visual scale. See Fetter, "A Progression of Human Figures," 10.

27. Less than five years from its initial production, the image was featured as part of the now-infamous *Cybernetic Serendipity* exhibition at the Institute of Contemporary Arts in London, and is currently available from Boeing's official print-on-demand

image repository as a framed print, stretched canvas, or wall mural. See William Fetter, "Boeing Computer Graphics," in *Cybernetic Serendipity: The Computer and the Arts*, ed. Jasia Reichardt (London: Praeger, 1969), 88–89.

28. Fetter continued to produce subsequent figures of varying complexity, including Second Man, Third Man and Woman, and Fourth Man and Woman. See Fetter, "A Progression of Human Figures."

29. See Kent C. Redmond and Thomas M. Smith, *From Whirlwind to MITRE: The R&D Story of the SAGE Air Defense Computer* (Cambridge, MA: MIT Press, 2000); Robert R. Everett, ed., "Special Issue: SAGE," *IEEE Annals of the History of Computing* 5, no. 4 (October–December 1983): 319–427.

30. As an abstract system, the SAGE project was widely considered a technical success, but in many ways it was already outdated by the time of its initial deployment in 1958, as the launch of Sputnik shifted the most feared military threat to the United States from long-range bombers to intercontinental ballistic missiles. See Committee on Innovations in Computing and Communications: Lessons from History and the National Research Council, *Funding a Revolution: Government Support for Computing Research* (Washington, DC: National Academies Press, 1999), 93.

31. There is evidence that the SAGE screens were also used to run programs for rudimentary artistic or representational drawings, including at least one documented pinup girl rendered sometime between 1956 and 1958. See Benj Edwards, "The Never-Before-Told Story of the World's First Comptuer Art (It's a Sexy Dame)," *Atlantic*, January 24, 2013, https://www.theatlantic.com/technology/archive/2013/01/the-never-before-told-story-of-the-worlds-first-computer-art-its-a-sexy-dame/267439/.

32. For a detailed account of the SAGE system, see Paul N. Edwards, *The Closed World: Computers and the Politics of Discourse in Cold War America* (Cambridge, MA: MIT Press, 1996).

33. See Rachel N. Weber, "Manufacturing Gender in Commercial and Military Cockpit Design," *Science, Technology, and Human Values* 22, no. 2 (1997): 235–253. For a comprehensive history of models and modeling in computer graphics, see Alana Staiti, "What's in a Model? A History of Human Modeling for Computer Graphics and Animation, 1961–1988" (PhD diss., Cornell University, 2018).

34. Fetter, "Computer Graphics," 20.

35. For a critical history of universal design, see Aimi Hamraie, *Building Access: Universal Design and the Politics of Disability* (Minneapolis: University of Minnesota Press, 2017).

36. This change is, in part, a shift in dimension. The move from 2D to 3D graphics that separates the 1950s from the 1960s is significant in our consideration of object simulation, but many of the two-dimensional applications listed above likewise follow

this same object logic. For a comprehensive history of three dimensionality in mathematics and engineering, see Jens Schröter, *3D: History, Theory and Aesthetics of the Transplane Image* (New York: Bloomsbury Publishing USA, 2014).

37. This distinction between computational images and graphical simulation is one of the principal reasons I am not discussing computational images produced through the collaborative research of artists and engineers working at research sites such as Bell Labs, or artist collectives and organizations like Experiments in Art and Technology, whose programs foregrounded experimental collaboration throughout the decade. The work of artists such as Lillian Schwartz, A. Michael Noll, Kenneth Knowlton, San VanDerBeek, Frieder Nake, and Charles Csuri are evocative for the many ways they anticipate the form and aesthetic of contemporary digital images while remaining firmly grounded in a tradition of modernist experimentation. Nonetheless, while these artists produced some of the earliest computational images, their works are largely disconnected from the technical structure of contemporary computer graphics and perhaps better understood as experimental precursors to the technology we know today. Likewise, there is already a rich body of scholarship in art history and media studies that examines the collaborative relationship between artists and engineers in this early period, while comparatively little writing exists on the technical history of computer graphics outside these artistic and experimental contexts. See Carolyn L. Kane, *Chromatic Algorithms: Synthetic Color, Computer Art, and Aesthetics after Code* (Chicago: University of Chicago Press, 2014); Zabet Patterson, *Peripheral Vision: Bell Labs, the SC 4020, and the Origins of Computer Art* (Cambridge, MA: MIT Press, 2015); Gloria Sutton, *The Experience Machine: Stan VanDerBeek's Movie-Drome and Expanded Cinema* (Cambridge, MA: MIT Press, 2015); Hannah Higgins and Douglas Kahn, *Mainframe Experimentalism: Early Computing and the Foundations of the Digital Arts* (Berkeley: University of California Press, 2012); Margit Rosen, ed., *A Little-Known Story about a Movement, a Magazine, and the Computer's Arrival in Art: New Tendencies and Bit International, 1961–1973* (Cambridge, MA: MIT Press, 2011); Andrew Johnston, *Pulses of Abstraction: Episodes from a History of Animation* (Minneapolis: University of Minnesota Press, 2020).

38. Steve Russell, Nolan Bushnell, and Stewart Brand, "Shall We Play a Game?: The Early Years of Computer Gaming" (video recording and discussion at the Computer History Museum, Mountain View, CA, May 7, 2002), accession no, 102695272.

39. Adele Goldberg, *Smalltalk-80: The Interactive Programming Environment* (Menlo Park, CA: Addison-Wesley Publishing Company, 1984).

40. Media theorist Casey Alt explores this transformation from computer as calculator to computer as medium in a series of essays on the development of object-oriented programming, though he does not identify computer graphics as the principal catalyst for this shift. See Casey Alt, "Objects of Our Affection: How Object Orientation Made Computers a Medium," in *Media Archeology: Approaches, Applications, and Implications*, ed. Erkki Huhtamo and Jussi Parikka (Berkeley: University of California Press, 2011),

278–301; Casey Alt, "The Materialities of Maya: Making Sense of Object-Orientation," *Configurations* 10, no. 3 (September 2002): 387–422.

41. The ontological weight of this claim is the subject of an emerging body of scholarship in media theory and philosophy on the existence and influence of digital objects, asking in what ways the object logic of computation engages, shapes, or transforms our understanding of object relations itself. Principal among these scholars are media theorists Yuk Hui and Alexander Galloway, but we might also include a range of new materialist philosophies that theorize objects as part of a relational system of communication. See Yuk Hui, *On the Existence of Digital Objects* (Minneapolis: University of Minnesota Press, 2016); Alexander Galloway, "The Poverty of Philosophy: Realism and Post-Fordism," *Critical Inquiry* 39, no. 2 (2013): 347–366; Brian Cantwell Smith, *On the Origin of Objects* (Cambridge, MA: MIT Press 1996). On the relationship between object-oriented programming and object-oriented philosophy, see Ian Bogost, "Object-Oriented P*: Philosophers vs. Programmers," July 16, 2009, http://www.bogost.com /blog/objectoriented_p.shtml; Dave Berry, "The New Bifurcation? Object-Oriented Ontology and Computation," *Stunlaw: Philosophy and Critique for a Digital Age*, June 4, 2012, http://stunlaw.blogspot.no/2012/06/new-bifurcation-object-oriented.html.

42. "A Brief History of Fort Douglas," Historic Fort Douglas at the University of Utah, July 10, 2010, https://web.archive.org/web/20100610082804/http://web.utah .edu/facilities/fd/history/history.html.

43. To accomplish this task, IPTO directors poured tens of millions of dollars into their vision for the future of computing over the subsequent decade, helping to found dozens of computer science departments across the country, including the program at the University of Utah. For a detailed history of the IPTO along with the collaborative efforts of the Department of Defense and university research centers, see Arthur L. Norberg, Judy E. O'Neill, and Kerry J. Freedman, *Transforming Computer Technology: Information Processing for the Pentagon, 1962–1986* (Baltimore: Johns Hopkins University Press, 2000).

44. J. C. R. Licklider, "Man-Computer Symbiosis," *IRE Transactions on Human Factors in Electronics* HFE-1 (March 1960): 4.

45. Arguably the IPTO's most famous contribution is funding and developing the early ARPANET under then director Lawrence Roberts—a technology that would ultimately develop into our modern internet. Less visible are the ways the IPTO's investment in computer graphics allowed for the kind of human-machine communication through graphical interfaces, software, and images we now take for granted. See Janet Abbate, *Inventing the Internet* (Cambridge, MA: MIT Press, 1999).

46. Thierry Bardini offers a parallel history of human-machine communication through the figure of Douglas Engelbart and the Stanford Research Institute in his comprehensive history *Bootstrapping*. Engelbart's now infamous demonstration at the 1968 Fall Joint Computer Conference—retroactively referred to as "The Mother

of All Demos"—was widely influential in crafting a vision for the future of computing. However, Engelbart's oN-Line System (NLS) is largely text based and procedural, not object oriented. See Thierry Bardini, *Bootstrapping: Douglas Engelbart, Coevolution, and the Origins of Personal Computing* (Palo Alto, CA: Stanford University Press, 2000).

47. Fletcher received his PhD in physics from Caltech in 1948. He was the son of the eminent Bell Labs scientist Harvey Fletcher, known as the "father of stereophonic sound" and credited with inventing the hearing aid. James Fletcher was a well-known research engineer in the aerospace industry, and had previously served as faculty at both Harvard and Princeton. He was appointed president of the University of Utah in 1964, and one of his first moves was to recruit Evans from the University of California at Berkeley. After serving at Utah from 1964 to 1971, Fletcher moved on to become the head of NASA from 1971 to 1977 and again for three years following the space shuttle Challenger disaster in 1986. "Hiring Recommendation from U of U Computer Committee to James Fletcher, May 18, 1965," box 18, folder 11, Coll. 0199, James Chipman Fletcher Presidential Records, Acc. 199, 1937–1971, University Archives and Records Management, University of Utah, J. Willard Marriott, Salt Lake City.

48. Born in 1924 to a prominent Mormon family, Evans was descended from one of the first colonial settler families of the Salt Lake Valley and could trace his heritage back to George Q. Cannon, an early member of the Quorum of the Twelve Apostles of the Church of Jesus Christ of Latter day Saints. David C. Evans, Peter Evans, Susan Evans Fudd, David Evans Jr., Gordon Fudd, Anna Evans Brown, Linda Evans, Joy Evans, Gail Shydell, Mary Evans, and Katherine Archer, "Oral History with Daniel Morrow," *Computerworld Honors* (April 18, 1996): 20. Note that this oral history was conducted with eleven members of the Evans family two years before David Evans's death from Alzheimer's in 1998.

49. By all accounts the Evans were happy in Berkeley, and prior to Fletcher's offer had no intention of leaving. In an oral history with the Evans family, David's wife, Joy, suggests that they expected to be in California for the rest of their lives, but when Fletcher made the offer to David, the family decided to "come home." It is unclear to what degree the free speech movement effected their decision, though Joy names it explicitly. She likewise notes that school desegregation created logistical challenges for the family, as the city of Berkeley chose to forgo busing in favor of sending each child of a particular grade to a different school, requiring parents to drive children to and from class each day. With seven children, the family found this impossible to maintain, and in her words, took the "cowardly way out" by moving over the hills to Lafayette and ultimately returning to Salt Lake in 1965. Evans et al., "Oral History with Daniel Morrow," 30.

50. "Letter from Vice President J. A. Adamson to David C. Evans, June 16, 1965," box 18, folder 12, Coll. 0199, James Chipman Fletcher Presidential Records, Acc. 199 1937–1971, University Archives and Records Management, University of Utah, J. Willard Marriott, Salt Lake City.

51. Ivan E. Sutherland, "Oral History with William Aspray," Charles Babbage Institute, Pittsburgh, May 1, 1989, 11.

52. Kelley J. P. Lindberg, "Pioneers on the Digital Frontier," *Continuum: The Magazine of the University of Utah* (Winter 2006–2007), https://continuum.utah.edu/back _issues/2006winter/feature3.html.

53. Utah was by no means the only research center invested in the development of computer graphics in this period, though it is arguably the most influential. Corporate research at GE, Boeing, and Bell Labs served a critical function in developing industry applications for graphical systems beginning in the 1950s. Likewise, MIT's Lincoln Laboratory was arguably the first academic center for graphical research, supporting the work of Steven Coons, Ivan Sutherland, and many others in the late 1950s and early 1960s, as discussed in chapter 3. Ohio State University's Computer Graphics Research Group and the Advanced Computing Center for the Arts and Design are also prominent in this period, and perhaps best known for the work of artist Charles Csuri, who developed early morphing techniques in the 1960s and was a prolific researcher for over thirty years. For a broad history of early graphical research, see Wayne E. Carlson, *Computer Graphics and Computer Animation: A Retrospective Overview* (Montreal: Pressbooks, 2017), https://ohiostate.pressbooks.pub/graphicshistory/.

54. While graphics was the department's focus, initially there were four specific areas of research: the computer-aided architectural design system project, headed by Stephen L. Macdonald, from the Department of Architecture; the left-ventricular dynamics project headed by Dr. Homer K. Warner from the Department of Biophysics; a group focused on "The Use of Graphics in the Solution of Partial-Differential Equations" headed by the director of the Computer Center, Louis A. Schmittroth; and Evans's computer graphics techniques division. David Evans, "Computer Science at the U of U," *Utechnic: University of Utah Engineering Publication* (May 1968): 12–13.

55. MIT Media Lab founder Nicholas Negroponte famously noted that researchers working in graphics and design in the 1960s were considered "sissy computer scientists, not the real thing." This quote reflects not only historical attitudes toward graphical research but also a culture of toxic masculinity within computer science broadly. Kate Torgovnick May, "Back to Tech's Future: Nicholas Negroponte at TED2014," *TEDBlog*, March 17, 2014, https://blog.ted.com/back-to-techs-future-nicholas-negroponte -at-ted2014/.

56. Gianna Walker, "The Inception of Computer Graphics at the University of Utah, 1960s–1970s" (notes from the annual meeting of the Association for Computing Machinery's SIGGRAPH Special Interest Group, September 27, 1994), https://web .archive.org/web/20020827134354/http://silicon-valley.siggraph.org/MeetingNotes /Utah.html.

57. This hands-off approach is perhaps best exemplified by the incredibly brief semi-annual reports written by Evans for the IPTO from 1966 to 1970. While the reports

grew in length and complexity as the program expanded, many are less than five pages, offering little in the way of justification, and instead favoring brief descriptions of hardware acquisitions and program goals. See Evans, *Graphical Man/Machine Communications*.

58. This is clearly reflected in the language of isolated frontiers and cowboy computing that is often evoked in interviews and oral histories with Utah faculty and students. While I am interested in this framing, along with the clear significance of Salt Lake City as a Mormon colonial settlement as well as the Mormon faith of many of the university's students and faculty, it is not my principal focus here. Certainly a set of claims can be made as to the reasons the Mormon context of Salt Lake City did not hinder technological development, unlike the rather-fraught relationship between many religious faiths and certain forms of scientific thought. Central among these would be Mormonism's broadly futurist and at times utopian faith driven by broad narratives of progress, coupled with its emergence in the nineteenth century as an explicitly modern and industrial era religion whose own origin narrative contains various technical devices, including the seer stones that Smith used to translate the Book of Mormon, commonly referred to as Urim and Thummim. We might also speculate on Evans's role as both a leader and mentor within the Mormon church and his drive to mentorship in the context of the Utah program, what is frequently referred to in Mormonism as "magnifying one's calling." These are important questions, and serve as a meaningful ground for the work that follows. For an examination of the relationship between Mormonism and media technology, see John Durham Peters, "Mormonism and Media," in *The Oxford Handbook of Mormonism*, ed. Terryl L. Givens and Philip L. Barlow (Oxford: Oxford University Press, 2015), 407–424.

59. As Sutherland recalls, the decision ultimately came down to a question of family, noting that "Joy Evans, Dave's wife, reasoned with him. She said, 'Dave, we have seven children and Ivan has only two. It would be much easier for Ivan to move to Salt Lake than for us to move to Boston.' And I believe that was the seed of the University of Utah phenomenon." H. Kent Bowen, "The University of Utah and the Computer Graphics Revolution" (unpublished case study, Harvard Business School, April 28, 2006), 5.

60. David C. Evans Papers, MS 625, box 2, folder 13, Special Collections, J. Willard Marriott Library, University of Utah.

Chapter 1

1. The epigraph above demonstrates the perspective transformation as expressed in the coordinate system of the observer's eye, where f is related to the "focal length" of an imaginary optical system that might be used to generate the view.

2. "Complete" in the sense of shaded and opaque. It had been possible to produce simple line drawings with a computer since at least 1960, but this is one of the

first graphical images to resemble the form of contemporary 3D computer graphics. The first experiments of this type at Utah took place one year prior in 1967, and consisted of simple shapes at varying degrees of resolution. See chapter 2.

3. David C. Evans, *Graphical Man/Machine Communications* (Salt Lake City: University of Utah National Technical Information Service, 1966), https://collections.lib .utah.edu/ark:/87278/s61n8j92.

4. Jim Blinn, quoted in *The Story of Computer Graphics*, directed by Frank Foster (Los Angeles: Association for Computing Machinery, 1999).

5. Ivan E. Sutherland, "The Ultimate Display," *Proceedings of the IFIP Conference* (1965): 508.

6. In this configuration, new media is in fact old media, the cinema is always already digital, and light, windows, frames, and interfaces are visual techniques that persist across time to encapsulate digital technologies within a broad regime of the visible. See David Norman Rodowick, *The Virtual Life of Film* (Cambridge, MA: Harvard University Press, 2009); Philip Rosen, *Change Mummified: Cinema, Historicity, Theory* (Minneapolis: University of Minnesota Press, 2001); Anne Friedberg, *The Virtual Window: From Alberti to Microsoft* (Cambridge, MA: MIT Press, 2009).

7. This problem is formulated early on as the "hidden line problem" or "hidden line algorithm" as early graphics were largely wireframe structures that needed only lines removed. Later algorithms would bring shading and other indicators of opacity, and so the problem is refigured as the "hidden surface algorithm" or, more broadly, "visibility problem." While it is true that hidden line algorithms differ from hidden surface algorithms in significant ways, each is concerned with the same broad conceptual problem. For the purpose of clarity, I have opted to use the term "hidden surface" throughout this chapter while emphasizing the specificity of each algorithm, and the way it deals with lines and/or surfaces.

8. Other significant early systems include Ivan Sutherland's Sketchpad software for CAD and Ken Knowlton's BEFLIX programming language. Significantly, none of these early ad hoc systems share a direct lineage with contemporary 3D computer graphical methods, which are based largely on polygonal modeling systems that were not yet possible given the hardware restrictions of the period. See Robert R. Everett, Charles A. Zraket, and Herbert D. Benington, "SAGE: A Data-Processing System for Air Defense," in *Papers and Discussions Presented at the December 9–13, 1957, Eastern Joint Computer Conference: Computers with Deadlines to Meet* (1957): 148–155; Ivan E. Sutherland, "Sketchpad: A Man-Machine Graphical Interface" (PhD diss., Massachusetts Institute of Technology, 1963); Kenneth C. Knowlton, "A Computer Technique for Producing Animated Movies," in *Proceedings of the April 21–23, 1964, Spring Joint Computer Conference* (New York: Association for Computing Machinery, 1964), 67–87; John Whitney, *Digital Harmony: On the Complementarity of Music and Visual Art* (Kingsport, TN: Kingsport Press, 1980); Zabet Patterson,

Peripheral Vision: Bell Labs, the SC 4020, and the Origins of Computer Art (Cambridge, MA: MIT Press, 2015).

9. For examples of the nineteenth-century history of visualization, see Jonathan Crary, *Techniques of the Observer: On Vision and Modernity in the Nineteenth Century* (Cambridge, MA: MIT Press, 1992); Erkki Huhtamo, *Illusions in Motion: Media Archaeology of the Moving Panorama and Related Spectacles* (Cambridge, MA: MIT Press, 2013).

10. The most prominent of these programs were Project MAC at MIT and Project Genie at Berkeley. Ivan E. Sutherland, "Oral History with William Aspray," Charles Babbage Institute, Pittsburgh, May 1, 1989), 6–8.

11. Advanced Research Projects Agency, "Graphic Control and Display of Computer Processes," Program Plan No. 439, March 1, 1965, 1, National Archives Branch Depository, Record Group (RG) 330-78-0013, box 1, folder: "Program Plans," FOIA Ref. 13-F-1248. Emphasis in the original.

12. In many ways this work was an extension of Licklider's early vision of human-computer symbiosis, allowing for new forms of graphical communication and control between a machine and its operator. J. C. R. Licklider, "Man-Machine Symbiosis," *IRE Transactions on Human Factors in Electronics* HFE-1 (March 1960): 4–11.

13. While the concentration of talent in particular universities was an asset for focused collaboration, it also created challenges for collaboration between ARPA-funded programs. This was in part the justification for ARPA's interest in time-sharing technology, and the funding and development of the ARPANET in 1969 under Taylor. If each research center functioned as a hub, by networking those hubs, those centers could tap into the expertise and technical resources of the others.

14. If a particular institution failed to coalesce as a center of excellence, it would be defunded and resources could be allocated elsewhere. This was the case with ARPA's computer graphics funding allocation, which was initially invested by Sutherland at the University of Michigan to fund a major graphics project called Research into the Conversational Use of Computers (CONCOMP). The objective of this project was to provide the theory and programs for a general network service system, which, through the use of computer graphics in a conversational mode, would allow the system engineer to specify specialized graphical problem-oriented language systems for the description and solution of diverse network problems. While the CONCOMP program had many successes and continued until 1970, the University of Michigan did not evolve into an IPTO center of excellence, and it was defunded by the IPTO in 1968. See Robert Taylor, "Oral History with Paul McJones," Computer History Museum, October 10–11, 2008, 16; K. B. Irani and A. W. Naylor, "Memo to: Professor B. Herzog. A Proposal for Research in Conversational Use of Computers for Systems Engineering Problems," September 30, 1966, RG 330–73-A-2108, FOIA Ref. 13-F-1248.

15. David C. Evans, "Computer Science at the U of U," *Utechnic: University of Utah Engineering Publication* (May 1968): 13.

16. Evans, *Graphical Man/Machine Communications*, 3.

17. Evans, "Computer Science at the U of U," 13.

18. Evans was not alone in this problem-solving formulation. Indeed it is a central concept for the modern sciences, and arguably the primary interest of the various branches of engineering, concerned as they are with the design, analysis, and development of technological solutions. Nonetheless, the trope of unsolved problems takes on a particular valence in computer graphics to become a kind of call to arms, mobilizing a disparate group of researchers to a clearly defined set of tasks. This formula begins as a brief six-page article written by Sutherland for the journal *Datamation* in 1966. Titled "Computer Graphics: Ten Unsolved Problems," the article became a critical framework for computer graphics researchers for over fifty years—a trope revisited time and time again as old problems were solved and new ones arose. The piece is one of Sutherland's most famous works, as it articulates a particular vision of the future for the field of computer graphics written by the then director of the IPTO and offers a set of key problems that suggest a trajectory researchers might follow. It should be noted that the article is often incorrectly cited as "Ten Unsolved Problems in Computer Graphics," which has since become the standard formatting for the phrase. See Ivan E. Sutherland, "Computer Graphics: Ten Unsolved Problems," *Datamation* 12, no. 5 (1966), 22–27; Jim Blinn, "Ten More Unsolved Problems in Computer Graphics," *IEEE Computer Graphics and Applications* 18, no. 5 (September 1998): 86–89; Martin Newell and Jim Blinn, "The Progression of Realism in Computer Generated Images," in *Proceedings of the 1977 ACM Annual Conference* (New York: Association for Computing Machinery, 1977), 444–448; Paul Heckbert, "Ten Unsolved Problems in Rendering" (Rendering Algorithms and Systems workshop at Graphics Interface 87, Toronto, April 1987); Marc Levoy, "Open Problems in Computer Graphics," last updated April 8, 1996, https://graphics.stanford.edu/courses/cs348b-96/open_problems.html; Jim Foley, "Getting There: The Ten Top Problems Left," *IEEE Computer Graphics and Applications* 20, no. 1 (January 2000): 66–68.

19. Crary, *Techniques of the Observer*, 1–2.

20. See David Bordwell and Kristin Thompson, *Film Art: An Introduction* (New York: McGraw-Hill College, 2003). *Film Art* remains the definitive introductory text for undergraduates to the field of cinema studies, and while its naturalization of computer-generated images and film form is perhaps expected, it is nonetheless telling.

21. Friedrich Kittler, *Optical Media* (Cambridge, UK: Polity Press, 2009), 228.

22. Of course, the construction of vision by computer graphics has many similarities with other visual media such as painting, which is not premised on the same claims to indexicality as film and photography. Likewise, we might reflect on the textual origins of the term *graphics* as a form of inscription, or the relationship between visuality and the production of knowledge broadly. What distinguishes

graphics here is the centrality of simulation in its construction of vision, along with the historical claim toward total simulation that marks its very origins, as discussed above. See Johanna Drucker, *Graphesis: Visual Forms of Knowledge Production* (Cambridge, MA: Harvard University Press, 2014).

23. This leads him to a counterintuitive conclusion: that the cinema was in fact a new media technology, as many of the formal techniques we now associate with digital media (compositing, sampling, binary, etc.) first structured this earlier media form. Lev Manovich, *The Language of New Media* (Cambridge, MA: MIT Press, 2001).

24. This work marks the beginning of a sea change in new media theory, but it was also the culmination of almost a decade of writing by Manovich in which the relationship between computer graphics and visual culture took center stage.

25. Here Manovich invokes Aristotle's rejection of Platonic realism and insistence on the particularity of individual objects. Lev Manovich, "The Mapping of Space: Perspective, Radar, and 3-D Computer Graphics," in *Computer Graphics Visual Proceedings*, ed. Thomas Linehan (New York: Association for Computing Machinery, 1993), http://manovich.net/content/04-projects/003-article-1993/01-article-1993.pdf.

26. Lev Manovich, "The Engineering of Vision from Constructivism to Computers" (PhD diss., University of Rochester, 1993).

27. Kittler, *Optical Media*, 75.

28. Jacques Lacan, "On the Gaze as *Objet Petit a*," in *The Four Fundamental Concepts of Psychoanalysis*, ed. Jacques-Alain Miller, trans. Alan Sheridan (New York: W. W. Norton and Company, 1981), 86.

29. James Elkins, *The Poetics of Perspective* (Ithaca, NY: Cornell University Press, 1996), 214.

30. Bernard Dionysius Geoghegan, "After Kittler: On the Cultural Techniques of Recent German Media Theory," *Theory, Culture, and Society* 30, no. 6 (November 2013): 67.

31. For a detailed discussion of *Kulturtechnik*, see Geoffrey Winthrop-Young, Ilinca Iurascu, and Jussi Parikka, eds., "Special Issue: Cultural Techniques," *Theory, Culture, and Society* 30, no. 6 (November 2013); Bernhard Siegert, *Cultural Techniques: Grids, Filters, Doors, and Other Articulations of the Real* (New York: Fordham University Press, 2015). For an analysis of competing perspectival modes in the history of digital image technologies, see Jacob Gaboury, "Perspective," in *Debugging Game History: A Critical Lexicon*, ed. Raiford Guins and Henry Lowood (Cambridge, MA: MIT Press, 2016), 359–368.

32. Erwin Panofsky, *Perspective as Symbolic Form*, trans. Christopher S. Wood (1927; New York: Zone Books, 1991).

33. Acknowledging the malleability of perspective as a governing regime has not led to a deprivileging of perspective as a critical lens through which to understand computer graphics, but rather a displacement of the privileged position of the perspectival subject in favor of a visual regime marked by the potentiality and multiplicity of perspectives. As Mark B. N. Hansen notes in his *New Philosophy for New Media,* "With the material fruition of the form of computer vision . . . we witness a marked deprivileging of the particular perspectival image in favor of a total and fully manipulable grasp of the entire dataspace, the whole repertoire of possible images it could be said to contain." Anne Friedberg gestures toward a similar genealogy in *The Virtual Window,* which tracks the development and transformation of the perspectival paradigm from the Renaissance to the modern graphical user interface, understood as an extension or multiplication of this broad visual tradition as opposed to a disruption of the primacy of the visual. In both formulations the fixity of perspectival subjectivity persists, even as we acknowledge the possibility of multiple embodied subject positions or the potential for multiple ways of picturing the world. See Mark B. N. Hansen, *New Philosophy for New Media* (Cambridge, MA: MIT Press 2004), 95; Anne Friedberg, *The Virtual Window: From Alberti to Microsoft* (Cambridge, MA: MIT Press, 2009).

34. Lawrence G. Roberts, "Machine Perception of Three-Dimensional Solids" (PhD diss., Massachusetts Institute of Technology, 1963).

35. This work was further elaborated by Timothy Johnson into Sketchpad III, the software demonstrated in the now-infamous educational film produced by the MIT Science Reporter in 1964. See Timothy E. Johnson, "Sketchpad III: A Computer Program for Drawing in Three Dimensions," in *Proceedings of the Spring 1963 Joint Computer Conference* (New York: Association for Computing Machinery, 1963, 347–353.

36. William J. Mitchell, *The Reconfigured Eye: Visual Truth in the Post-Photographic Era* (Cambridge, MA: MIT Press, 1994), 118.

37. Roberts, "Machine Perception," 2.

38. James J. Gibson, *The Perception of the Visual World* (Boston: Houghton Mifflin, 1950).

39. Zabet Patterson, "Visionary Machines: A Genealogy of the Digital Image" (PhD diss., University of California at Berkeley, 2007), 45.

40. Gibson, *The Perception of the Visual World,* 6.

41. Roberts, "Machine Perception," 13.

42. The early introduction of perspective into computer visualization is unsurprising given that the construction of Renaissance perspective is itself a procedural, mathematical, and even algorithmic process, "a translation of psychophysiological space into mathematical space; in other words, an objectification of the subjective." Panofsky, *Perspective as Symbolic Form,* 66.

43. In the dissertation's section on hidden line removal, Roberts notes that as far as he knows, "no one has ever devised a procedure for determining hidden line segments." He also remarks this was the most difficult and time-consuming aspect of his program, as well as the most significant. Roberts, "Machine Perception," 62.

44. Evans, *Graphical Man/Machine Communications*.

45. This culling logic can be seen across a number of applications, whereby a scene is restricted in various ways to be made legible to the output of a graphical display. One of the earliest examples of this logic is the cropping of an image to the dimensions of a particular screen or window. These *clipping algorithms* are used to determine what objects should be visible in a particular render so that any object that falls outside the frame is not shown. This process saves the unnecessary calculation of objects that cannot be seen from the viewing position of a virtual camera, such that the world of a scene disappears just beyond the edge of the frame and must be rendered into being in real time to match a viewer's gaze. One of the earliest implementations of a clipping algorithm was in Sutherland's Sketchpad software, but the most influential work on clipping was published by Sutherland and Robert Sproull at the end of the 1960s. See Sutherland, "Sketchpad"; Robert F. Sproull and Ivan E. Sutherland, "A Clipping Divider," in *Proceedings of the December 9–11, 1968, Fall Joint Computer Conference, Part I* (New York: Association for Computing Machinery, 1968), 765–775.

46. Sutherland, "Computer Graphics: Ten Unsolved Problems," 26.

47. Ivan E. Sutherland, "Computer Displays," *Scientific American* 222, no. 6 (June 1970): 73.

48. Ivan E. Sutherland, Robert F. Sproull, and Robert Schumacker, "A Characterization of Ten Hidden-Surface Algorithms," *Computing Surveys* 6, no. 1 (1974): 1–55.

49. Sutherland, Sproull, and Schumacker, "A Characterization of Ten Hidden-Surface Algorithms," 19.

50. A raster screen consists of a structure of pixels or points of color that when viewed together at a distance form a coherent image. This includes early television screens and almost all computer and HDTV screens. Early computer graphics prior to the 1970s were largely based on vector graphics, which "paint" a series of lines on a display rather than calculate a shade or color for each individual pixel. Image-space algorithms similar to those described here are therefore indicative of the shift, at this time, from vector- to raster-based graphics in the field of computer science. See chapter 2.

51. John Warnock, "A Hidden Surface Algorithm for Computer Generated Halftone Pictures" (PhD diss., University of Utah, 1969).

52. While the z-buffer concept is most often attributed to Catmull, it was simultaneously developed by Wolfgang Straßer at the Technischen Universität Berlin in apparent isolation from research at the University of Utah. See Edwin Catmull, "A

Subdivision Algorithm for Computer Display of Curved Surfaces" (PhD diss., University of Utah, 1974); Wolfgang Straßer, "Schnelle kurven-und flächendarstellung auf grafischen sichtgeräten" (PhD diss., Technischen Universität Berlin, 1974).

53. An alternate solution that is still used by some systems is known as the painter's algorithm, in reference to the painting technique whereby distant parts of a scene are painted before parts that are closer, thereby covering those areas of distant parts that are occluded by objects in the foreground. The algorithm is less efficient than z-buffering methods as it requires polygon values to be calculated for background objects that are later occluded by objects in the foreground. It is an extremely simple solution, if not as efficient for complex renders. It should be noted that, despite its name, this technique does not model any common technique for painting, and would more accurately be called a "depth priority" algorithm.

Chapter 2

1. For a detailed analysis of contemporary screen technology, including contemporary pixel techniques for raster displays, see Sean Cubitt, *The Practice of Light: A Genealogy of Visual Technologies from Prints to Pixels* (Cambridge, MA: MIT Press, 2014), 95–100. Kittler controversially discusses computer graphics from another perspective: the ontology of the pixel. See Friedrich Kittler, "Computer Graphics: A Semi-Technical Introduction," trans. Sara Ogger, *Grey Room* 2 (Winter 2001): 30–45.

2. Anne Friedberg, *The Virtual Window: From Alberti to Microsoft* (Cambridge, MA: MIT Press, 2009). See also the discussion of the screen and grid in Hubert Damisch, *The Origin of Perspective*, trans. John Goodman (Cambridge, MA: MIT Press, 1995); Jonathan Crary, *Techniques of the Observer: On Vision and Modernity in the Nineteenth Century* (Cambridge, MA: MIT Press, 1992).

3. This biological metaphor is central to the naturalization of technical imagery. See Vílem Flusser, *Into the Universe of Technical Images* (1986), trans. Nancy Ann Roth (Minneapolis: University of Minnesota Press, 2011), esp. 23–32; Brandon Hookway, *Interface* (Cambridge, MA: MIT Press, 2014).

4. As Montfort suggests, "The screen is often portrayed as an essential aspect of all creative and communicative computing—a fixture, perhaps even a basis, for new media." Nick Montfort, "Continuous Paper: Print Interfaces and Early Computer Writing" (paper presented at ISEA 2004, Helsinki, August 20, 2004), http://nickm.com/writing/essays/continuous_paper_isea.html. Most graphical output was likewise limited to point plotter drawings, used primarily for CAD and in early experiments in computer art. See Christoph Klütsch, *Computergrafik: Ästhetische Experimente zwischen zwei Kulturen: Die Anfänge der Computerkunst in den 1960er Jahren* (Berlin: Springer, 2007).

5. Montfort, "Continuous Paper."

6. For a primer on the scanning principles at work in early television systems, see R. W. Burns, *Television: An International History of the Formative Years* (London: Institution of Engineering and Technology, 1998); Doron Galili, *Seeing by Electricity: The Emergence of Television, 1878–1939* (Durham, NC: Duke University Press, 2020).

7. For a detailed history of radar in the context of the computer screen, see Bernard Dionysius Geoghegan, "An Ecology of Operations: Vigilance, Radar, and the Birth of the Computer Screen," *Representations* 147, no. 1 (2019): 59–95.

8. While all contemporary computer and television screens now function using a pixel-based raster grid, vector and raster graphic displays coexisted alongside one another well into the 1980s, with vector displays particularly prevalent in popular early arcade cabinets such as those used for *Asteroids* (1979), *Star Castle* (1980), and *Lunar Lander* (1980). Each technology produced its own affordances and limitations, and in turn each shaped the limits of what kinds of graphical images were possible. See Nick Montfort and Ian Bogost, "Random and Raster: Display Technologies and the Development of Video Games," *IEEE Annals of the History of Computing* 31, no. 3 (2009): 34–42.

9. Interactive graphics predate the widespread commercialization of the frame buffer concept and were developed for programs such as Sutherland's Sketchpad as early as 1962. Nonetheless, these real-time interactive graphics were highly limited in their use and restricted to the large-scale, multimillion-dollar computing machines on which they ran.

10. In this, Laposky follows in the long-standing tradition of "visual music" that reaches back to the start of the twentieth century. See Aimee Mollaghan, *The Visual Music Film* (London: Palgrave Macmillan, 2015); Ben F. Laposky, *Electronic Abstractions* (Cherokee, IA: Sanford Museum, 1953), 15.

11. Ben F. Laposky, "Oscillons: Electronic Abstractions," *Leonardo* 2, no. 4 (October 1969): 348.

12. Laposky, "Oscillons," 352.

13. Randi Martin, "Laposky Cited for Tracing History in Computer Art," *Cherokee Daily Times*, January 7, 1972, 1; Alison Drain, "Laposky's Lights Make Visual Music," *Symmetry* 4, no. 3 (April 2007): 32.

14. Most notable for her use of the oscilloscope is artist Mary Ellen Bute, but Laposky's work is also often contextualized within the history of computer art in both the United States and Europe. See Mary Ellen Bute, "Abstronics: An Experimental Filmmaker Photographs the Esthetics of the Oscillograph," *Films in Review New York: National Board of Review of Motion Pictures* 5 (1952): 263–266.

15. Of Laposky's original 102 mounted images, 101 remain in the collection of the Sanford Museum. None of the 10,000 negatives Laposky claimed to have taken have

been found, and he kept no records of the control settings he used to make them. While Laposky suggested the pieces could be displayed in any number of ways, including as active waveforms, much like Nam June Paik's cathode ray pieces such as *TV Crown* (1965), all that remains of the cathode ray sculptures are the photographs that document their initial form. For more on Paik's *TV Crown*, see Gregory Zinman, *Making Images Move: Handmade Cinema and the Other Arts* (Berkeley: University of California Press, 2020), 249–280.

16. By the year 2000, each US household had an average of 2.43 television CRTs, not including computer screens and other CRT displays. "More Than Half the Homes in U.S. Have Three or More TVs," Nielsen, July 20, 2009, http://www.nielsen.com/us/en /insights/news/2009/more-than-half-the-homes-in-us-have-three-or-more-tvs.html.

17. The first flat-panel plasma display was developed by Donald L. Bitzer, H. Gene Slottow, and Robert Willson in 1964 at the University of Illinois at Urbana-Champagne, and was used in the PLATO computer system throughout the 1960s and 1970s. See Donald L. Bitzer and H. Gene Slottow, "The Plasma Display Panel: A Digitally Addressable Display with Inherent Memory," in *Proceedings of the November 7–10, 1966, Fall Joint Computer Conference* (New York: Association for Computing Machinery, 1966), 541–547; Benjamin Gross, *The TVs of Tomorrow: How RCA's Flat-Screen Dreams Led to the First LCDs* (Chicago: University of Chicago Press, 2018); Joy Lisi Rankin, *A People's History of Computing in the United States* (Cambridge, MA: Harvard University Press, 2018).

18. In the late 1990s, CRTs were one of the largest sources of lead in municipal solid waste, leading numerous states to ban their incineration or disposal in landfills in the early 2000s. See Hai-Yong Kang and Julie M. Schoenung, "Electronic Waste Recycling: A Review of U.S. Infrastructure and Technology Options," *Resources, Conservation, and Recycling* 45, no. 4 (December 2005): 368–400. The archiving of electronic images is also relevant here. For a paradigmatic discussion of preservation techniques for Paik's work, see John Anderson, "Nam June Paik: Preserving the Human Televisions," *Art in America*, February 5, 2013, http://www.artinamericamagazine.com /news-features/news/nam-june-paik-smithsonian/.

19. For a useful primer on the life and death of the CRT and other electronic waste, see Josh Lepawsky, *Reassembling Rubbish: Worlding Electronic Waste* (Cambridge, MA: MIT Press, 2018).

20. This is by necessity an oversimplification of this process, and ignores details such as video interlacing and the development of color television. Likewise the number of scan lines on a television set differs by region, and the history of scan line standardization is its own topic worthy of a study. The most prominent divergence is likely the incompatibility of NTSC (525 scan lines) and PAL (576 scan lines) standards. See Susan Murray, *Bright Signals: A History of Color Television* (Durham, NC: Duke University Press, 2018).

21. On the history of the computer screen in the context of radar technology, see Charlie Gere, "Genealogy of the Computer Screen," *Visual Communication* 5, no. 2 (2006): 141–152; Geoghegan, "An Ecology of Operations."

22. The ability to display an entire letter with a single projection of the electron beam allowed Charactron CRTs to display a relatively large amount of text. Charactron systems could display up to fifty characters horizontally at a rate of ten to twenty thousand characters per second. Due to the size of the CRT character matrix, each tube was limited to a specific set of sixty-four characters and shapes, though an operator could change fonts or character sets by physically removing and reinstalling a different tube—a process that took several minutes. See Peter A. Keller, *The Cathode-Ray Tube: Technology, History, and Applications* (New York: Palisades Press, 1991); Ben Ferber, "The Use of the Charactron with ERA 1103," in *AIEE-IRE '56 (Western): Papers Presented at the February 7–9, 1956, Joint ACM–AIEE-IRE Western Computer Conference* (New York: Association for Computing Machinery, 1956), 34–36.

23. The tube was most prominently used for the visual displays of the SAGE air defense system beginning in 1958, but was also the display that allowed for early graphical experiments using the Stromberg-Carlson 4020 computer at Bell Labs by artist-researchers including A. Michael Noll, Lillian Schwartz, and Kenneth Knowlton. For more on the SAGE system, see Paul N. Edwards, *The Closed World: Computers and the Politics of Discourse in Cold War America* (Cambridge, MA: MIT Press,1996). For a discussion of SAGE in the context of midcentury artistic and visual cultures in the United States and Canada, see Kenneth White, "Strangeloves: From/De la région centrale, Air Defense Radar Station Moisie, and Media Cultures of the Cold War," *Grey Room* 58 (2015): 50–82. For a detailed study of the Stromberg Carlson 2040 and early graphical experimentation at Bell Labs, see Zabet Patterson, *Peripheral Vision: Bell Labs, the SC 4020, and the Origins of Computer Art* (Cambridge, MA: MIT Press, 2015).

24. While in the United States we continue to use Zworykin's term "cathode ray tube," it is called the *Braunsche Röhre* in German-speaking countries and *Buraun-kan* in Japan.

25. See Albert Abramson, *Zworykin, Pioneer of Television* (Chicago: University of Illinois Press, 1995); Albert Abramson, *The History of Television, 1880 to 1941* (London: McFarland and Company, 1987).

26. While the cathode ray oscilloscope would become the most prominent technical form oscillography would take, the visualization of waveforms was accomplished early on through a wide range of techniques, from hand plotting and automated paper drawing, to photography and mirrored projection. See Nehemiah Hawkins, *Hawkins Electrical Guide* (New York: Theodore Audel, 1914).

27. The other widely influential and historically significant use of the CRT during this period was in radar display, starting with the work of meteorologist Robert

Watson-Watt in 1922. Radar technology existed prior to this moment, but the widespread use of radar displays in World War II is one explanation for their adoption by war-trained engineers for computer graphics in the postwar period. For work on the history of radar, see Jim Brown, *Radar: How It All Began* (Cambridge, UK: Janus Publishing, 1996); Robert Buderi, *The Invention That Changed the World: How a Small Group of Radar Pioneers Won the Second World War and Launched a Technical Revolution* (New York: Simon and Schuster, 1996); S. S. Swords, *Technical History of the Beginnings of Radar* (London: Institute of Engineering and Technology, 1986); Louis Brown, *A Radar History of World War II: Technical and Military Imperatives* (Bristol, UK: Institute of Physics Publishing, 1999).

28. Early vector display systems were often modified oscilloscope displays, but later custom vector displays used magnetic force to move and shift the direction of the electron beam, and were widely used in arcade cabinets and other display technologies throughout the 1970s and 1980s. Montfort and Bogost, "Random and Raster," 35.

29. Specialized circuits were required to convert the digital signals of these early computers into analog signals for calligraphic display. See Ivan E. Sutherland, "Computer Displays," *Scientific American* 222, no. 6 (June 1970): 60.

30. In digital imaging and computer graphics, aliasing is the appearance of distortion artifacts when representing a high-resolution image at a lower resolution, or displaying curved or irregular shapes on a raster screen. Antialiasing techniques are used to minimize these effects, which are often referred to as "jaggies" for their jagged, steplike appearance. See Frank Crow, "The Aliasing Problem in Computer-Generated Shaded Images," *Communications of the ACM* 20, no. 11 (1977): 799–805; Lance Williams, "Pyramidal Parametrics," in *Proceedings of the 10th Annual Conference on Computer Graphics and Interactive Techniques* (New York: Association for Computing Machinery, 1983): 1–11; Robert L. Cook, Thomas Porter, and Loren Carpenter, "Distributed Ray Tracing," in *Proceedings of the 11th Annual Conference on Computer Graphics and Interactive Techniques* (New York: Association for Computing Machinery, 1984), 137–145.

31. In contrast, storage tube vector graphics terminals were designed to maintain a single image on the screen without the need to refresh the beam, thereby avoiding the problem of image flicker. Many storage tube vector systems used two electron guns: one to draw the image, and another to "bathe" the entire screen with electrons at a lower intensity, preserving its screen image indefinitely. This limited the screen's utility, though, as in order to erase any part of an image, the entire screen would need to be cleared. Despite these limitations storage tube systems did dramatically reduce the cost of graphical hardware, allowing more researchers access to graphical systems than ever before.

32. The goal for computer graphics from its initial formalization by the US Department of Defense in the mid-1960s included realistic shading, lighting, and object opacity,

along with fully interactive screen images—all of which would require raster display technology. These stated goals are outlined in internal and public-facing publications of the period, including Advanced Research Projects Agency, "Graphic Control and Display of Computer Processes," Program Plan No. 439, March 1, 1965, 1, National Archives Branch Depository, RG 330-78-0013, box 1, folder: "Program Plans," FOIA Ref. 13-F-1248; Robert W. Taylor, "Accomplishments in Calendar Year 1967, Internal Memorandum for the Acting Deputy Director, ARPA," January 5, 1968, 2–3, National Archives Branch Depository, RG 330-74-107, box 1, folder: "Internal Memoranda 1968 through 1970," FOIA Ref. 13-F-1248; Sutherland, "Computer Displays"; Frank D. Skinner, "Computer Graphics: Where Are We?," *Datamation* 12 (May 1966): 28–31; J. C. R. Licklider, "Computer Graphics as a Medium of Artistic Expression," in *Computers and Their Potential Application in Museums* (New York: Arno, 1968), 273–302.

33. For Bernhard Siegert, the grid is one of many cultural techniques that reproduce, displace, process, and reflect the distinctions fundamental to a given culture over time. See Bernhard Siegert, *Cultural Techniques: Grids, Filters, Doors, and Other Articulations of the Real* (New York: Fordham University Press, 2015), 97–120.

34. Hannah Higgins, *The Grid Book* (Cambridge, MA: MIT Press, 2009).

35. Rosalind Krauss, "Grids," *October* 9 (Summer 1979): 50.

36. Higgins, *The Grid Book*, 6.

37. Siegert, *Cultural Techniques*, 98, quoting Michel Foucault, "Why Study Power: The Question of the Subject," in *Beyond Structuralism and Hermeneutics*, ed. Hubert L. Dreyfus and Paul Rabinow (Chicago: University of Chicago Press, 1982), 208.

38. In contrast, cinema's ability to sample and store time in discrete form (twenty-four frames per second) arguably positions it more closely with the temporality of the digital. See Lev Manovich, *The Language of New Media* (Cambridge, MA: MIT Press, 2001), 50–51.

39. This problem does not disappear with the introduction of the frame buffer, as the analog form of the electron beam in any CRT display requires the conversion of digital information into analog signal for output and visualization. See Sutherland, "Computer Displays," 60.

40. As Sutherland notes, "The calligraphic display has the advantage that information to be displayed can be stored in computer memory in any order, whereas information for a raster display must first be sorted from top to bottom and from left to right so that it can be put on screen in the correct sequence. . . . The task of sorting information from top to bottom and from left to right for presentation on raster displays has largely precluded their use for anything but presentations of text. In principal, however, a raster display has the potential of producing pictures with a range of light and dark tones, in color if desired, that provide a realism unequalled by the line drawings of a calligraphic display." Sutherland, "Computer Displays," 57.

41. "Bitmap" is a general term for the mapping of some domain into bits. In computer graphics, a bitmap gives a way to store the location of a binary image, though a true bitmap image has only two bit settings, 0 or 1, black or white. "Pixmap" refers to a map of pixels where each pixel may store more than two colors and thereby more than one bit per pixel. The term "bitmap" is sometimes used for all pixelated bit mapping, but at this early moment it was not possible to map a full range of colors into a pixmap, so the distinction is inconsequential.

42. To be clear, there is no difference between the physical memory used for a frame buffer and other forms of RAM, only that the frame buffer treats that memory as a screen-like grid for the purposes of storage and interaction. Alvy Ray Smith, "Digital Paint Systems: An Anecdotal and Historical Overview," *IEEE Annals of the History of Computing* 23, no. 2 (April–June 2001): 12.

43. Friedrich Kittler, *Optical Media* (Cambridge, UK: Polity Press, 2009), 32.

44. Miller is best known for her work with Max Matthews on the digital synthesis of sound, which led in 1961 to a fully synthesized version of the song "Daisy Bell"—also known as "Bicycle Built for Two"—that so inspired Arthur C. Clark on a visit to Bell Labs that he incorporated it into his novel *2001: A Space Odyssey* (1968). Joan Miller, personal communication with Alvy Ray Smith, Bell Labs, Murray Hill, NJ, July 1978, cited in Alvy Ray Smith, "Tint Fill," *ACM SIGGRAPH Computer Graphics* 13, no. 2 (1979): 276–282. On the development of one of the earliest experimental frame buffer systems, known as the Brookhaven Raster Display, see Drora Ophir, S. Rankowitz, Barry J. Shepherd, and Robert J. Spinrad, "BRAD: The Brookhaven Raster Display," *Communications of the ACM* 11, no. 6 (June 1968): 415.

45. Noll and others at Bell Labs had worked in the early 1960s to produce raster graphics via Ken Knowlton's BEFLIX programming language, but these were not real-time graphics intended to be seen and interacted with on a CRT display. Rather, they were filmed off a special CRT device and viewed later as film projections. See Patterson, *Peripheral Visions*, 52–54.

46. A. Michael Noll, "Scanned-Display Computer Graphics," *Communications of the ACM* 14, no. 3 (March 1970): 146–148.

47. When discussing most computer graphics systems, one generally needs to consider five bit depths: one, three, eight, twenty-four, and thirty-two. These correspond, respectively, to 2 colors (black and white), 8 colors, 256 colors, 16.7 million colors, and 16.7 million colors plus 256 levels of transparency. The 8-bit, or 256-color, systems made digital painting a real tool for color video and general artistic applications. The 24- and 32-bit paint systems are required for higher-quality film use. The difference between 24- and 32-bit systems is the availability of an extra channel—the "alpha channel"—that always carries transparency information for all images.

48. The hardware for the initial frame buffer took up three refrigerator-size racks and cost almost a quarter of a million dollars. Smith, "Digital Paint Systems," 5, 12.

49. Richard Shoup, "SuperPaint: An Early Frame Buffer Graphics System," *IEEE Annals of the History of Computing* 23, no. 2 (April–June 2001): 34.

50. This failed vision was one of many prominent mistakes made by Xerox in this period, during which it developed and failed to commercialize numerous contemporary technologies, including the personal computer itself. See Douglas K. Smith and Robert C. Alexander, *Fumbling the Future: How Xerox Invented, Then Ignored, the first Personal Computer* (New York: William Morrow and Company, 1988).

51. James Kajiya, Ivan E. Sutherland, and Edward C. Cheadle, "A Random-Access Video Frame Buffer," in *Proceedings of the IEEE Conference on Computer Graphics* (Piscataway, NJ: IEEE, 1975), 1–6.

52. This period marks the earliest instance of experimentation with pixel resolution for rendered objects. Chris Wylie, Gorgon Romney, David Evans, and Alan Erdahl, "Half-Tone Perspective Drawings by Computer," in *Proceedings of the November 14–16, 1967, Fall Joint Computer Conference* (New York: Association for Computing Machinery, 1967), 49–58.

53. Only one year later, at the International Federation for Information Processing conference in Edinburgh, a team of researchers presented a paper demonstrating a dramatic increase in the range and quality of three-dimensional rendered objects, though computation and display time was still on the order of several dozen seconds per image. Gordon Romney, Gary Watkins, and David Evans, "Real-Time Display of Computer Generated Half-Tone Perspective Pictures," in *Information Processing 68: Proceedings of IFIP Congress 1968, Edinburgh, UK* (Laxenburg, Austria: International Federation for Information Processing, 1968), 973–978.

54. Color images could be achieved using a color map, which simulated a 24-bit color depth on an 8-bit system using a color lookup table.

55. While the department had limited funding for visiting artists, one faculty member's work was dedicated exclusively to artistic applications of computer graphics: the paper-folding artist and architect Ronald Resch. See Ronald D. Resch, "The Topological Design of Sculptural and Architectural Systems," in *Proceedings of the June 4–8, 1973, National Computer Conference and Exposition* (New York: Association for Computing Machinery, 1973), 643–650.

56. Smith, "Digital Paint Systems," 14.

57. Schure was deeply invested in being the first to develop a fully digital animated film and thus often asked his research team what it needed to stay ahead. Not long after acquiring the first E&S frame buffer, Smith told Schure in passing that what they really needed was two additional frame buffers to assemble a complete RGB buffer. This would allow them to produce a true dynamic color range with full antialiasing. Within several weeks, Schure had purchased not two but rather five additional buffers at $60,000 each. Combined with the original buffer, this made for a total of $360,000—the contemporary equivalent of more than $1,600,000—spent

on little more than an offhand request. This made NYIT the first studio capable of producing images in full 24-bit color. Alvy Ray Smith, interview by author, Berkeley, CA, August 20, 2012; "Letter to Alexander Schure from David C. Evans, October 2, 1975," David C. Evans Papers, MS 625, box 105, folder 9, Special Collections, J. Willard Marriott Library, University of Utah.

58. Schure's animation team initially produced a feature-length adaptation of the Paul Tripp song "Tubby the Tuba" using conventional animation methods, though it was poorly received and a commercial flop. Following this failure, Schure looked to computational techniques to reduce expenses and streamline production. See Edwin Catmull, "The Problems of Computer-Assisted Animation," *ACM SIGGRAPH Computer Graphics* 12, no. 3 (1978): 348–353; Alexander Schure, dir., *Tubby the Tuba* (Los Angeles: Embassy Pictures, 1975), 35 mm.

59. For more on the history of Pixar, see David Price, *The Pixar Touch: The Making of a Company* (New York: Vintage, 2009).

60. Edwin Catmull, "A Subdivision Algorithm for Computer Display of Curved Surfaces" (PhD diss., University of Utah, 1974), 6.

61. The term is used in Paul Nipkow's 1884 patent for his mechanical-scanning television and by Hermann Voge (1874) in reference to the point in the focal plane of a camera lens where rays from an object point converge. See Richard F. Lyon, "A Brief History of 'Pixel,'" in *Proceedings Volume 6069, Digital Photography II* (San Jose, CA: Electronic Imaging, 2006); Richard F. Lyon, "Pixels and Me" (lecture at the Computer History Museum, Mountain View, CA, March 23, 2005), https://youtu .be/D6n2Esh4jDY. For an alternate history of the pixelated image in nineteenth-century painting, see Carol Armstrong, "Seurat's Media, or a Matrix of Materialities," *Grey Room* 58 (Winter 2015): 6–25.

62. Tom Kilburn, "Mark I" (presentation at the Manchester Science Museum, May 23, 1991), reported in "Early Computers at Manchester University," *Computer Resurrection: The Bulletin of the Computer Conservation Society* 1, no. 4 (Summer 1992), http://www.cs.man.ac.uk/CCS/res/res04.htm#g.

63. As Smith notes in his history of early memory tube technology, Kilburn's initial account of the development of the CRT memory concept attributes its invention to the Radiation Laboratory at MIT. Only later does he suggest that the visit merely served as inspiration for Williams's own invention. See Alvy Ray Smith, "The Dawn of Digital Light," *IEEE Annals of the History of Computing* 38, no. 4 (2016): 74–91; Frederic Williams and Tom Kilburn, "A Storage System for Use with Binary-Digital Computing Machines," *Proceedings of the IEE—Part III: Radio and Communication Engineering* 96, no. 40 (1949): 81–98.

64. John von Neumann, "First Draft of a Report on the EDVAC," *IEEE Annals of the History of Computing* 15, no. 4 (1993; June 30, 1945): 27–75. Von Neumann was

not alone in developing the idea of stored program architecture. While he is most often credited with the concept, many computer historians consider it inaccurate to refer to electronic stored program digital computers as "von Neumann machines" because of the significant contributions of figures such as Alan Turing, Konrad Zuse, J. Prespert Eckert, and John Mauchly. See B. Randell, "On Alan Turing and the Origins of Digital Computers," in *Machine Intelligence 7*, ed. Bernard Meltzer and Donald Michie (Edinburgh: Edinburgh University Press, 1972), 10.

65. These include the Z3 (Germany in 1941), Harvard Mark 1 (the United States in 1944), and ENIAC (the United States in 1946).

66. Wendy Chun describes this not as an omission but rather an intentional methodological decision on the part of von Neumann, suggesting it reflects the "axiomatic" (black boxing) method of his general theory of natural and artificial automatons as well as his work on game theory. See Wendy Hui Kyong Chun, *Programmed Visions: Software and Memory* (Cambridge, MA: MIT Press, 2011), 132.

67. Eckert describes this process technologically as a "short-range human device" for memory. See J. Presper Eckert Jr., "A Survey of Digital Computer Memory Systems," *Proceedings of the IEEE* 85, no. 1 (January 1997): 186.

68. One likely outgrowth of the blinking lights of the Williams-Kilburn CRT is the "blinkenlights" effect of early mainframe computers, in which blinking lights were used to indicate the computer was working and had not ceased to function. The earliest computers tended to fail midcomputation. To show whether the machine was working, a set of lights was sometimes added that indicated the condition of the address bus, data bus, and (sometimes) control bus. If the lights were blinking, the computer was doing something. If the lights stopped in a pattern, the computer had stopped doing anything, and the problem might be found at the binary address displayed by the lights. These displays were useful because many programs might take days to complete, and the outcome would be known only when the machine spat out a card with an eighty-character answer. While the lights became quickly outdated as technology improved, they often remain as a skeuomorphic indication of computation in action. See "Blinkenlights," Jargon File, version 4.4.6, October 25, 2003, http://jargon-file.org/archive/jargon-4.4.6.dos.txt.

69. Nonetheless, many systems used an additional CRT as an output device that could display the results of a calculation or the image from any of its storage tubes as a binary array. Researchers could physically view the bits of data stored in the machine at any given time to determine the state of a calculation or debug a program that failed to run. Turing termed this visual inspection "peeking," and PEEK and POKE are still used as commands in the BASIC programming language to read and set the contents of a memory cell at a specified address. Matthew G. Kirschenbaum, *Mechanisms: New Media and the Forensic Imagination* (Cambridge, MA: MIT Press, 2008), 254–256.

70. Alvy Ray Smith has recently explored this early history of what he calls "digital light," making a strong distinction between early digital images made with points of light or pixels, and images that are the product of graphical calculation—that is, computer graphics. Smith, "The Dawn of Digital Light."

71. As early as 1945, Eckert developed yet failed to implement an electronic CRT memory, writing bits to a screen but failing to read or keep them refreshed for use in computation. Perhaps the earliest CRT developed for both memory and picture display was the Haeff tube, developed in 1947 by Andrew V. Haeff while working at the US Naval Research Laboratory in Washington, DC; it was the first tube able to store and display graphics and text on an electronic screen for an unlimited period of time. See J. Presper Eckert Jr., Herman Lukoff, and Gerald Smoliar, "A Dynamically Regenerated Electrostatic Memory System," *Proceedings of the IRE* 38 (1950): 498–510. This is a revision of the talk presented at the 1949 IRE Convention on March 8, 1949, in New York. See also B. Jack Copeland, Andre A. Haeff, Peter Gough, and Cameron Wright, "Screen History: The Haeff Memory and Graphics Tube," *IEEE Annals of the History of Computing* 39, no. 1 (2017): 9–28.

72. Fred Joseph Gruenberger, "The History of the Jonniac," Memorandum RM-5654-PR, RAND Corporation, October 1968, 25–27.

73. Recent research by Smith calls into question the dates ascribed to this work at MIT given that the images Taylor used to illustrate the working of the Whirlwind tubes appear to be from 1952. See Smith, "The Dawn of Digital Light."

74. Jan Hurst, Michael S. Mahoney, Norman H. Taylor, Douglas T. Ross, and Robert M. Fano, "Retrospectives I: The Early Years in Computer Graphics at MIT, Lincoln Lab and Harvard," in *SIGGRAPH '89 Panel Proceedings: July 31–August 4, 1989* (New York: Association for Computing Machinery, 1989), 19–38 .

75. Hurst et al., "Retrospectives I," 20.

76. For a detailed account of the Whirlwind I computer, see Kent C. Redmond and Thomas M. Smith, *Project Whirlwind: History of a Pioneer Computer* (Bedford, MA: Digital Press, 1980).

77. This was followed slightly later by a "2048 DIGIT STORE" image at twice the resolution. Unlike the research team at MIT, however, Williams and Kilburn's team made no further efforts to research graphical representation. Frederic Williams and Tom Kilburn, "A Storage System for Use with Binary-Digital Computing Machines," *Proceedings of the IEE—Part III: Radio and Communication Engineering* 96, no. 40 (1949): 82.

78. Hurst et al., "Retrospectives I," 22.

79. The weaving of these planes was often the work of female technicians, as was the wiring of circuits and other manual technical labor. See Sadie Plant, *Zeros and*

Ones: Digital Women and the New Technoculture (New York: Doubleday, 1997); Lisa Nakamura, "Indigenous Circuits: Navajo Women and the Racialization of Early Electronic Manufacture," *American Quarterly* 66, no. 4 (2014): 919–941.

Chapter 3

1. These effects are most commonly packaged into software suites such as Pixar's RenderMan, distilling photo-realistic simulation into an on-demand, drag-and-drop operation. See Alan Warburton, *Goodbye Uncanny Valley*, October 2017, 14:38, https:// alanwarburton.co.uk/goodbye-uncanny-valley.

2. Lev Manovich, "Assembling Reality: Myths of Computer Graphics," *Afterimage* 20, no. 2 (1992): 12–14.

3. For a history and theory of proxy objects generally, see Dylan Mulvin, *Proxies: The Cultural Work of Standing In* (Cambridge, MA: MIT Press, 2021).

4. See Dylan Mulvin and Jonathan Sterne, "Scenes from an Imaginary Country: Test Images and the American Color Television Standard," *Television and New Media* 17, no. 1 (2016): 21–43; Genevieve Yue, "The China Girl on the Margins of Film," *October* 153 (Summer 2015): 96–116; Rebecca Hall, "Leader Ladies Project," Chicago Film Society, https://www.chicagofilmsociety.org/projects/leaderladies/.

5. Utah graduate Gordon Romney has claimed that the first complex (non-square) object ever rendered was a Soma Cube in 1968. The cube is exemplary as it is comprised of simple primitives but models the process of assembling complex shapes out of smaller objects. Gordon Romney, "First Rendering: A History of 3D Rendering through a Look at the Contributions of Gordon Romney, Alan Erdahl, Edwin Catmull and James Blinn," accessed November 5, 2020, https://firstrender.net.

6. The most common solution to this problem was the use of wireframe models composed of a series of curved surfaces approximated by a succession of line segments, producing a polygon mesh that gave the appearance of a smooth curve. Henri Gouraud, "Computer Display of Curved Surfaces" (PhD diss., University of Utah, 1971), 4. Systems that allowed for rudimentary curvature include: Mathematical Applications Group Inc., "3-D Simulated Graphics," *Datamation* 14 (February1968): 69; Paul G. Comba, "A Procedure for Detecting Intersections of Three Dimensional Objects," IBM New York Scientific Center, Rep. 39.020, January 1967; Ruth A. Weiss, "Be Vision: A Package of IBM 7090 Fortran Programs to Draw Orthographic Views of Combinations of Planes and Quadratic Surfaces," *Journal of the Association for Computing Machinery* 13 (April 1966): 194–204.

7. This history reaches back to the Roman Empire, when ships were built using rib templates that could be used and reused over and over again. Drawn templates did not become popular until the seventeenth century, when the classical "spline" was likely invented and named in England. The earliest available mention of a spline

appears in Henri-Louis Duhamel du Monceau, *Eléments de l'architecture navale ou traité pratique de la construction des vaissaux* (Paris: Chez C.-A. Jombert, 1752). For a detailed history, see Gerald Farin, Josef Hoschek, and Myung-Soo Kim, *Handbook of Computer Aided Geometric Design* (Amsterdam: North Holland Publishing Company, 2002), 1–21.

8. A contemporary tool that was used for smaller-scale drawings was the French curve, which consisted of a number of templates made out of metal, wood, or plastic composed of numerous different curves. The tools came in a wide variety of shapes and forms, but the Burmester set of three curves are the most common. Many of the curves resemble the shape of a pistol, and the French name for the devices is *le pistolet*.

9. Other early names used include "dogs" or "rats." See Isaac Jacob Schoenberg, "Contributions to the Problem of Approximation of Equidistant Data by Analytic Functions," *Quarterly of Applied Mathematics* 4 (1946): 45–99, 112–141.

10. Spline devices also helped bend the wood for pianos, violins, and other string instruments. See A. Robin Forrest, foreword to *An Introduction to Splines for Use in Computer Graphics and Geometric Modeling*, ed. Richard Bartels, John Beatty, and Brian Barsky (Burlington, MA: Morgan Kaufmann Publishers, 1995), vii.

11. The first academic reference to mathematical splines appears in Schoenberg, "Contributions to the Problem of Approximation of Equidistant Data," 45–99. See also Carl de Boor, "On Calculating with B-Splines," *Journal of Approximation Theory* 6 (1972), 50–62; James Ferguson, "Multivariable Curve Interpolation," *Journal of the Association for Computing Machinery* 11, no. 2 (1964), 221–228; M. Sabin, *Offset Parametric Surfaces*, Technical Report VTO/MS/149 (London: British Aircraft Corporation, 1968); M. Sabin, *Parametric Splines in Tension*, Technical Report VTO/MS/160 (London: British Aircraft Corporation, 1970); M. Sabin, *Trinomial Basis Functions for Interpolation in Triangular Regions (Bézier Triangles)* (London: British Aircraft Corporation, 1971).

12. Paul de Casteljau, *Courbes et surfaces à poles* (Paris: A. Citroën, 1963); Pierre Bézier, "Definition numèrique des courbes et surfaces I," *Automatisme* 11 (1966): 625–632; Pierre Bézier, "Definition numèrique des courbes et surfaces II," *Automatisme* 12 (1967): 17–21.

13. Bézier's work on splines was further generalized in the 1960s into what are known as b-splines or basis splines, and NURBS, or nonuniform rational basis splines, which allow for the more precise, individual manipulation of each curve along a given path. While I will continue to use the term "Bézier curve" moving forward to describe a set of mathematical processes to approximate natural curvature, I am depicting processes that are also largely true of b-splines and NURBS. While I do not wish to minimize important differences between these methods for reproducing curvature, I will note that they each emerge from the same historical tradition

described here, and all three curves are often present as options in modern graphical software platforms.

14. Pierre Bézier, "Example of an Existing System in the Motor Industry: The Unisurf System," *Proceedings of the Royal Society of London. Series A, Mathematical and Physical Sciences* 321, no. 1545 (February 9, 1971): 207–218.

15. For more on this history, see Donald E. Knuth, "Mathematical Typography," *Bulletin (New Series) of the American Mathematical Society* 1, no. 2 (March 1979): 337–372.

16. It should be noted that the display of curvature is one of the earliest forms of computational visualization, though in a dramatically different form. Some of the earliest experimentation with computer visualization was done through the manipulation of oscilloscopes, which could be used to produce and transform simple geometric waveforms (sine waves, etc.) as well as read and visualize analog signal voltages (see chapter 2). In some ways, this transformation is indicative of a larger shift from analog to digital forms of visualization, in which continuous and irregular shapes such as curves become difficult to describe computationally.

17. The key difference is the significance of interpolation to the process of transforming dimensions. While smooth lines can be approximated and formed from a relatively small number of data points, it becomes necessary when moving to surfaces in three dimensions to make certain assumptions about the consistency of a given object and interpolate its shape between a limited number of data points. While it is possible to construct objects using a massive number of data points that re-create its surface with great accuracy, such a procedure would be impractical and—particularly in the 1970s—computationally quite difficult. As such, it was necessary to interpolate between lines and data points to form surfaces that may be built into structures.

18. The most prestigious award granted in the field of computer graphics is the ACM SIGGRAPH's Steven A. Coons Award, given in odd-numbered years to an individual to honor that person's lifetime contribution to computer graphics and interactive techniques. The award was founded in 1983, three years after Coons's death, and at the time of this writing, eight of the nineteen recipients were at one point in time Utah faculty or students.

19. For a detailed history of the MIT CAD Project, see Daniel Cardozo Llach, *Builders of the Vision: Software and the Imagination of Design* (New York: Routledge, 2015), 49–72.

20. Timothy E. Johnson, "Sketchpad III: A Computer Program for Drawing in Three Dimensions," in *Proceedings of the Spring 1963 Joint Computer Conference* (New York: Association for Computing Machinery, 1963); Steven Anson Coons, "Surfaces for Computer-Aided Design of Space Forms," Project MAC, Massachusetts Institute of Technology, Cambridge, June 1967.

21. For Coons, this research was meant to facilitate the production of sculptured parts by designers with little or no experience in computing. The goal was to allow

a designer to quickly and simply produce a virtual prototype that could then be transformed to match the desired shape and complexity. As such, it is a system built not to digitize existing physical objects but instead facilitate and replace the process by which objects are designed and produced. Nonetheless, it does so through the digitization of existing methods for the design of shapes that thus far had presented a great challenge to computing: complex curves and surfaces.

22. Coons, "Surfaces for Computer-Aided Design," iii.

23. Coons's report was produced as part of the Project on Mathematics and Computation (Project MAC), which was funded largely by the Department of Defense, and responsible for several groundbreaking innovations in operating systems, artificial intelligence, and the theory of computation. For more on the military origins of CAD and computer graphics, see Tim Lenoir, "All but War Is Simulation: The Military-Entertainment Complex," *Configurations* 8, no. 3 (2000): 289–335.

24. While the geometric splines formalized by Coons, Bézier, and others were extremely useful in the design of vehicles and other sculpted parts, they were limited to surfaces comprised of simple curving lines. As such, many complex surfaces are now modeled as a polygon mesh using a subdivision surface algorithm.

25. I mark 1974 as the year in which CAD crystallized as a field of research as it is the year in which the first International Conference on Computer Aided Geometric Design was held at the University of Utah. Organized by Utah faculty member Richard Riesenfeld, the conference brought together key researchers in the field for the first time, including Bézier and Coons. The event is often credited as the origin of computer-aided geometric design as a distinct field, and its proceedings were subsequently published in a widely influential volume. See Robert E. Barnhill, ed., *Computer Aided Geometric Design: Proceedings of a Conference Held at the University of Utah, Salt Lake City, Utah, March 18–21, 1974* (San Diego: Academic Press, 1974).

26. The "normal" of an object is a line that runs perpendicular to its surface. In a sense, it is the inverse of a tangent line or plane to a given point on a surface, in that it forms a ninety-degree angle with the tangent. See R. S. Rougelotand and R. Shoemaker, *G.E. Real Time Display*, NASA Report, NAS 9–3916 (Syracuse, NY: General Electric Company, 1969); Arthur Appel, "Some Techniques for Shading Machine Renderings of Solids," *Sprint Joint Computer Conference, 1968* (New York: Association for Computing Machinery, 1968), 37–45; John Warnock, "A Hidden Surface Algorithm for Computer Generated Halftone Pictures" (PhD diss., University of Utah, 1969).

27. Frank Crow, unpublished email interview with Peter Shirley, November 8, 1996.

28. Gary S. Watkins, "A Real Time Visible Surface Algorithm," no. UTEC-CSC-70–101, University of Utah School of Computing, Salt Lake City, June 1970.

29. Stockham had been hired by Evans from MIT in 1969, and would ultimately replace Evans as department chair following his move into industry in the early

1970s. Stockham's principal interest was signal processing, where he would lay the groundwork for the entire field of audio and image digitization and restoration. An avid fan of the famous Italian tenor Enrico Caruso, part of what drove Stockham's research was a desire to create a digital master of the few existing audio recordings of Caruso's voice made in the era before microphone-based recording. This led him to develop a technique for blind deconvolution that led to the rerelease of digitally remastered Caruso recordings in 1975, after which Stockham founded Soundstream, Inc., the first digital audio recording company in the United States. In the 1980s, the company sought to capitalize on digital audio by developing a consumer-grade digital player that used "a business card style memory device that would play back the 1812 Overture at 50 kHz," but this technology ultimately lost out to the joint effort of Sony and Philips to set the compact disc as an industry standard. See Jacob Gaboury, "Sounding Silence," *continent.* 5, no. 3 (2016), http://www.continentcontinent.cc/index.php/continent/article/view/261; James Lehning, "'Raising the State of the Art': Commercializing Innovation in Digital Sound," *Media History* (2018): 1–13; Thomas G. Stockham, Thomas M. Cannon, and Robert B. Ingebretsen, "Blind Deconvolution through Digital Signal Processing," *Proceedings of the IEEE* 63, no. 4 (1975): 678–692; Simon Barber, "Soundstream: The Introduction of Commercial Digital Recording in the United States, "*ASARP: Journal on the Art of Record Production* 7 (November 2012), http://arpjournal.com/2140/soundstream-the -introduction-of-commercial-digital-recording-in-the-united-states/.

30. Isabelle Bellin, "Images de synthèse: palme de la longévité pour l'ombrage de Gouraud," Interstices, September 15, 2008, https://interstices.info/images-de-synthese -palme-de-la-longevite-pour-lombrage-de-gouraud/.

31. Gouraud, "Computer Display of Curved Surfaces."

32. Phong was born in Hanoi in 1942 on the eve of the First Indochina War. While Vietnam had been a French colony since the mid-nineteenth century, the ensuing conflict between the Viet Minh and French ultimately led to the dissolution of French Indochina on July 20, 1954. That same year, Phong's family moved from Hanoi in the north to Saigon in the south, where he attended the Lycée Jean Jacques Rousseau. In 1964, he moved to France and was admitted to the Grenoble Institute of Technology, where he received his *Licence en Sciences* in 1966 and his *Diplôme d'Ingénieur* from the École nationale supérieure d'électronique, d'électrotechnique, d'informatique, d'hydraulique et des télécommunications in Toulouse in 1968. Phong then joined the Institut national de recherche en informatique et en automatique as a researcher in computer science, working in the development of operating systems for digital computers before being recruited by Sutherland to the University of Utah in 1971. Phong died of cancer shortly after accepting a tenure-track position at Stanford in 1975, and as such, there is relatively little work documenting his life and research. "Tenure Letter of Recommendation to E.J. McClusky," David C. Evans Papers, MS 625, box 1, folder 2, Special Collections, J. Willard Marriott Library, University of Utah.

33. Bui Tuong Phong, "Illumination for Computer-Generated Images" (PhD diss., University of Utah, 1973).

34. Phong, "Illumination for Computer-Generated Images," 38–72. For a history and theory of lighting algorithms, see Friedrich Kittler, "Computer Graphics: A Semi-Technical Introduction," trans. Sara Ogger, *Grey Room* 2 (Winter 2001): 30–45.

35. Frank Crow, "The Origins of the Teapot," *IEEE Computer Graphics and Animation* 7, no. 1 (January 1987), 8. Crow completed his dissertation research under Sutherland and is best known for his work on antialiasing. While less prominent in this book, he was a significant researcher and instructor at many of the institutions that make up this history, including the New York Institute of Technology, Ohio State University, Xerox PARC, Apple, and NVIDIA. See Frank Crow, "The Aliasing Problem in Computer-Generated Shaded Images," *Communications of the ACM* 20, no. 11 (1977): 799–805.

36. Robert Joseph McDermott, "Robert Remembers: The VW Bug," *Utah Teapot: Quarterly Newspaper for the Alumni and Friends of the University of Utah School of Computing* (Fall 2003): 7. McDermott was one of few students to work under Ronald Resch at Utah, and is perhaps most famous for writing an algorithm to cast a periodic b-spline curve that was used to define and manufacture the Vegreville egg, a giant pysanka sculpture in the town of Vegreville, Alberta, that was the first physical structure designed entirely with computer-aided geometric modeling software. See Robert Joseph McDermott, "Geometric Modelling in Computer-Aided Design" (PhD diss., University of Utah, 1980); Robert Joseph McDermott, "A Ukrainian Easter Egg Monument Stands for Thirty Years," in *Proceedings of the 2005 Bridges Conference, Renaissance Banff: Mathematics, Music, Art, Culture*, ed. Reza Sarhangi and Robert V. Moody (Bridges Organization, 2005), 109–116; James F. Blinn. "The World's Largest Easter Egg and What Came Out of It," *IEEE Computer Graphics and Applications* 8, no. 2 (March 1988): 16–23; Andrew Witt and Eliza Pertigkiozoglou, *Computation as Design: Ron Resch and the New Media of Geometry* (Montreal: Canadian Centre for Architecture, 2019).

37. McDermott, "Robert Remembers," 7.

38. Edwin Catmull, "A System for Computer Generated Movies," in *ACM '72 Proceedings of the ACM Annual Conference* (New York: Association for Computing Machinery, 1972), 1:429.

39. This technique was frequently used prior to the widespread adoption of 3D scanning technology.

40. Edwin Catmull and Fred Parke, *Halftone Animation* (1972), 16 mm, http://vimeo .com/16292363. Parke completed a dissertation on the computer-generated animation of faces under Robert Stephenson, Ivan Sutherland, and Richard Riesenfeld, and subsequently went on to work at NYIT. He later worked for IBM and is now

emeritus faculty at Texas A&M in the Department of Visualization. See Frederic Parke, *Computer Generated Animation of Faces*, Technical Report UTEC-CSs-72–120 (Salt Lake City: University of Utah, 1972); Frederic Parke, "A Parametric Model for Human Faces" (PhD diss., University of Utah, 1974); Jacob Gaboury, "Virtual Bodies and Empty Signifiers: On Fred Parke and Miley Cyrus," Rhizome, January 20, 2014, https://rhizome.org/editorial/2014/jan/20/fred-parke-and-miley-cyrus/.

41. The one major exception to this is Edward E. Zajac's 1963 scientific visualization of a two-giro gravity attitude control system, though this film does not use contemporary polygon-based rendering techniques and is not fully shaded. Edward E. Zajac, "Computer-Made Perspective Movies as a Scientific and Communication Tool," *Communications of the ACM 7*, no. 3 (1964): 169–170, https://techchannel.att.com/embed/index.cfm?mediaID=11107&w=560&h=315.

42. John M. Miller, "Futureworld," Turner Classic Movies, http://www.tcm.com/this-month/article/245820%7C0/Futureworld.html.

43. "Letter to Martin E. Newell, June 15, 1972," David C. Evans Papers, MS 625, box 5, folder 2, Special Collections, J. Willard Marriott Library, University of Utah; "Quarterly Report: Graphical Man/Machine Communications (Contract Number F 30602–70-C-0300) 1970–1973," University of Utah Department of Computer Science records, account 051, box 1, folder 11, University Archives and Records Management, University of Utah, J. Willard Marriott Library, Salt Lake City.

44. Martin Newell, "Modeling by Computer," unpublished draft essay, January 31, 1975, David C. Evans Papers, MS 625, box 140, folder 21, 4, Special Collections, J. Willard Marriott Library, University of Utah; Martin Newell, "The Utilization of Procedure Models in Digital Image Synthesis" (PhD diss., University of Utah, 1975).

45. The dissertation also includes a pawn set and checkerboard floor that are among the earliest iconic images in computer graphics, with examples dating back as far as 1968. Pawns are simple uniform shapes that can be easily modeled, and the grid of a chessboard is a useful means of demonstrating the depth, perspective, and distortion of objects in a scene.

46. The Zion's Cooperative Mercantile Institution was founded by Brigham Young on October 9, 1868, and for many years claimed the title of "America's First Department Store." It was sold to the May Department Stores Company (now Macy's, Inc.) in 1999.

47. Crow, "The Origins of the Teapot."

48. The teapot is one of the first 3D computer-generated objects that was rendered as a sculptured surface with Bézier curves rather than as a set of polygons.

49. A common anecdote suggests that before the teapot model was included as a standard object in most rendering software, many researchers would memorize the

numbers and could recite them in order. This seems largely apocryphal, as the numbers were easily stored in a file to be accessed without rote memorization.

50. The teapot is categorized as one of "various objects defined using Bézier patches" and part of a fully rendered "table setting." Newell, "The Utilization of Procedure Models," 84, 86.

51. Jim Blinn and Martin Newell, "Texture and Reflection in Computer Generated Images," *Communications of the ACM* 19, no. 10 (October 1976): 542–547; Edwin Catmull, "Computer Display of Curved Surfaces," in *Proceedings of the IEEE Conference on Computer Graphics* (New York: Association for Computing Machinery, 1975), 11–17.

52. Crow, "The Origins of the Teapot," 8.

53. Jen Grey, "TEATIME at Boston ACM SIGGRAPH 2006," *ACM SIGGRAPH Computer Graphics* 40, no. 3 (November 2006). See also Marc J. Ball, "The Teapot as Object and Icon," ACM SIGGRAPH 2006 exhibition, https://www.siggraph.org//s2006/main.php?f=conference&p=teapot.

54. Ann-Sophie Lehmann, "Taking the Lid off the Utah Teapot," *Zeitschrift für Medien- und Kulturforschung* 1 (2012): 173–174.

55. In an email correspondence with the author, Blinn contradicts Crow's suggestion that the teapot was scaled multiple times, suggesting it was scaled once for ARPA and this became the now iconic model. Jim Blinn, email correspondence with the author, May 21, 2020; Mike Seymour, "Founders Series: Industry Legend Jim Blinn," fxguide, July 24, 2012, http://www.fxguide.com/featured/founders-series-industry -legend-jim-blinn/; Crow, "The Origins of the Teapot," 9.

56. While I have been unable to corroborate this early 1986 date through archival sources, at the latest the Bézier patches for the full tea set were posted by a user named Juhana Kouhia on October 25, 1991, to NIC.FUNET.FI, an FTP server hosted via the Finnish University and Research Network. See Russ Fish, "Teapot Subdivision," 1998, http://www.cs.utah.edu/gdc/projects/alpha1/help/man/html/model_repo/model _teapot/model_teapot.html.

57. Since the digitization and standardization of the teapot, many other standard graphical objects have followed suit. Subsequent objects are generally more complex or produced using different methods that allow for unique forms of testing. The Stanford bunny, developed by Greg Turk and Matt Levoy in 1994, consists of data describing 69,451 triangles determined by 3D scanning a ceramic figurine of a rabbit. Three-dimensional scanning was in its infancy in the early 1990s, and the bunny suffers from many of the problems inherent to this method of digitization, such as holes in its data that must be compensated for in any algorithm applied to it. The Stanford dragon is a similar model developed in 1996 also using 3D scanning technology, with data describing 871,414 triangles. A third modern standard—a

cartoonish orangutan face named "Suzanne" after the monkey in the 2001 Kevin Smith film *Jay and Silent Bob Strike Back*—is much closer to a modern Utah teapot in its simplicity. With only five hundred faces, it can be used to quickly test basic material, animation, rigs, texture, and lighting setups, and is also used as a joke image in demos and games.

58. James Arvo and David Kirk, "Fast Ray Tracing by Ray Classification," *Proceeding: SIGGRAPH '87 Proceedings of the 14th Annual Conference on Computer Graphics and Interactive Techniques* (New York: ACM SIGGRAPH, 1987), 55–64.

59. The screen saver has a small chance of spawning the teapot, and there are numerous threads on the Web devoted to stories of teapot spottings and time wasted waiting for the teapot to appear.

60. John Lasseter, dir., *Toy Story* (1995; Emeryville, CA: Pixar Animation Studios, 2016), Blu-ray Disc; Matt Groening, dir., "Treehouse of Horror VI," *The Simpsons* (New York: Twentieth Century Fox, 1995), TV.

61. These teapots are highly prized by SIGGRAPH attendees, with people lining up for hours to receive one. There is also a strong secondary market for the teapots on eBay, where they can sell for several hundreds of dollars.

62. Erwin Panofsky, "Jan van Eyck's Arnolfini Portrait," *Burlington Magazine for Connoisseurs* 64, no. 372 (March, 1934): 117–119, 122–127.

63. Channeling philosopher Alfred North Whitehead, media theorist Matthew Fuller has suggested that standard objects operate as "ideally isolated systems" that function in ignorance of that which is incompatible with its standard—a restriction of the world to that which can be made meaningfully legible. Matthew Fuller, *Media Ecologies: Materialist Energies in Art and Technoculture* (Cambridge, MA: MIT Press, 2005).

64. Newell, "Modeling by Computer," 3.

65. This process whereby the domestic is transformed to suit the disciplinary needs of a technical practice is by no means unique to computer graphics. For example, the now-ubiquitous breadboard used in the prototyping of electronics derives its name from the kitchen breadboards repurposed by radio amateurs in the early twentieth century.

66. Gouraud, "Computer Display of Curved Surfaces," 55.

67. See Jennifer S. Light, "When Computers Were Women," *Technology and Culture* 40, no. 3 (1999): 455–483; Janet Abbate, *Recoding Gender: Women's Changing Participation in Computing* (Cambridge, MA: MIT Press, 2012); Marie Hicks, *Programmed Inequality: How Britain Discarded Women Technologists and Lost Its Edge in Computing* (Cambridge, MA: MIT Press, 2017); Nathan Ensmenger, *The Computer Boys Take Over: Computers, Programmers, and the Politics of Technical Expertise* (Cambridge, MA: MIT Press, 2012).

68. For a detailed history of 3D models for computer graphics, see Alana Staiti, "What's in a Model? A History of Human Modeling for Computer Graphics and Animation, 1961–1988" (PhD diss., Cornell University, 2018).

Chapter 4

1. Kay, "The Early History of Smalltalk," 515.

2. Kay, "The Early History of Smalltalk," 516.

3. While Simula is widely considered to be the first object-oriented programming language, this distinction elides the simultaneous development of several other arguably object-oriented systems, as I describe in this chapter. Moreover, Simula is not considered a "true" object-oriented language since it largely functions as an extension of Algol 60 and is not conceived of as object-oriented from the "bottom up." It is for this reason that I treat object orientation not as a concept that emerges with a particular language but rather as a structuring paradigm with multiple overlapping origins.

4. Kay, "The Early History of Smalltalk," 516.

5. Kay, "The Early History of Smalltalk," 514–515.

6. H. Kent Bowen, "The University of Utah and the Computer Graphics Revolution" (unpublished case study, Harvard Business School, April 28, 2006).

7. For a history of Kay's work in developing the personal computer as a multimedia object, see Lev Manovich, *Software Takes Command* (New York: Bloomsbury, 2013), 55–106.

8. Alan Kay, "The Reactive Engine" (PhD diss., University of Utah, 1969).

9. The most prominent examples of object-oriented programming languages include C++ and Java, but object-oriented principles are found in many mixed-paradigm languages such as Python and Ruby.

10. While Smalltalk is often viewed as the quintessential object-oriented language, it is important to recall that it was more influential than practical insofar as it was never widely adopted for personal computing and education as Kay envisioned. Indeed, object-oriented programming did not truly rise to prominence until the growth of the windowed graphical user interface in the late 1980s, the release of Microsoft's C++-driven COM architecture in the early 1990s, and the rise to prominence of Sun's Java language in the mid-1990s. As such, object orientation should be understood as an evolutionary paradigm that emerges from and diffuses into a broad technical field.

11. Grady Booch, *Object-Oriented Analysis and Design with Applications*, 3rd ed. (Boston: Addison-Wesley Professional, 2007).

12. The system functioned using a rudimentary form of encapsulation, perhaps the most basic precondition of an object-like structure. Joline Zepcevski, "Complexity and Verification: The History of Programming as Problem Solving" (PhD diss., University of Minnesota, 2012), 239; Kay, "The Early History of Smalltalk," 514.

13. C. Gordon Bell, J. Craig Mudge, and John E. McNamara, *Computer Engineering: A DEC View of Computer Design* (Bedford, MA: Digital Press, 1978).

14. "Toward a Machine with Interactive Skills," in *Understanding Computers: Computer Images* (New York: Time-Life Books, 1986), 31.

15. This marks one of the earliest interactive solutions to the problem of "clipping," where the computer must be able to tell when an object extends beyond the edge of the screen and should therefore not be shown (see chapter 1). Sketchpad solved this problem in such a way that objects outside the frame of the screen remained in memory and would reappear if the user zoomed out over the display.

16. Ivan E. Sutherland, dir., *Sketchpad* (Cambridge, MA: MIT Lincoln Laboratory, 1962), film, https://youtu.be/3wrn9cxlgls. A second film was produced by the MIT Science Reporter for local television in 1964, and is often conflated on YouTube and other online video-sharing sites with Sutherland's original film. This film, however, does not feature the original system as Sutherland designed it but instead is an updated version called Sketchpad III, which has the addition of simple 3D graphics thanks to modifications made by Timothy Johnson as part of his MA thesis. Due to a general resemblance between Sutherland and Johnson, images of Johnson demonstrating the Sketchpad system are frequently mistaken with images of Sutherland himself. The video also features an interview with Sutherland's adviser, Steven Coons. See Russell Morash, dir., *Computer Sketchpad* (Cambridge, MA: MIT Science Reporter, July 1964), film, https://youtu.be/6orsmFndx_o.

17. This cartographic zoom is reminiscent of, but presages, Charles and Ray Eames's short film *The Powers of Ten* (1977), in which identical structures seem to appear at vastly different scales. An earlier version of that film was completed in 1968, five years after Sutherland's *Sketchpad*. See Charles Eames and Ray Eames, dirs., *Powers of Ten* (New York: IBM, 1977), film.

18. "Toward a Machine with Interactive Skills," 35.

19. Architecture historian Matthew Allen has made a strong case for the emergence of the computer screenshot as a technical and cultural practice among researchers at MIT's Computer Aided Design Project in the early 1960s largely as a tool for exemplifying the interactive potential of graphical computing using programs such as Sutherland's Sketchpad. These early screenshots fulfilled the explicit need of reproducing interactive simulations such that they could be seen by those without access to the multimillion-dollar research systems they required in order to run. Somewhat ironically, what screenshots captured here was not stillness but rather interaction,

such that these images were in many ways responsible for shaping the technological imaginary of interactive computing that would ultimately evolve into the machines we use today. Matthew Allen, "Representing Computer-Aided Design: Screenshots and the Interactive Computer circa 1960," *Perspectives on Science* 24, no. 6 (2016): 637–668.

20. The machine was based on the earlier TX-0 machine, also developed by Clark and in use at MIT throughout the 1960s. Initially Clark had planned a TX-1 machine, but it was scrapped due to its complexity and redesigned as the TX-2.

21. Years later, Clark told Sutherland figuratively that he had designed the TX-2 for Sketchpad long before Sutherland had even arrived. Ivan E. Sutherland, "Looking Back: The TX-2 Computer and Sketchpad," *Lincoln Laboratory Journal* 11, no. 1 (2012): 82.

22. Separating the TX-2 from the era of personal computing are several decades of time-shared computing, in which multiple users relied on terminals to connect them with a single mainframe machine.

23. "Toward a Machine with Interactive Skills," 34.

24. Ivan E. Sutherland, "Sketchpad: A Man-Machine Graphical Communication System," in *Proceedings of the AFIPS 1963 Spring Joint Computer Conference, May 21–23 1963* (Baltimore: Spartan Books, 1963), 333.

25. Ivan E. Sutherland, "Sketchpad: A Man-Machine Graphical Interface" (PhD diss., Massachusetts Institute of Technology, 1963), 89.

26. See Kay, "The Early History of Smalltalk," 517; Gottfried Wilhelm Leibniz, *Philosophical Essays*, ed. Daniel Garber and Roger Areiw (New York: Hackett, 1989); Baruch Spinoza, "The Ethics," in *The Ethics and Other Works*, ed. and trans. Edwin Curley (Princeton, NJ: Princeton University Press, 1994), part 1, def. 5; Gilles Deleuze, *Spinoza: Practical Philosophy* (San Francisco: City Lights Books, 1988), 122.

27. This *modularity* is one of the five "principles of new media" that Manovich defines in *The Language of New Media* (2001). Here he associates it with the rise in the 1970s of structured programming languages, which follow a distinct organizational logic from object-oriented languages, and grow in popular use prior to object-oriented languages and systems. Nonetheless, this modular logic can be found in both, emerges first in object-oriented systems, and differentiates both from earlier procedural models. Lev Manovich, *The Language of New Media* (Cambridge, MA: MIT Press, 2001), 30.

28. While design systems were not developed until the 1960s, techniques for computer-aided manufacturing through the numerical control of milling machines can be traced back to the late 1940s at MIT. For a comprehensive history, see J. Francis Reintjes, *Numerical Control: Making a New Technology* (Oxford: Oxford University Press, 1991).

29. Fred N. Krull, "The Origin of Computer Graphics within General Motors," *IEEE Annals of the History of Computing* 16, no. 3 (1994): 40.

30. Edwin L. Jacks, "A Laboratory for the Study of Man-Machine Communication," in *Proceedings of the October 27–29, 1964, Fall Joint Computer Conference, Part I* (New York: Association for Computing Machinery, 1964), 343–344.

31. Krull, "The Origin of Computer Graphics," 41.

32. The initial name of the research group was Digital Design, but it was changed to avoid any misunderstanding that the team was involved in the design of digits. This confusion over the use of the word "digital" will be familiar to many digital media theorists and researchers.

33. Edwin L. Jacks, "A Laboratory for the Study of Man-Machine Communication," *Proceedings of the October 27–29, 1964, Fall Joint Computer Conference, Part I* (New York: Association for Computing Machinery 1964), 344.

34. Krull, "The Origin of Computer Graphics," 42.

35. The system developed for line digitization is truly innovative and well ahead of its time. In particular its treatment of irregular curves based on parametric models predates Coons's foundational research by several years. For a detailed account of the line-scanning system, see Fred N. Krull and James E. Foote, "A Line Scanning System Controlled from an On-Line Console," in *Proceedings of the October 27–29, 1964, Fall Joint Computer Conference, Part I* (New York: Association for Computing Machinery, 1964), 397–410.

36. Jacks, "A Laboratory for the Study," 349.

37. Krull, "The Origin of Computer Graphics," 46.

38. Jacks, "A Laboratory for the Study," 349.

39. During its development phase, the name NOMAD stood for "Non-Operational Michigan Algorithm Decoder," but was changed to "Newly Operational" once the system was up and running.

40. Krull, "The Origin of Computer Graphics," 48.

41. Casey Alt, "Objects of Our Affection: How Object Orientation Made Computers a Medium," in *Media Archeology: Approaches, Applications, and Implications*, ed. Erkki Huhtamo and Jussi Parikka (Berkeley: University of California Press, 2011), 278–301.

42. Alan Kay and Adele Goldberg, *Personal Dynamic Media*, Learning Research Group, Technical Report No. SSL-76–1 (Palo Alto, CA: Xerox Palo Alto Research Center, 1976), 4.

43. Tim Rentsch, "Object Oriented Programming," *ACM SIGPLAN Notices* 17 (September 1982): 52.

44. For a detailed discussion of the connection between Xerox, NeXT, and contemporary graphical user interfaces, see Hansen Hsu, "The Deep History of Your Apps: Steve Jobs, NeXTSTEP, and Early Object-Oriented Programming," *Computer History Museum Blog*, March 15, 2016, https://computerhistory.org/blog/the-deep-history-of -your-apps-steve-jobs-nextstep-and-early-object-oriented-programming/.

45. This is why current Mac OS X programs are low-level programmed in Objective C, which is more closely related to Smalltalk than it is to Stoustrup's C++. In 2014, however, Apple announced a shift to a new programming language called Swift, which builds on the functionality of Objective C while updating it with many of the features that were difficult to graft onto an existing language such as NeXTSTEP.

46. Kay has done considerable work to formalize this narrative and his role within it, which has led to a number of hagiographic treatments of his life and work to the exclusion of the broader field of practice from which object orientation was developed. See Kay, "The Early History of Smalltalk."

47. Edwin Catmull, "A System for Creating Computer Generated Movies," in *ACM '72 Proceedings of the ACM Annual Conference* (New York: Association for Computer Machinery, 1972), 422–423.

48. Later efforts to generalize this work at Utah as a set of "object description languages" was begun by Sutherland and Newell in 1973, though it is unclear if it was formalized into a distinct language or ended with the failure of the Electric Picture Company. "Memo to ONR File: Object Description Languages," David C. Evans Paper, MS 625, box 63, folder 27, Special Collections, J. Willard Marriott Library, University of Utah.

49. Catmull, "A System for Creating Computer Generated Movies," 424.

50. Alt outlines some of these connections, though not in a historical context, in an earlier article on the Maya modeling interface. See Casey Alt, "The Materialities of Maya: Making Sense of Object-Orientation," *Configurations* 10, no. 3 (September 2002): 387–422.

51. "A Proposal for CAORF, July 30 1973," David C. Evans Papers, MS 625, box 62, folder 7–8, Special Collections, J. Willard Marriott Library, University of Utah.

52. See Tim Lenoir, "All but War Is Simulation: The Military-Entertainment Complex," *Configurations* 8, no. 3 (2000): 289–335; Tim Lenoir and Luke Caldwell, *The Military-Entertainment Complex* (Cambridge, MA: Harvard University Press, 2018).

53. Tekla S. Perry, "PostScript Prints Anything: A Case History," *IEEE Spectrum* 25, no. 5 (1988): 43.

54. The company was located in a research park adjacent to campus in what was once the Fort Douglas military garrison, founded in 1862 to protect the overland mail route and telegraph lines running from Salt Lake City to San Francisco. Many

of the Utah program's students' first industry jobs were at E&S, and the university contracted out to E&S for several collaborations that drew funds from ARPA contracts and used university facilities. "Proposal to Advanced Research Projects Agency from the Evans & Sutherland Computer Corporation: A Program to Build and Operate a Real Time Shaded Picture Generating System," David C. Evans Papers, MS 625, box 89, folder 3, Special Collections, J. Willard Marriott Library, University of Utah.

55. The company would also build simulators for commercial airlines and even simulators to train astronauts for space flight.

56. While it is tempting to read into this religious iconography given the LDS system's name and the religion of many of its developers, the LDS Church does not use the cross or crucifix as symbols of faith, as many Mormons view crucifixion-related symbols as emphasizing the death of Jesus rather than his life and resurrection.

57. These fully interactive systems were extremely successful, but the graphics themselves were still fairly rudimentary as functional solutions to many key problems had not yet been produced. For several years, E&S relied on "night vision" systems that simulated plane takeoff and landing at night using distant points of light and a flat runway. These simulators served an important market since night flying is one of the most difficult training scenarios for pilots, but with the added benefit that there was no need to simulate mountains, trees, and other objects if they couldn't be seen. Redifon was established by the company Rediffusion in 1948 as a manufacturer of navel and later flight telecommunications equipment. In 1981, the company's name was changed to Rediffusion Simulation to capitalize on the name it shared with other Rediffusion subsidiaries.

58. Susan Lammers, *Programmers at Work, Vol. 1.* (Redmond, WA: Microsoft Press, 1986), http://programmersatwork.wordpress.com/john-warnock/.

59. Perry, "PostScript Prints Anything," 43.

60. Ivan Sutherland, "A Proposal for CAORF," David C. Evans Papers, MS 625, box 62, folder 7, 4, Special Collections, J. Willard Marriott Library, University of Utah.

61. John Warnock, "The Origins of PostScript," *IEEE Annals of the History of Computing* 40, no. 3 (2018): 69.

62. Perry, "PostScript Prints Anything," 43.

63. The Design System was based in part on the Burroughs B5500 and B6500 computers Gaffney had used as a graduate student at the University of Illinois. It had an interactive, stack-oriented architecture, with simple commands for pushing and popping arguments onto and from the stack, and a rich dictionary for lookups. "The Design System," David C. Evans Papers, MS 625, box 63, folder 6–10, Special Collections, J. Willard Marriott Library, University of Utah.

64. "JOY User's Manual," David C. Evans Papers, MS 625, box 48, folder 23, Special Collections, J. Willard Marriott Library, University of Utah.

65. For an outline of the origins of the PostScript language at Xerox PARC, see Adobe Press, *PostScript Language Reference Manual*, 1st ed. (Boston: Addison-Wesley Longman Publishing Co., 1985).

66. John Warnock, "Adobe Co-Founder John Warnock on the Competitive Advantages of Aesthetics and the 'Right' Technology," interview with Knowledge@Wharton, January 20, 2010, http://knowledge.wharton.upenn.edu/article/adobe-co-founder-john-warnock-on-the-competitive-advantages-of-aesthetics-and-the-right-technology/.

67. Brian Reid, reid@Glacier, "PostScript and Interpress: A Comparison," [fa.laser-lovers], March 2, 1985, https://groups.google.com/forum/m/#!topic/fa.laser-lovers/H3us4h8S3Kk.

68. Steven J. Harrington and Robert R. Buckley, *Interpress: The Source Book* (New York: Simon and Schuster, 1988).

69. Warnock, "Adobe Co-Founder John Warnock."

70. Rudy VanderLans, ed., *Emigre* (San Francisco, 1984–2005); Marvin Scott Jarrett, *Ray Gun* (Santa Monica, CA, 1992–2000).

71. Adobe PageMaker was originally Aldus PageMaker, but still relied on PostScript even in its earliest implementations.

Chapter 5

1. The acronym "GPU" wasn't popularized until the late 1990s, when it was used extensively by NVIDIA to advertise its GeForce line of graphics processors. Likewise, the abbreviation is sometimes conflated with graphics cards or video cards, expansion cards that generate a feed of output images to a display, and include the GPU as part of their architecture. The graphics card is therefore part of this history, but its development runs in parallel with the GPU itself and is tied more explicitly to the development of graphical user interfaces for personal computing in the early 1990s. That said, the GPU is often used to refer to the graphics card as a whole. See "NVIDIA Launches the World's First Graphics Processing Unit: GeForce 256," ResponseSource, August 31, 1999, https://pressreleases.responsesource.com/news/3992/nvidia-launches-the-world-s-first-graphics-processing-unit-geforce-256/.

2. This basic pipeline model is now more commonly referred to as the geometry pipeline, with the full graphics pipeline including extra steps that use programmable shaders for additional effects. Likewise, while specific pipelines can vary depending on hardware systems and application programming interfaces, all pipelines must perform each of these basic operations in some capacity in order to render an image.

3. Vertices are the most basic primitive to be stored, but other geometric data might also be stored here such as characters. The same basic principle applies to this process of translation between spaces.

4. William M. Newman and Robert F. Sproull, *Principles of Interactive Computer Graphics* (New York: McGraw-Hill, Inc., 1979).

5. Clipping can occur along near- and far-clip planes too, so that anything that is determined to be behind the viewing window or too far away from it is also left unrendered. This process of preemptive removal is also known as "culling."

6. The processing power for GPUs is measured in floating point operations per second, or FLOPS. For comparison, the Sony Playstation 4 Pro and Microsoft Xbox One X are each capable of 4.2 and 6.0 teraflops, respectively. Initial specifications for the next generation of consoles promise as high as 12.0 teraflops, which is 12 trillion FLOPS.

7. Time-sharing offers a similar solution to the problem of CPU inefficiency, and was a prominent area for research during the 1960s and 1970s alongside computer graphics. Yet unlike graphical processing, time-sharing simply splits up and reallocates processing time for multiple users of a single system. The sequential nature of that system remains unchanged; it simply redistributes the available processing time across multiple users or terminals.

8. This is also the reason graphical applications are some of the most energy-demanding tasks a computer can perform, with screen use the single-largest energy drain in any graphical system.

9. Ed Fries, "Fixing Color Gotcha," Ed Fries: The Game Is Not Over, May 25, 2016, https://edfries.wordpress.com/2016/05/25/fixing-color-gotcha/.

10. Nick Montfort and Ian Bogost, *Racing the Beam: The Atari Video Computer System* (Cambridge, MA: MIT Press, 2009), 27–30.

11. Examples include the National Bureau of Standards' Machine for Automatic Graphics Interface to a Computer or MAGIC (1964) and the Information Displays, Inc. IDIIOM (1967) terminal, among others. See D. E. Rippy and D. E. Humphries, "Magic: A Machine for Automatic Graphics Interface to a Computer," in *Proceedings of the November 30–December 1, 1965, Fall Joint Computer Conference, Part I* (New York: Association for Computing Machinery, 1965), 819–830; William H. Ninke, "Graphic 1: A Remote Graphical Display Console System," in *Proceedings of the November 30–December 1, 1965, Fall Joint Computer Conference, Part I* (New York: Association for Computing Machinery, 1965), 839–846; Don Bissell, "Was the IDIIOM the First Stand-alone CAD Platform?," *IEEE Annals of the History of Computing* 2 (1998): 14–19.

12. These terms were somewhat loosely defined in this period, with "display list" and "display file" used interchangeably. Likewise, "display generator" was a common term

for what would become the display processor in more complex machines, and display file generators were often programs used to interpret information in a database to produce a display file for processing. The shift is one in complexity, and from interpretation to stand-alone computation.

13. Ivan E. Sutherland, "Computer Displays," *Scientific American* 222, no. 6 (June 1970): 60.

14. Carl Machover, "Graphic CRT Terminals: Characteristics of Commercially Available Equipment," in *Proceedings of the November 14–16, 1967, Fall Joint Computer Conference* (New York: Association for Computing Machinery, 1967), 150–152.

15. Ivan E. Sutherland and Theodore H. Myer, "On the Design of Display Processors," *Communications of the ACM* 11, no. 6 (June 1968): 411.

16. Of course, recursion is one of the central concepts of computer science as it allows for the possibility of defining an infinite set of objects by a finite statement—an object whose definition requires a selfsame invocation of the object as a whole. Indeed, the problem of infinite recursion is present at the very moment that computation is first formalized in the incomputability of Turing's halting problem, but computer science has since mobilized recursion in the service of complexity as a procedural means of subdividing the world into smaller instances of the same problem. Alan Turing, "On Computable Numbers, with an Application to the Entscheidungsproblem," *Proceedings of the London Mathematical Society* 2, no. 42 (1937): 230–265.

17. Matt Pharr, Wenzel Jakob, and Greg Humphreys, *Physically Based Rendering: From Theory to Implementation* (Cambridge, MA: Morgan Kaufmann, 2016), 48.

18. Blinn's law is sometimes also formulated as "All frames take 45 minutes." Neither "law" is a direct quote from Blinn, though in an email correspondence he clarified that he likely made this observation sometime in the 1980s, after which it took on "a life of its own." While render times can vary widely, Blinn's law remains largely true today, and researchers continue to use Blinn's law as exemplar and straw man in contemporary writing. Jim Blinn, email correspondence with the author, September 27, 2020.

19. The name was Sutherland's idea, for which he asked the approval of Evans. Ivan E. Sutherland and Bert Sutherland, "Mom Loved Him Best: Bert and Ivan Sutherland" (discussion moderated by Robert F. Sproull, Computer History Museum, February 3, 2004), https://www.computerhistory.org/collections/catalog/102695308.

20. "Toward a Machine with Interactive Skills," in *Understanding Computers: Computer Images* (New York: Time-Life Books, 1986), 37.

21. After Utah acquired an LDS-1 for its graphics lab in 1970, Evans noted a dramatic rise in the speed and flexibility of its graphical output, attributed explicitly to this shift from general-purpose to graphical processing. "Quarterly Report: Graphical Man/Machine Communications (Contract Number F 30602–70-C-0300)

1970–1973," University of Utah Department of Computer Science records, account 051, box 1, folder 11, University Archives and Records Management, University of Utah, J. Willard Marriott Library, Salt Lake City.

22. The LDS-1 clipping divider was based on a system developed by Sutherland and Sproull at Harvard in 1967 under contract with the Department of Defense and Office of Naval Research. Robert F. Sproull and Ivan E. Sutherland, "A Clipping Divider," in *Proceedings of the December 9–11, 1968, Fall Joint Computer Conference, Part I* (New York: Association for Computing Machinery, 1968).

23. The LDS-1 installed footprint measured sixty-nine by sixty-seven by thirty-four inches. The first LDS-1 system was sold to Bolt, Beranek, and Newman in August 1969 for use in studies of aircraft displays, automobile handling characteristics, air traffic control, and human-computer interaction. "LDS-1 Press Release, December 1969," David C. Evans Papers, MS 625, box 54, folder 1, Special Collections, J. Willard Marriott Library, University of Utah.

24. "LDS-1 Manual," David C. Evans Papers, MS 625, box 54, folder 15, 2, Special Collections, J. Willard Marriott Library, University of Utah.

25. This is likely the first implementation of a graphics pipeline and first use of the term "pipeline" to describe this process. This pipeline structure can be traced to earlier nongraphical machines such as the ILLIAC II (1962), though these implementations exist more as logical structures than true hardware pipelining. Likewise the metaphor of pipelining grew in prominence in the late 1970s for its use in supercomputer architectures.

26. "LDS-1 Manual."

27. "Quarterly Report," 4.

28. This subroutine calculation is also present to a lesser degree in earlier systems that utilized display lists and display generators. See David E. Weisberg, "The Engineering Design Revolution: The People, Companies and Computer Systems That Changed Forever the Practice of Engineering," 2008, http://cadhistory.net/.

29. "Quarterly Report," 4.

30. Within three years of the LDS-1's release, E&S quickly adapted the systems developed for it into the Picture System line of terminals, which the company continued to develop throughout the 1970s and 1980s, and which enjoyed wide success across a range of commercial contexts. "Key Design Features of the Picture System, 1974," David C. Evans Papers, MS 625, box 60, folder 8, Special Collections, J. Willard Marriott Library, University of Utah.

31. VLSI was preceded by "large-scale integration," a term first used in the mid-1970s to describe early microchips like the IBM MCS-4. This in turn gave rise to the terms "small-scale integration" and "medium-scale integration" to depict earlier developments in integrated circuit design in the 1960s.

32. The name Moore's law refers to Gordon Moore's 1965 observations in *Electronics* magazine, but the "law" was explicitly named by Carver Mead in 1970 in the context of his work on circuit design at Caltech. While Moore is most often credited with this prediction, a similar claim was made by Engelbart as early as 1959. There is also mixed evidence that Moore's law may be coming to an end, due largely to the physical restrictions of silicon at the microscopic level. See Gordon Moore, "Cramming More Components onto Integrated Circuits," *Electronics* 38, no. 8 (1965): 114–117; Douglas Engelbart, "Microelectronics and the Art of Similitude," in *Solid-State Circuits Conference. Digest of Technical Papers. 1960 IEEE International* (New York: IEEE, 1960), 3:76–77. For a discussion of VLSI and the establishment of Moore's law within technical and popular discourse, see Ethan Mollick, "Establishing Moore's Law," *IEEE Annals of the History of Computing* 28, no. 3 (2006): 62–75.

33. Marco Casale-Rossi, "The Heritage of Mead & Conway: What Has Remained the Same, What Has Changed, What Was Missed, and What Lies Ahead," *Proceedings of the IEEE* 102, no. 2 (2014): 114–119.

34. This is the first annual report of the Intel Corporation as a publicly traded company. "1971 Annual Report" (Santa Clara, CA: Intel Corporation, 1971), 4, https://www.intel.com/content/www/us/en/history/history-1971-annual-report.html.

35. The first published use of the term "Silicon Valley" is credited to Dan Hoefler, who used the phrase in a series of articles published in the weekly trade newspaper *Electronic News*, the first of which appeared in the paper's January 11, 1971, issue. The phrase grew in prominence in the early 1980s after the establishment of the semiconductor industry over the course of the previous decade. See Timothy J. Sturgeon, "How Silicon Valley Came to Be," in *Understanding Silicon Valley: The Anatomy of an Entrepreneurial Region*, ed. Martin Kenney (Palo Alto, CA: Stanford University Press, 2000), 15–47.

36. Ivan Sutherland, "THE ELECTRIC PICTURE COMPANY (Draft)," David C. Evans Papers, MS 625, box 9, folder 21, Special Collections, J. Willard Marriott Library, University of Utah.

37. "Computer Science—a Timely Idea," *Engineering and Science Magazine*, January–February 1977, 27.

38. Ivan E. Sutherland, Carver Mead, and Thomas E. Everhart, *Basic Limitations in Microcircuit Fabrication Technology*, ARPA Report R-1956-ARPA (Santa Monica, CA: Rand Corporation, November 1976).

39. Ivan E. Sutherland, "The Problem: How to Build Digital Electronic Circuits from Now to 1985," letter to William. R. Sutherland, January 26, 1976, http://ai.eecs.umich.edu/people/conway/VLSI/BackgroundContext/IvanSutherlandLetter1-26-76.PDF; William Sutherland, *Management of Industrial Research: Exploring the Unknown Technical Future* (Menlo Park, CA: Sun Microsystems, July 2008), https://ai.eecs.umich.edu/people/conway/Memoirs/VLSI/Files/Management_of_Industrial_Research.pdf.

40. William Sutherland, "The On-line Graphical Specification of Computer Procedures" (PhD diss., Massachusetts Institute of Technology, 1966). After PARC, Ivan formed the company Sutherland, Sproull and Associates, which was later purchased by Sun Microsystems to form the basis for its research division Sun Labs, which Bert would manage from 1992 to 1998. One of the laboratory's most famous developments is the widely used object-oriented programming language Java in 1995.

41. Lynn Conway, "The 'Sutherland Letter' of 1976: Notes by Lynn Conway," December 31, 2012, http://ai.eecs.umich.edu/people/conway/VLSI/BackgroundCon text/Sutherland_Letter.html.

42. Michael A. Hiltzik, *Dealers of Lightning: Xerox PARC and the Dawn of the Computer Age* (New York: Harper Business, 1999), 311–312.

43. This collaboration went both ways, with research collaboration at PARC and pedagogical collaboration at Caltech. Throughout fall 1976, Sproull and Kay flew down to Los Angeles from San Francisco one day a week to teach courses on computer graphics and the philosophy of computing, respectively. "Computer Science—a Timely Idea," 28.

44. Sutherland's departure from computer graphics research was quite sudden. Following the publication of the "Ten Hidden Surface Algorithms" paper with Bob Sproull in 1974, Sutherland determined that hidden surface removal was essentially a sorting problem and became disinterested in future research. Describing the moment in an oral history made in 1989, he notes in a characteristically unceremonious way, "That seemed to me to sort of tidy up a loose end, and I stopped doing graphics for good—have not done any since." Ivan E. Sutherland, "Oral History with William Aspray," Charles Babbage Institute, Pittsburgh, May 1, 1989, 37.

45. Sutherland, "The Problem," 1.

46. Sutherland, "The Problem," 4. Circuit design is central to the development of CAD systems going back to Sutherland's Sketchpad and was also central to research teams at Bell Labs working in the late 1960s. See Owen Murphy, prod., *Incredible Machine* (Murray Hill, NJ: Bell Laboratories, 1968), film, https://techchannel.att.com /play-video.cfm/2011/4/22/AT&T-Archives-Incredible-Machine.

47. Friedrich Kittler, "There Is No Software," *CTheory*, ed. Arthur Kroker and Marilouise Kroker (1995), http://www.ctheory.net/articles.aspx?id=74.

48. For a discussion of photolithography and microprocessor design, see Kyle Stine, "Critical Hardware: The Circuit of Image and Data," *Critical Inquiry* 45, no. 3 (2019): 762–786.

49. Douglas G. Fairbairn and J. Rowson, "ICARUS: An Interactive Integrated Circuit Layout Program," in *Proceedings of the 15th Conference on Design Automation* (New York: IEEE Press, 1978), 188–192.

50. See Douglas G. Fairbairn, *Video Ethnography of 'ICARUS' on the Xerox Alto*, Computer History Museum, December 12, 2017, https://www.youtube.com/watch ?v=BauuOoB6EIU.

51. Ron Ayres, "IC Specification Language," in *Proceedings of the 16th Design Automation Conference (DAC '79)* (New York: IEEE Press, 1979), 307–309. The Caltech Intermediate Form provides a limited set of graphics primitives that are useful for describing the two-dimensional shapes on the different layers of a chip. Robert F. Sproull, Richard Lyon, and Stephen Trimberger, *The Caltech Intermediate Form for LSI Layout Description, California Institute of Technology Silicon Structures Project*, Technical Report 2686 (Pasadena: California Institute of Technology, 1980).

52. Lynn Conway, "Reminiscences of the VLSI Revolution," *IEEE Solid-State Circuits Magazine* 4, no. 4 (2012): 8–10.

53. Carver Mead and Lynn Conway, *Introduction to VLSI Systems* (Reading, MA: Addison-Wesley, 1980). For a contemporary reflection on the impact of Mead and Conway's work on VLSI, see Lynn Conway, "Impact of the Mead-Conway Innovations in VLSI Chip Design and Implementation Methodology," November 16, 2007, http://ai.eecs.umich.edu/people/conway/Impact/Impact.html.

54. Despite Sutherland's encouragement, Conway was hesitant to move into a more public role at MIT, as she had been fired early in her career when she underwent a gender transition while working at IBM in the late 1960s. Conway did not publicly come out as transgender until the early 2000s and feared being outed while working at PARC. Conway, "Impact of the Mead-Conway Innovations," 12.

55. Conway, "Reminiscences of the VLSI Revolution," 15.

56. Mead was openly against the project as he worried it would lead ARPA to take credit for the VLSI work being developed at PARC. Conway, "Reminiscences of the VLSI Revolution."

57. James Clark, interview by John Hennessey, StanfordOnline, June 26, 2013, https://www.youtube.com/watch?v=gXuOH9B6kTM.

58. James Clark, "3-D Design of Free-form B-spline Surfaces" (PhD diss., University of Utah, 1974).

59. This was not the first attempt to use VLSI to solve common graphical problems. In 1977, Sutherland and Mead wrote a proposal to E&S about the development of integrated circuits for hidden surface computation. "Integrated Circuits for the Hidden Surface Computation," David C. Evans Papers, MS 625, box 9, folder 24, Special Collections, J. Willard Marriott Library, University of Utah.

60. In fact, this early model was a prototype for a much larger architecture that is perhaps the true predecessor to the GPU, developed in 1981 and called the "Geometry System." See James Clark, "Special Feature: A VLSI Geometry Processor for Graphics,"

Computer 13, no. 7 (1980): 59–68; James Clark, "The Geometry Engine: A VLSI Geometry System for Graphics," *ACM SIGGRAPH Computer Graphics* 16, no. 3 (1982): 127–133.

61. Clark, "Special Feature," 59.

62. Sproull and Sutherland, "A Clipping Divider."

63. In order to produce the Geometry Engine on a single chip, Clark was forced to abandon Sutherland and Sproull's parallel clipping algorithm in favor of a sequential plane-at-a-time method, as described in Sutherland and Gary Hodgman's "Reentrant Polygon Clipping." The system is still defined by its parallel structure, although it simply calculates these procedures along a sequential pipeline configuration for each geometric primitive. Ivan E. Sutherland and Gary W. Hodgman, "Reentrant Polygon Clipping," *Communications of the ACM* 17, no. 1 (1974): 32–42.

64. Clark initially planned to found a company with Martin Newell—then working at Xerox PARC—and call it Clark and Newell, Incorporated. The two believed they were at the forefront of a new wave in graphical hardware design, but ultimately Newell remained at PARC. "Handwritten Meeting Notes," Vernon Russell Anderson Papers, M1222, box 5, unlabeled folder, Stanford University Library Special Collections, Stanford, CA.

65. IRIS GL was a proprietary graphics library used by SGI throughout the 1980s. In the early 1990s, the company removed its proprietary code to transform IRIS GL into the OpenGL public standard application programming interface used in almost all contemporary graphics applications. OpenGL is most typically used to interact with a GPU to achieve hardware-accelerated rendering. https://www.opengl.org/.

66. "Business Proposal, 'Clark and Newell, Incorporated,'" Vernon Russell Anderson Papers, M1222, box 5, unlabeled folder, Stanford University Library Special Collections, Stanford, CA.

67. The equivalent of $93,000 in 2019. Craig Olson, "40% Discount on GRAPHICS UNIX WORKSTATIONS," August 9, 1984, http://www.sgistuff.net/hardware/systems/iris1000.html.

68. Hiltzik, *Dealers of Lightning*, 301.

69. The June 1992 SGI employee newsletter notes that "all of the computers in the computer room are running real-world applications that are used today in the scientific community. There's nothing fake about them." "All Hands, June 1992," Computer History Museum Special Collections, *Silicon Graphics, Inc.*, Catalog Number: 102709252, Lot Number: X4680.2008, https://www.computerhistory.org/collections/catalog/102709252.

70. These films include *Babe* (1995), *Independence Day* (1996), *Titanic* (1997), *What Dreams May Come* (1998), *The Matrix* (1999), *Gladiator* (2000), *The Lord of the Rings:*

The Fellowship of the Ring (2001), and *The Lord of the Rings: The Return of the King* (2002).

71. "e3.quest.txt," Kurt Akeley Papers, SC628, box 6, folder "Nintendo 64," Stanford University Archives Special Collections, Stanford, CA.

72. SGI was by no means the only workstation or GPU producer in the field. A parallel history could be told of the growth of graphic and video card technologies for the personal computer, whose development is more explicitly mapped onto the growth of graphical user interfaces and Microsoft Windows in the 1990s. Most early chips in this history emerge from the game industry and use LSI techniques for highly specialized machines. More general-purpose chips emerge in the early 1980s, the most significant of which is perhaps the NEC μPD7220 video interface controller from 1982, capable of drawing lines, circles, arcs, and character graphics onto a bit-mapped display. Likewise, the Texas Instruments TMS34010 from 1986 was the first programmable graphics processor integrated circuit, and the IBM 8514 from 1987 is the first personal computer, mass-market, fixed-function graphics accelerator.

73. Despite this advertising rhetoric, the GeForce 256 was more a leap in performance than an entirely new product form, though it did offer the first complete graphics pipeline available in hardware for the personal computer. While the terms "graphics processor" and even "graphics processing unit" have been in use since at least the 1980s, the 256 is the first explicit naming of what we now recognize as the modern GPU for personal computing. At the time, NVIDIA defined the GPU as "a single-chip processor with integrated transform, lighting, triangle setup/clipping, and rendering engines that is capable of processing a minimum of 10 million polygons per second." "NVIDIA Launches."

74. The museum has since built a research facility across the bay in Fremont, CA.

75. "Big Challenges in Computer City," Computer History Museum Special Collections, *Silicon Graphics, Inc.*, Catalog Number: 102639077, 1996, VHS, https://www.computerhistory.org/collections/catalog/102639077.

76. Both Conway and Hiltzik single out Clark's Geometry Engine as one of the key technologies to emerge from PARC's VLSI research. Conway, "Reminiscences of the VLSI Revolution," 24–27.

77. With regard to cinema, Philip Rosen has described this process as "change mummified." Philip Rosen, *Change Mummified: Cinema, Historicity, Theory* (Minneapolis: University of Minnesota Press, 2001), 301–349. On the media episteme of the twentieth century, see Friedrich Kittler, *Gramophone, Film, Typewriter* (Palo Alto, CA: Stanford University Press, 1999).

78. The GeForce 3 was used in Microsoft's first Xbox console, whereas the PlayStation 2 used a custom-vector DSP for hardware-accelerated vertex processing—commonly referred to VU0/VU1.

79. Early incarnations of shader execution engines were not general purpose and could not execute arbitrary pixel code, but by October 2002, with the introduction of the ATI Radeon 9700, pixel and vertex shaders could implement looping and lengthy floating-point calculations. While early devices necessitated the translation of data into graphical form in order to take advantage of the processing speeds of these general-purpose GPUs, subsequent developments and customized hardware have since eliminated the need for this translation.

80. Leaving aside the ontological implications of reimagining the world as a computable task, there is a growing body of work on the environmental costs of computing, of which GPU-enabled systems play a primary role. See Nathan Ensmenger, "The Environmental History of Computing," *Technology and Culture* 59, no. 4 (2018): S7-S33; Ingrid Burrington, "The Environmental Toll of a Netflix Binge," *Atlantic* 16 (2015), https://www.theatlantic.com/technology/archive/2015/12/there-are-no-clean -clouds/420744/.

Coda

1. The ad campaign for the New Beetle in many ways resembled the Y2K aesthetic of Apple's iMac advertisements of the period, complete with colorful pastel finishes against a blank white background. The 1998 model likewise sought to mimic the now-iconic minimal advertising of the original Beetle with the simple slogan: "Curves Are Back."

2. Bridle's sentiment in the epigraph that opens this chapter is often repeated but largely anecdotal. One of the earliest documented examples of an architect noting the visibility of software in the built environment comes from Greg Lynn, who was asked in an interview with Richard Weinstein in 2000 whether the attributes of style are inherent in the operation of a particular software program, and whether different programs tend to meet the different styles. His reply is worth quoting at length: "When I was shopping for a toothbrush, I was frustrated because all of the available toothbrushes I was looking at appeared to be designed in AutoCad, and I didn't want to put that aesthetic in my mouth. Then I found a toothbrush that looked like it was designed in Alias, a program that I liked to use at the time. A month later there was an article in ID Magazine about toothbrush design, and the brand I didn't want was in fact designed in AutoCad, and I bought the one designed in Alias." Greg Lynn, interview with Richard Weinstein, *Constructs* (Spring 2000): 5.

3. "Building 3D with IKEA," CGSociety, 2014, https://web.archive.org/web/201 40901100414/http://www.cgsociety.org/index.php/CGSFeatures/FeaturePrintable /building_3d_with_ikea.

4. In contrast with the uncanniness often attributed to digital scenes, these images exude a sense of comfort and familiarity. This is a striking reversal of the uncanny

(*Unheimlichkeit*) with the homely (*heimelig*), creating images of an ideal but unreal domesticity.

5. Martin Enthed, *IKEA, VR, AR, and Meatballs*, November 14, 2017, https://vimeo .com/243860738.

6. Ivan E. Sutherland, "The Ultimate Display," *Proceedings of the IFIP Conference* (1965): 506–508.

7. IKEA is currently experimenting with virtual reality and mixed-reality applications for its digital models, including experimental virtual reality in some European showrooms that include physical chairs placed in the room with virtual reality users such that they may quite literally sit. A free-to-play *IKEA VR Experience* on the Steam video game digital distribution platform was released in 2016 and was one of the top downloaded titles of that year. IKEA Communications AB, *IKEA VR Experience*, 2016, https://store.steampowered.com/app/447270/IKEA_VR_Experience/.

8. This process allows each space to be highly localized, translating mundane domesticity for different regional markets, and offering offer up modular configurations of individual spaces tailored to taste and preference. ChaosGroupTV, *Putting the CGI in IKEA: How V-Ray Helps Visualize Perfect Home*, March 22, 2018, https:// youtu.be/bJFlslL1wFI.

9. Apple Inc., "Apple Unveils Apple Watch—Apple's Most Personal Device Ever," Apple, September 14, 2014, https://www.apple.com/newsroom/2014/09/09Apple-Un veils-Apple-Watch-Apples-Most-Personal-Device-Ever/.

10. Apple Inc., "Apple Watch Reveal," 2014, https://www.youtube.com/watch ?v=dVYajpN4Qzc.

11. Moore, "Cramming More Components Onto Integrated Circuits" (1965).

12. Whether this law is accurate or logical is questionable, as its goal seems to be to propose the inevitability of a coming age of "Discrete AI" that will replace GPU computing rather than serving as an accurate historical descriptor. See Usman Prizada, "Intel CREATE Event at SIGGRAPH 2019: New High Performance Raytracing Engine, Raja's Law, Xe GPU Collabs and More," WCCF Tech, August 1, 2019, https://wccftech .com/intel-create-event-siggraph-2019-rajas-law/.

13. The massive growth in Amazon Web Services and related systems is perhaps the primary vector for this processing, outside the graphical calculation of a user's computer, phone, or other device. For a historical and political account of cloud services, see Tung-Hui Hu, *A Prehistory of the Cloud* (Cambridge, MA: MIT Press, 2015).

14. As the artist Hito Steyerl suggests, "Images are now routinely transitioning beyond screens into a different state of matter. They surpass the boundaries of data channels and manifest materially. They incarnate as riots or products, as lens flares, high-rises, or pixelated tanks. Images become unplugged and unhinged and start

crowding off-screen space." Hito Steyerl, "Too Much World: Is the Internet Dead?," *e-flux journal* 49 (November 2013), https://www.e-flux.com/journal/49/60004/too -much-world-is-the-internet-dead/.

15. The essay is primarily a reflection on the term "post-internet," with relatively little discussion of the term "image object." Along with Gene McHugh and Marisa Olson, Vierkant was one of the principal figures in this period thinking through the concept of the postinternet, which has joined related terms such as the "post-digital" and "post-cinema" to describe the media of our historical present. See Artie Vierkant, "The Image Object Post-Internet," JstChillin, 2010, http://jstchillin.org/artie/pdf /The_Image_Object_Post-Internet_us.pdf; Michael Connor, "What's Postinternet Got to Do with Net Art?," Rhizome.org, November 1, 2013, https://rhizome.org/editorial /2013/nov/1/postinternet/; Gene McHugh, *Post Internet* (Brescia, IT: LINK Editions, 2014); Marisa Olson, "Postinternet: Art after the Internet," *Foam Magazine* 19 (Winter 2011–2012): 59–63; Florian Cramer, "What Is 'Post-Digital'?," *A Peer-Reviewed Journal About* 3, no. 1 (2014), https://aprja.net/article/download/116068/165295; Shane Denson and Julia Leyda, ed., *Post-Cinema: Theorizing 21st-Century Film* (Falmer, UK: REFRAME Books, 2016), https://reframe.sussex.ac.uk/post cinema/.

16. Vierkant, "The Image Object Post-Internet," 3.

Bibliography

Abbate, Janet. *Inventing the Internet*. Cambridge, MA: MIT Press, 1999.

Abbate, Janet. *Recoding Gender: Women's Changing Participation in Computing*. Cambridge, MA: MIT Press, 2012.

Abramson, Albert. *The History of Television, 1880 to 1941*. London: McFarland and Company, 1987.

Abramson, Albert. *Zworykin, Pioneer of Television*. Chicago: University of Illinois Press, 1995.

Adobe Press. *PostScript Language Reference Manual*. 1st ed. Boston: Addison-Wesley Longman Publishing Co., 1985.

Advanced Research Projects Agency. "Graphic Control and Display of Computer Processes." Program Plan No. 439, March 1, 1965, 1. National Archives Branch Depository, Record Group 330-78-0013, box 1, folder: "Program Plans." FOIA Ref. 13-F-1248.

"All Hands, June 1992." Computer History Museum Special Collections. *Silicon Graphics, Inc.* Catalog Number: 102709252. Lot Number: X4680.2008. https://www.computerhistory.org/collections/catalog/102709252.

Allen, Matthew. "Representing Computer-Aided Design: Screenshots and the Interactive Computer circa 1960." *Perspectives on Science* 24, no. 6 (2016): 637–668.

Alt, Casey. "The Materialities of Maya: Making Sense of Object-Orientation." *Configurations* 10, no. 3 (September 2002): 387–422.

Alt, Casey. "Objects of Our Affection: How Object Orientation Made Computers a Medium." In *Media Archaeology: Approaches, Applications, and Implications*, edited by Erkki Huhtamo and Jussi Parikka, 278–301. Berkeley: University of California Press, 2011.

Anderson, John. "Nam June Paik: Preserving the Human Televisions." *Art in America*, February 5, 2013. http://www.artinamericamagazine.com/news-features/news/nam-june-paik-smithsonian/.

Appel, Arthur. "Some Techniques for Shading Machine Renderings of Solids." In *Sprint Joint Computer Conference, 1968*, 37–45. New York: Association for Computing Machinery, 1968.

Apple Inc. "Apple Unveils Apple Watch—Apple's Most Personal Device Ever." Apple, September 14, 2014. https://www.apple.com/newsroom/2014/09/09Apple-Unveils -Apple-Watch-Apples-Most-Personal-Device-Ever/.

Apple Inc. "Apple Watch Reveal." 2014. https://www.youtube.com/watch?v=dVYajp N4Qzc.

Armstrong, Carol. "Seurat's Media, or a Matrix of Materialities." *Grey Room* 58 (Winter 2015): 6–25.

Arvo, James, and David Kirk. "Fast Ray Tracing by Ray Classification." In *Proceeding: SIGGRAPH '87 Proceedings of the 14th Annual Conference on Computer Graphics and Interactive Techniques*, 55–61. New York: ACM SIGGRAPH, 1987.

Ayres, Ron. "IC Specification Language." In *Proceedings of the 16th Design Automation Conference (DAC '79)*, 307–309. New York: IEEE Press, 1979.

Barber, Simon. "Soundstream: The Introduction of Commercial Digital Recording in the United States." *ASARP: Journal on the Art of Record Production* 7 (November 2012). http://arpjournal.com/2140/soundstream-the-introduction-of-commercial-digital -recording-in-the-united-states/.

Bardini, Thierry. *Bootstrapping: Douglas Engelbart, Coevolution, and the Origins of Personal Computing*. Palo Alto, CA: Stanford University Press, 2000.

Barnhill, Robert E., ed. *Computer Aided Geometric Design: Proceedings of a Conference Held at the University of Utah, Salt Lake City, Utah, March 18–21, 1974*. San Diego: Academic Press, 1974.

Barr, Marc J. "The Teapot as Object and Icon." ACM SIGGRAPH 2006 exhibition. https://www.siggraph.org//s2006/main.php?f=conference&p=teapot.

Bateson, Gregory. *Steps to an Ecology of Mind: Collected Essays in Anthropology, Psychiatry, Evolution, and Epistemology*. Chicago: University of Chicago Press, 1972.

Bell, C. Gordon, J. Craig Mudge, and John E. McNamara. *Computer Engineering: A DEC View of Computer Design*. Bedford, MA: Digital Press, 1978.

Bellin, Isabelle. "Images de synthèse: palme de la longévité pour l'ombrage de Gouraud." Interstices, September 15, 2008. https://interstices.info/images-de-synthese -palme-de-la-longevite-pour-lombrage-de-gouraud/.

Berry, Dave. "The New Bifurcation? Object-Oriented Ontology and Computation." *Stunlaw: Philosophy and Critique for a Digital Age*, June 4, 2012. http://stunlaw .blogspot.no/2012/06/new-bifurcation-object-oriented.html.

Bézier, Pierre. "Definition numèrique des courbes et surfaces I." *Automatisme* 11 (1966): 625–632.

Bézier, Pierre. "Definition numèrique des courbes et surfaces II." *Automatisme* 12 (1967): 17–21.

Bézier, Pierre. "Example of an Existing System in the Motor Industry: The Unisurf System." *Proceedings of the Royal Society of London. Series A, Mathematical and Physical Sciences* 321, no. 1545 (February 9, 1971): 207–218.

"Big Challenges in Computer City." Computer History Museum Special Collections. *Silicon Graphics, Inc.* Catalog Number: 102639077. 1996. VHS. https://www.computer history.org/collections/catalog/102639077.

Bissell, Don. "Was the IDIIOM the First Stand-alone CAD Platform?" *IEEE Annals of the History of Computing* 2 (1998): 14–19.

Bitzer, Donald L., and H. Gene Slottow. "The Plasma Display Panel: A Digitally Address-able Display with Inherent Memory." In *Proceedings of the November 7–10, 1966, Fall Joint Computer Conference*, 541–547. New York: Association for Computing Machinery, 1966.

"Blinkenlights." Jargon File, version 4.4.6, October 25, 2003. http://www.catb.org /~esr/jargon/html/B/blinkenlights.html.

Blinn, Jim. "Ten More Unsolved Problems in Computer Graphics." *IEEE Computer Graphics and Applications* 18, no. 5 (September 1998): 86–89.

Blinn, Jim. "The World's Largest Easter Egg and What Came Out of It." *IEEE Computer Graphics and Applications* 8, no. 2 (March 1988): 16–23.

Blinn, Jim, and Martin Newell. "Texture and Reflection in Computer Generated Images." *Communications of the ACM* 19, no. 10 (October 1976): 542–547.

Bogost, Ian. "Object-Oriented P*: Philosophers vs. Programmers." July 16, 2009. http://www.bogost.com/blog/objectoriented_p.shtml.

Booch, Grady. *Object-Oriented Analysis and Design with Applications*. 3rd ed. Boston: Addison-Wesley Professional, 2007.

Bordwell, David, and Kristin Thompson. *Film Art: An Introduction*. New York: McGraw-Hill College, 2003.

Bowen, H. Kent. "The University of Utah and the Computer Graphics Revolution." Unpublished case study, Harvard Business School, April 28, 2006.

Bridle, James. "#sxaesthetic." Presentation at South by Southwest, March 15, 2012. http://booktwo.org/notebook/sxaesthetic/.

"A Brief History of Fort Douglas." Historic Fort Douglas at the University of Utah, July 10, 2010. https://web.archive.org/web/20100610082804/http://web.utah.edu/facilities /fd/history/history.html.

Brown, Jim. *Radar: How It All Began*. Cambridge, UK: Janus Publishing, 1996.

Brown, Louis. *A Radar History of World War II: Technical and Military Imperatives*. Bristol, UK: Institute of Physics Publishing, 1999.

Buderi, Robert. *The Invention That Changed the World: How a Small Group of Radar Pioneers Won the Second World War and Launched a Technical Revolution*. New York: Simon and Schuster, 1996.

"Building 3D with IKEA." CGSociety, 2014. https://web.archive.org/web/20140 901100414/http://www.cgsociety.org/index.php/CGSFeatures/FeaturePrintable /building_3d_with_ikea.

Burns, R. W. *Television: An International History of the Formative Years*. London: Institution of Engineering and Technology, 1998.

Burrington, Ingrid. "The Environmental Toll of a Netflix Binge." *Atlantic* 16 (2015). https://www.theatlantic.com/technology/archive/2015/12/there-are-no-clean-clouds /420744/.

Bute, Mary Ellen. "Abstronics: An Experimental Filmmaker Photographs the Esthetics of the Oscillograph." *Films in Review New York: National Board of Review of Motion Pictures* 5 (1952): 263–266.

Cardoso Llach, Daniel. *Builders of the Vision: Software and the Imagination of Design*. New York: Routledge, 2015.

Carlson, Wayne E. *Computer Graphics and Computer Animation: A Retrospective Overview*. Montreal: Pressbooks, 2017. https://ohiostate.pressbooks.pub/graphicshistory/.

Casale-Rossi, Marco. "The Heritage of Mead & Conway: What Has Remained the Same, What Has Changed, What Was Missed, and What Lies Ahead." *Proceedings of the IEEE* 102, no. 2 (2014): 114–119.

Catmull, Edwin. "Computer Display of Curved Surfaces." In *Proceedings of the IEEE Conference on Computer Graphics*. New York: Association for Computing Machinery, 1975.

Catmull, Edwin. "The Problems of Computer-Assisted Animation." *ACM SIGGRAPH Computer Graphics* 12, no. 3 (1978): 348–353.

Catmull, Edwin. "A Subdivision Algorithm for Computer Display of Curved Surfaces." PhD diss., University of Utah, 1974.

Catmull, Edwin. "A System for Computer Generated Movies." In *ACM '72 Proceedings of the ACM Annual Conference* 1:422–431. New York: Association for Computing Machinery, 1972.

Catmull, Edwin, and Fred Parke. *Halftone Animation*. 1972. 16 mm. http://vimeo .com/16292363.

ChaosGroupTV. *Putting the CGI in IKEA: How V-Ray Helps Visualize Perfect Home.* March 22, 2018. https://youtu.be/bJFlslL1wFI.

Chun, Wendy Hui Kyong. "Introduction: Did Somebody Say New Media?" In *New Media, Old Media: A History and Theory Reader*, edited by Wendy Hui Kyong Chun and Thomas Keenan, 1–10. New York: Routledge, 2006.

Chun, Wendy Hui Kyong. *Programmed Visions: Software and Memory.* Cambridge, MA: MIT Press, 2011.

Clark, James. "The Geometry Engine: A VLSI Geometry System for Graphics." *ACM SIGGRAPH Computer Graphics* 16, no. 3 (1982): 127–133.

Clark, James. Interview by John Hennessey. StanfordOnline, June 26, 2013. https://www.youtube.com/watch?v=gXuOH9B6kTM.

Clark, James. "Special Feature: A VLSI Geometry Processor for Graphics." *Computer* 13, no. 7 (1980): 59–68.

Clark, James. "3-D Design of Free-form B-spline Surfaces." PhD diss., University of Utah, 1974.

Comba, Paul G. "A Procedure for Detecting Intersections of Three Dimensional Objects." IBM New York Scientific Center. Rep. 39.020, January 1967.

Committee on Innovations in Computing and Communications: Lessons from History and the National Research Council. *Funding a Revolution: Government Support for Computing Research.* Washington, DC: National Academies Press, 1999.

"Computer Science—a Timely Idea." *Engineering and Science Magazine*, January–February 1977, 26–28.

Connor, Michael. "What's Postinternet Got to Do with Net Art?" Rhizome.org, November 1, 2013. https://rhizome.org/editorial/2013/nov/1/postinternet/.

Conway, Lynn. "Impact of the Mead-Conway Innovations in VLSI Chip Design and Implementation Methodology." November 16, 2007. http://ai.eecs.umich.edu/people/conway/Impact/Impact.html.

Conway, Lynn. "Reminiscences of the VLSI Revolution." *IEEE Solid-State Circuits Magazine* 4, no. 4 (2012): 8–10.

Conway, Lynn. "The 'Sutherland Letter' of 1976: Notes by Lynn Conway." December 31, 2012. http://ai.eecs.umich.edu/people/conway/VLSI/BackgroundContext/Sutherland_Letter.html.

Cook, Robert L., Thomas Porter, and Loren Carpenter. "Distributed Ray Tracing." In *Proceedings of the 11th Annual Conference on Computer Graphics and Interactive Techniques*, 137–145. New York: Association for Computing Machinery, 1984.

Coons, Steven Anson. "Surfaces for Computer-Aided Design of Space Forms." Project MAC, Massachusetts Institute of Technology, Cambridge, June 1967.

Coons, Steven Anson. "The Uses of Computers in Technology." *Scientific American* 215, no. 3 (1966): 176–191.

Copeland, B. Jack, Andre A. Haeff, Peter Gough, and Cameron Wright. "Screen History: The Haeff Memory and Graphics Tube." *IEEE Annals of the History of Computing* 39, no. 1 (2017): 9–28.

Cramer, Florian. "What Is 'Post-Digital'?" *A Peer-Reviewed Journal About* 3, no. 1 (2014). https://aprja.net/article/download/116068/165295.

Crary, Jonathan. *Techniques of the Observer: On Vision and Modernity in the Nineteenth Century*. Cambridge, MA: MIT Press, 1992.

Crow, Frank. "The Aliasing Problem in Computer-Generated Shaded Images." *Communications of the ACM* 20, no. 11 (1977): 799–805.

Crow, Frank. "The Origins of the Teapot." *IEEE Computer Graphics and Animation* 7, no. 1 (January 1987): 8–19.

Cubitt, Sean. *The Practice of Light: A Genealogy of Visual Technologies from Prints to Pixels*. Cambridge, MA: MIT Press, 2014.

Damisch, Hubert. *The Origin of Perspective*. Translated by John Goodman. Cambridge, MA: MIT Press, 1995.

Darley, Andrew. *Visual Digital Culture: Surface Play and Spectacle in New Media Genres*. New York: Routledge, 2000.

David C. Evans Papers. MS 625. Special Collections, J. Willard Marriott Library, University of Utah.

de Boor, Carl. "On Calculating with B-Splines." *Journal of Approximation Theory* 6 (1972): 50–62.

de Casteljau, Paul. *Courbes et surfaces à poles*. Paris: A. Citroën, 1963.

Deleuze, Gilles. *Spinoza: Practical Philosophy*. San Francisco: City Lights Books, 1988.

Denson, Shane, and Julia Leyda, eds. *Post-Cinema: Theorizing 21st-Century Film*. Falmer, UK: REFRAME Books, 2016. https://reframe.sussex.ac.uk/post-cinema/.

Drain, Alison. "Laposky's Lights Make Visual Music." *Symmetry* 4, no. 3 (April 2007): 32–33.

Drucker, Johanna. *Graphesis: Visual Forms of Knowledge Production*. Cambridge, MA: Harvard University Press, 2014.

du Monceau, Henri-Louis Duhamel. *Elémens de l'architecture navale ou traité pratique de la construction des vaisseaux*. Paris: Chez C.-A. Jombert, 1752.

Eames, Charles, and Ray Eames, dirs. *Powers of Ten*. New York: IBM, 1977. Film.

Eckert, J. Presper, Jr. "A Survey of Digital Computer Memory Systems." *Proceedings of the IEEE* 85, no. 1 (January 1997): 184–197. Originally published in *Proceedings of the Institute of Radio Engineers* 41 (October 1953).

Eckert, J. Presper, Jr., Herman Lukoff, and Gerald Smoliar. "A Dynamically Regenerated Electrostatic Memory System." *Proceedings of the IRE* 38 (1950): 498–510.

Edwards, Benj. "The Never-Before-Told Story of the World's First Comptuer Art (It's a Sexy Dame)." *Atlantic*, January 24, 2013. https://www.theatlantic.com/technology /archive/2013/01/the-never-before-told-story-of-the-worlds-first-computer-art-its-a -sexy-dame/267439/.

Edwards, Paul N. *The Closed World: Computers and the Politics of Discourse in Cold War America*. Cambridge, MA: MIT Press, 1996.

Eguchi, Katsuya, dir. *Star Fox*. Kyoto: Nintendo Entertainment, 1993. ROM cartridge.

Elkins, James. *The Poetics of Perspective*. Ithaca, NY: Cornell University Press, 1996.

Engelbart, Douglas. "Microelectronics and the Art of Similitude." In *Solid-State Circuits Conference. Digest of Technical Papers. 1960 IEEE International*, 3:76–77. New York: IEEE, 1960.

Ensmenger, Nathan. *The Computer Boys Take Over: Computers, Programmers, and the Politics of Technical Expertise*. Cambridge, MA: MIT Press, 2012.

Ensmenger, Nathan. "The Environmental History of Computing." *Technology and Culture* 59, no. 4 (2018): S7-S33.

Enthed, Martin. *IKEA, VR, AR, and Meatballs*. November 14, 2017. https://vimeo .com/243860738.

Evans, David C. "Computer Science at the U of U." *Utechnic: University of Utah Engineering Publication* (May 1968): 12–18.

Evans, David C. *Graphical Man/Machine Communications*. Salt Lake City: University of Utah National Technical Information Service, 1966. https://collections.lib.utah .edu/ark:/87278/s61n8j92.

Evans, David C., Peter Evans, Susan Evans Fudd, David Evans Jr., Gordon Fudd, Anna Evans Brown, Linda Evans, Joy Evans, Gail Shydell, Mary Evans, and Katherine Archer. "Oral History with Daniel Morrow." *Computerworld Honors* (April 18, 1996): 1–37.

Everett, Robert R. "Special Issue: SAGE." *IEEE Annals of the History of Computing* 5, no. 4 (October–December 1983): 319–427.

Everett, Robert R., Charles A. Zraket, and Herbert D. Benington. "SAGE: A Data-Processing System for Air Defense." In *Papers and Discussions Presented at the December*

9–13, 1957, Eastern Joint Computer Conference: Computers with Deadlines to Meet (1957): 148–155.

Fairbairn, Douglas G. *Video Ethnography of 'ICARUS' on the Xerox Alto.* Computer History Museum, December 12, 2017. https://www.youtube.com/watch?v=BauuOoB6EIU.

Fairbairn, Douglas G., and J. Rowson. "ICARUS: An Interactive Integrated Circuit Layout Program." In *Proceedings of the 15th Conference on Design Automation*, 188–192. New York: IEEE Press, 1978.

Farin, Gerald, Josef Hoschek, and Myung-Soo Kim. *Handbook of Computer Aided Geometric Design*. Amsterdam: North Holland Publishing Company, 2002.

Ferber, Ben. "The Use of the Charactron with ERA 1103." In *AIEE-IRE '56 (Western): Papers Presented at the February 7–9, 1956, Joint ACM–AIEE-IRE Western Computer Conference*, 34–36. New York: Association for Computing Machinery, 1956.

Ferguson, James. "Multivariable Curve Interpolation." *Journal of the Association for Computing Machinery* 11, no. 2 (1964): 221–228.

Fetter, William. "Boeing Computer Graphics." In *Cybernetic Serendipity: The Computer and the Arts*, edited by Jasia Reichardt, 88–89. London: Praeger, 1969.

Fetter, William. "Computer Graphics." *Design Quarterly* 66–67 (1966): 14–23.

Fetter, William. "A Progression of Human Figures Simulated by Computer Graphics." *IEEE Computer Graphics and Applications* 2, no. 9 (1982): 9–13.

Fish, Russ. "Teapot Subdivision." 1998. http://www.cs.utah.edu/gdc/projects/alpha1 /help/man/html/model_repo/model_teapot/model_teapot.html.

Flusser, Vílem. *Into the Universe of Technical Images* (1986). Translated by Nancy Ann Roth. Minneapolis: University of Minnesota Press, 2011.

Foley, Jim. "Getting There: The Ten Top Problems Left." *IEEE Computer Graphics and Applications* 20, no. 1 (January 2000): 66–68.

Forrest, A. Robin. Foreword to *An Introduction to Splines for Use in Computer Graphics and Geometric Modeling*, edited by Richard Bartels, John Beatty, and Brian Barsky, vii–viii. Burlington, MA: Morgan Kaufmann Publishers, 1995.

Foster, Frank, dir. *The Story of Computer Graphics*. Los Angeles: Association for Computing Machinery, 1999.

Foucault, Michel. "Why Study Power: The Question of the Subject." In *Michel Foucault: Beyond Structuralism and Hermeneutics*, edited by Hubert L. Dreyfus and Paul Rabinow, 208–228. Chicago: University of Chicago Press, 1982.

Friedberg, Anne. *The Virtual Window: From Alberti to Microsoft*. Cambridge, MA: MIT Press, 2009.

Fries, Ed. "Fixing Color Gotcha." Ed Fries: The Game Is Not Over, May 25, 2016. https://edfries.wordpress.com/2016/05/25/fixing-color-gotcha/.

Fuller, Matthew. *Media Ecologies: Materialist Energies in Art and Technoculture.* Cambridge, MA: MIT Press, 2005.

Fuller, Matthew. *Software Studies: A Lexicon.* Cambridge, MA: MIT Press, 2008.

Gaboury, Jacob. "Other Places of Invention: Computer Graphics at the University of Utah." In *Communities of Computing: Computer Science and Society in the ACM*, edited by Thomas J. Misa, 259–285. San Rafael, CA: Morgan and Claypool, 2016.

Gaboury, Jacob. "Perspective." In *Debugging Game History: A Critical Lexicon*, edited by Raiford Guins and Henry Lowood, 359–368. Cambridge, MA: MIT Press, 2016.

Gaboury, Jacob. "Sounding Silence." *continent.* 5, no. 3 (2016). http://www.continent continent.cc/index.php/continent/article/view/261.

Gaboury, Jacob. "Virtual Bodies and Empty Signifiers: On Fred Parke and Miley Cyrus." Rhizome, January 20, 2014. https://rhizome.org/editorial/2014/jan/20/fred-parke-and-miley-cyrus/.

Galili, Doron. *Seeing by Electricity: The Emergence of Television, 1878–1939.* Durham, NC: Duke University Press, 2020.

Galloway, Alexander. *The Interface Effect.* Cambridge, UK: Polity Press, 2012.

Galloway, Alexander. "The Poverty of Philosophy: Realism and Post-Fordism." *Critical Inquiry* 39 (Winter 2013): 347–366.

Geoghegan, Bernard Dionysius. "After Kittler: On the Cultural Techniques of Recent German Media Theory." *Theory, Culture, and Society* 30, no. 6 (November 2013): 66–82.

Geoghegan, Bernard Dionysius. "An Ecology of Operations: Vigilance, Radar, and the Birth of the Computer Screen." *Representations* 147, no. 1 (2019): 59–95.

Gere, Charlie. "Genealogy of the Computer Screen." *Visual Communication* 5, no. 2 (2006): 141–152.

Gibson, James J. *The Perception of the Visual World.* Boston: Houghton Mifflin, 1950.

Gitelman, Lisa. *Always Already New: Media, History, and the Data of Culture.* Cambridge, MA: MIT Press, 2008.

Gitelman, Lisa, and Geoffrey B. Pingree, eds. *New Media, 1740–1915.* Cambridge, MA: MIT Press, 2004.

Goldberg, Adele. *Smalltalk-80: The Interactive Programming Environment.* Menlo Park, CA: Addison-Wesley Publishing Company, 1984.

Gouraud, Henri. "Computer Display of Curved Surfaces." PhD diss., University of Utah, 1971.

Grey, Jen. "TEATIME at Boston ACM SIGGRAPH 2006." *ACM SIGGRAPH Computer Graphics* 40, no. 3 (November 2006).

Groening, Matt, dir. "Treehouse of Horror VI." *The Simpsons*. New York: Twentieth Century Fox, 1995. TV.

Gross, Benjamin. *The TVs of Tomorrow: How RCA's Flat-Screen Dreams Led to the First LCDs*. Chicago: University of Chicago Press, 2018.

Gruenberger, Fred Joseph. "The History of the Jonniac." Memorandum RM-5654-PR, RAND Corporation, October 1968, 25–27.

Hall, Rebecca. "Leader Ladies Project." Chicago Film Society. https://www.chicagofilmsociety.org/projects/leaderladies/.

Hamraie, Aimi. *Building Access: Universal Design and the Politics of Disability*. Minneapolis: University of Minnesota Press, 2017.

Hansen, Mark B. N. *New Philosophy for New Media*. Cambridge, MA: MIT Press, 2004.

Harrington, Steven J., and Robert R. Buckley. *Interpress: The Source Book*. New York: Simon and Schuster, 1988.

Hawkins, Nehemiah. *Hawkins Electrical Guide*. New York: Theodore Audel, 1914.

Heckbert, Paul. "Ten Unsolved Problems in Rendering." Rendering Algorithms and Systems workshop at Graphics Interface 87, Toronto, April 1987.

Heidegger, Martin. "The Thing." In *Poetry, Language, Thought*, translated by Albert Hofstadter, 161–184. New York: Harper and Row, 2001.

Hicks, Marie. *Programmed Inequality: How Britain Discarded Women Technologists and Lost Its Edge in Computing*. Cambridge, MA: MIT Press, 2017.

Higgins, Hannah. *The Grid Book*. Cambridge, MA: MIT Press, 2009.

Higgins, Hannah, and Douglas Kahn, eds. *Mainframe Experimentalism: Early Computing and the Foundations of the Digital Arts*. Berkeley: University of California Press, 2012.

Hiltzik, Michael A. *Dealers of Lightning: Xerox PARC and the Dawn of the Computer Age*. New York: Harper Business, 1999.

Hinterwaldner, Inge. *The Systemic Image: A New Theory of Interactive Real-Time Simulations*. Cambridge, MA: MIT Press, 2017.

Hookway, Brandon. *Interface*. Cambridge, MA: MIT Press, 2014.

Hsu, Hansen. "The Deep History of Your Apps: Steve Jobs, NeXTSTEP, and Early Object-Oriented Programming." *Computer History Museum Blog*, March 15, 2016. https://computerhistory.org/blog/the-deep-history-of-your-apps-steve-jobs-nextstep-and-early-object-oriented-programming/.

Hu, Tung-Hui. *A Prehistory of the Cloud*. Cambridge, MA: MIT Press, 2015.

Huhtamo, Erkki. *Illusions in Motion: Media Archaeology of the Moving Panorama and Related Spectacles*. Cambridge, MA: MIT Press, 2013.

Huhtamo, Erkki, and Jussi Parikka, eds. *Media Archaeology: Approaches, Applications, and Implications*. Berkeley: University of California Press, 2011.

Hui, Yuk. *On the Existence of Digital Objects*. Minneapolis: University of Minnesota Press, 2016.

Hurst, Jan, Michael S. Mahoney, Norman H. Taylor, Douglas T. Ross, and Robert M. Fano. "Retrospectives I: The Early Years in Computer Graphics at MIT, Lincoln Lab and Harvard." *SIGGRAPH '89 Panel Proceedings: July 31–August 4, 1989* (New York: Association for Computing Machinery, 1989), 19–38.

IKEA Communications AB. *IKEA VR Experience*. 2016. https://store.steampowered .com/app/447270/IKEA_VR_Experience/.

Irani, K. B., and A. W. Naylor. "Memo to: Professor B. Herzog. A Proposal for Research in Conversational Use of Computers for Systems Engineering Problems." September 30, 1966, RG 330–73-A-2108. FOIA Ref. 13-F-1248.

Jacks, Edwin L. "A Laboratory for the Study of Man-Machine Communication." In *Proceedings of the October 27–29, 1964, Fall Joint Computer Conference, Part I*, 343–344. New York: Association for Computing Machinery, 1964.

James Chipman Fletcher Presidential Records, Acc. 199. University Archives and Records Management. University of Utah, J. Willard Marriott, Salt Lake City.

Jarrett, Marvin Scott. *Ray Gun*. Santa Monica, CA, 1992–2000.

Johnson, Timothy E. "Sketchpad III: A Computer Program for Drawing in Three Dimensions." In *Proceedings of the Spring 1963 Joint Computer Conference*, 347–353. New York: Association for Computing Machinery, 1963.

Johnston, Andrew. *Pulses of Abstraction: Episodes from a History of Animation*. Minneapolis: University of Minnesota Press, 2020.

Kajiya, James, Ivan E. Sutherland, and Edward C. Cheadle. "A Random-Access Video Frame Buffer." In *Proceedings of the IEEE Conference on Computer Graphics*, 1–6. Piscataway, NJ: IEEE, 1975.

Kane, Carolyn. *Chromatic Algorithms: Synthetic Color, Computer Art, and Aesthetics after Code*. Chicago: University of Chicago Press, 2014.

Kang, Hai-Yong, and Julie M. Schoenung. "Electronic Waste Recycling: A Review of U.S. Infrastructure and Technology Options." *Resources, Conservation, and Recycling* 45, no. 4 (December 2005): 368–400.

Kay, Alan. *Doing with Images Makes Symbols: Communicating with Computers.* Stanford, CA: University Video Communications, 1987. https://archive.org/details/AlanKeyD1987.

Kay, Alan. "The Early History of Smalltalk." In *HOPL-II: The Second ACM SIGPLAN Conference on History of Programming Languages* (New York: Association for Computing Machinery, 1993), 511–598.

Kay, Alan. "The Reactive Engine." PhD diss., University of Utah, 1969.

Kay, Alan, and Adele Goldberg. *Personal Dynamic Media.* Learning Research Group, Technical Report No. SSL-76–1. Palo Alto, CA: Xerox Palo Alto Research Center, 1976.

Keller, Peter A. *The Cathode-Ray Tube: Technology, History, and Applications.* New York: Palisades Press, 1991.

Kilburn, Tom. "Mark I." Presentation at the Manchester Science Museum, May 23, 1991. Reported in "Early Computers at Manchester University," *Computer Resurrection: The Bulletin of the Computer Conservation Society* 1, no. 4 (Summer 1992). http://www.cs.man.ac.uk/CCS/res/res04.htm#g.

Kirschenbaum, Matthew G. *Mechanisms: New Media and the Forensic Imagination.* Cambridge, MA: MIT Press, 2008.

Kittler, Friedrich. "Computer Graphics: A Semi-Technical Introduction." Translated by Sara Ogger. *Grey Room* 2 (Winter 2001): 30–45.

Kittler, Friedrich. *Gramophone, Film, Typewriter.* Palo Alto, CA: Stanford University Press, 1999.

Kittler, Friedrich. *Optical Media.* Cambridge, UK: Polity Press, 2009.

Kittler, Friedrich. "There Is No Software." *CTheory*, edited by Arthur Kroker and Marilouise Kroker (1995). http://www.ctheory.net/articles.aspx?id=74.

Klütsch, Christoph. *Computergrafik: Ästhetische Experimente zwischen zwei Kulturen: Die Anfänge der Computerkunst in den 1960er Jahren.* Berlin: Springer, 2007.

Knowlton, Kenneth C. "A Computer Technique for Producing Animated Movies." In *Proceedings of the April 21–23, 1964, Spring Joint Computer Conference*, 67–87. New York: Association for Computing Machinery, 1964.

Knuth, Donald E. "Mathematical Typography." *Bulletin (New Series) of the American Mathematical Society* 1, no. 2 (March 1979): 337–372.

Krauss, Rosalind. "Grids." *October* 9 (Summer 1979): 50–64.

Krull, Fred N. "The Origin of Computer Graphics within General Motors." *IEEE Annals of the History of Computing* 16, no. 3 (1994): 40–56.

Krull, Fred N., and James E. Foote. "A Line Scanning System Controlled from an On-Line Console." In *Proceedings of the October 27–29, 1964, Fall Joint Computer Conference, Part I*, 397–410. New York: Association for Computing Machinery, 1964.

Kurt Akeley Papers. SC628. Stanford University Archives Special Collections, Stanford, CA.

Lacan, Jacques. "On the Gaze as *Objet Petit a*." In *The Four Fundamental Concepts of Psychoanalysis*. Edited by Jacques-Alain Miller. Translated by Alan Sheridan, 67–122. New York: W. W. Norton and Company, 1981.

Lammers, Susan. *Programmers at Work, Vol. 1*. Redmond, WA: Microsoft Press, 1986. http://programmersatwork.wordpress.com/john-warnock/.

Laposky, Ben F. *Electronic Abstractions*. Cherokee, IA: Sanford Museum, 1953.

Laposky, Ben F. "Oscillons: Electronic Abstractions." *Leonardo* 2, no. 4 (October 1969): 345–354.

Lasseter, John, dir. *Toy Story*. 1995; Emeryville, CA: Pixar Animation Studio, 2016. Blu-ray Disc.

Lehmann, Ann-Sophie. "Taking the Lid off the Utah Teapot." *Zeitschrift für Medien- und Kulturforschung* 1 (2012): 169–184.

Lehning, James. "'Raising the State of the Art': Commercializing Innovation in Digital Sound." *Media History* (2018): 1–13.

Lehning, James. "Technological Innovation, Commercialization, and Regional Development: Computer Graphics in Utah, 1965–1978." *Information and Culture* 51, no. 4 (2016): 479–499.

Leibniz, Gottfried Wilhelm. *Philosophical Essays*, edited by Daniel Garber and Roger Areiw. New York: Hackett, 1989.

Lenoir, Tim. "All but War Is Simulation: The Military-Entertainment Complex." *Configurations* 8, no. 3 (2000): 289–335.

Lenoir, Tim, and Luke Caldwell. *The Military-Entertainment Complex*. Cambridge, MA: Harvard University Press, 2018.

Lepawsky, Josh. *Reassembling Rubbish: Worlding Electronic Waste*. Cambridge, MA: MIT Press, 2018.

Levoy, Marc. "Open Problems in Computer Graphics." Last updated April 8, 1996, https://graphics.stanford.edu/courses/cs348b-96/open_problems.html.

Licklider, J. C. R. "Computer Graphics as a Medium of Artistic Expression." In *Computers and Their Potential Application in Museums*, 273–302. New York: Arno, 1968.

Licklider, J. C. R. "Man-Computer Symbiosis." *IRE Transactions on Human Factors in Electronics* HFE-1 (March 1960): 4–11.

Light, Jennifer S. "When Computers Were Women." *Technology and Culture* 40, no. 3 (1999): 455–483.

Lindberg, Kelley J. P. "Pioneers on the Digital Frontier." *Continuum: The Magazine of the University of Utah* (Winter 2006–2007). http://www.continuum.utah.edu /2006winter/feature3.html.

Lynn, Greg. Interview with Richard Weinstein. *Constructs* (Spring 2000): 5.

Lyon, Richard F. "A Brief History of 'Pixel.'" In *Proceedings Volume 6069, Digital Photography II.* San Jose, CA: Electronic Imaging, 2006.

Lyon, Richard F. "Pixels and Me." Lecture at the Computer History Museum, Mountain View, CA, March 23, 2005. https://youtu.be/D6n2Esh4jDY.

Machover, Carl. "Graphic CRT Terminals: Characteristics of Commercially Available Equipment." In *Proceedings of the November 14–16, 1967, Fall Joint Computer Conference,* 150–152. New York: Association for Computing Machinery, 1967.

Manovich, Lev. "Assembling Reality: Myths of Computer Graphics." *Afterimage* 20, no. 2 (1992): 12–14.

Manovich, Lev. "The Engineering of Vision from Constructivism to Computers." PhD diss., University of Rochester, 1993.

Manovich, Lev. *The Language of New Media.* Cambridge, MA: MIT Press, 2001.

Manovich, Lev. "The Mapping of Space: Perspective, Radar, and 3-D Computer Graphics." In *Computer Graphics Visual Proceedings,* edited by Thomas Linehan. New York: Association for Computing Machinery, 1993. http://manovich.net/content/04 -projects/003-article-1993/01-article-1993.pdf.

Manovich, Lev. *Software Takes Command.* New York: Bloomsbury Academic, 2013.

Martin, Randi. "Laposky Cited for Tracing History in Computer Art." *Cherokee Daily Times,* January 7, 1972, 1.

Mathematical Applications Group Inc. "3-D Simulated Graphics." *Datamation* 14 (February 1968): 69.

May, Kate Torgovnick. "Back to Tech's Future: Nicholas Negroponte at TED2014." *TEDBlog,* March 17, 2014. https://blog.ted.com/back-to-techs-future-nicholas-negro ponte-at-ted2014/.

McDermott, Robert Joseph. "Geometric Modelling in Computer-Aided Design." PhD diss., University of Utah, 1980.

McDermott, Robert Joseph. "Robert Remembers: The VW Bug." *Utah Teapot: Quarterly Newspaper for the Alumni and Friends of the University of Utah School of Computing* (Fall 2003): 7.

McDermott, Robert Joseph. "A Ukrainian Easter Egg Monument Stands for Thirty Years." In *Proceedings of the 2005 Bridges Conference, Renaissance Banff: Mathematics,*

Music, Art, Culture, edited by Reza Sarhangi and Robert V. Moody, 109–116. Bridges Organization, 2005.

McHugh, Gene. *Post Internet*. Brescia, IT: LINK Editions, 2014.

McPherson, Tara. "US Operating Systems at Mid-Century: The Intertwining of Race and UNIX." In *Race after the Internet*, edited by Lisa Nakamura and Peter A. Chow-White, 21–37. New York: Routledge, 2013.

Mead, Carver, and Lynn Conway. *Introduction to VLSI Systems*. Reading, MA: Addison-Wesley, 1980.

Miller, John M. "Futureworld." Turner Classic Movies. http://www.tcm.com/this-month/article/245820%7C0/Futureworld.html.

Mitchell, William J. *The Reconfigured Eye: Visual Truth in the Post-Photographic Era*. Cambridge, MA: MIT Press, 1994.

Mollaghan, Aimee. *The Visual Music Film*. London: Palgrave Macmillan, 2015.

Mollick, Ethan. "Establishing Moore's Law." *IEEE Annals of the History of Computing* 28, no. 3 (2006): 62–75.

Montfort, Nick. "Continuous Paper: Print Interfaces and Early Computer Writing." Paper presented at ISEA 2004, Helsinki, August 20, 2004. http://nickm.com/writing/essays/continuous_paper_isea.html.

Montfort, Nick, and Ian Bogost. *Racing the Beam: The Atari Video Computer System*. Cambridge, MA: MIT Press, 2009.

Montfort, Nick, and Ian Bogost. "Random and Raster: Display Technologies and the Development of Videogames." *IEEE Annals of the History of Computing* 31, no. 3 (2009): 34–43.

Moore, Gordon. "Cramming More Components onto Integrated Circuits." *Electronics* 38, no. 8 (1965): 114–117.

Morash, Russell, dir. *Computer Sketchpad*. Cambridge, MA: MIT Science Reporter, July 1964. Film. https://youtu.be/6orsmFndx_o.

"More Than Half the Homes in U.S. Have Three or More TVs." Nielsen, July 20, 2009. http://www.nielsen.com/us/en/insights/news/2009/more-than-half-the-homes-in-us-have-three-or-more-tvs.html.

Mulvin, Dylan. *Proxies: The Cultural Work of Standing In*. Cambridge, MA: MIT Press, 2021.

Mulvin, Dylan, and Jonathan Sterne. "Scenes from an Imaginary Country: Test Images and the American Color Television Standard." *Television and New Media* 17, no. 1 (2016): 21–43.

Murphy, Owen, prod. *Incredible Machine*. Murray Hill, NJ: Bell Laboratories, 1968. Film. https://techchannel.att.com/play-video.cfm/2011/4/22/AT&T-Archives-Incredible-Machine.

Murray, Susan. *Bright Signals: A History of Color Television*. Durham, NC: Duke University Press, 2018.

Nakamura, Lisa. "Indigenous Circuits: Navajo Women and the Racialization of Early Electronic Manufacture." *American Quarterly* 66, no. 4 (2014): 919–941.

Nake, Frieder. "Oberfläche & Unterfläche / Vom Zeichnen aus großer Ferne." Paper presented at Node 10 Forum for Digital Arts, Frankfurt, November 15–20, 2010. http://node10.vvvv.org/events/lecture-day.

Newell, Martin. "Modeling by Computer." Unpublished draft essay, January 31, 1975, 4. David C. Evans Papers, MS 625, box 140, folder 21, Special Collections, J. Willard Marriott Library, University of Utah.

Newell, Martin. "The Utilization of Procedure Models in Digital Image Synthesis." PhD diss., University of Utah, 1975.

Newell, Martin, and Jim Blinn. "The Progression of Realism in Computer Generated Images." In *Proceedings of the 1977 ACM Annual Conference*, 444–448. New York: Association for Computing Machinery, 1977.

Newman, William M., and Robert F. Sproull. *Principles of Interactive Computer Graphics*. New York: McGraw-Hill, Inc., 1979.

"1971 Annual Report." Santa Clara, CA: Intel Corporation, 1971. https://www.intel.com/content/www/us/en/history/history-1971-annual-report.html.

Ninke, William H. "Graphic 1: A Remote Graphical Display Console System." In *Proceedings of the November 30–December 1, 1965, Fall Joint Computer Conference, Part I*, 839–846. New York: Association for Computing Machinery, 1965.

Noll, A. Michael. "Scanned-Display Computer Graphics." *Communications of the ACM* 14, no. 3 (March 1970): 146–148.

Nooney, Laine. "A Pedestal, a Table, a Love Letter: Archaeologies of Gender in Videogame History." *Game Studies* 13, no. 2 (2013). http://gamestudies.org/1302/articles/nooney.

Norberg, Arthur L., Judy E. O'Neill, and Kerry J. Freedman. *Transforming Computer Technology: Information Processing for the Pentagon, 1962–1986*. Baltimore: Johns Hopkins University Press, 2000.

North, Dan. *Performing Illusions: Cinema, Special Effects, and the Virtual Actor*. New York: Wallflower Press, 2008.

North, Dan, Bob Rehak, and Michael S. Duffy, eds. *Special Effects: New Histories, Theories, Contexts*. London: British Film Institute, 2015.

"NVIDIA Launches the World's First Graphics Processing Unit: GeForce 256." Response-Source, August 31, 1999. https://pressreleases.responsesource.com/news/3992/nvidia-launches-the-world-s-first-graphics-processing-unit-geforce-256/.

Olson, Craig. "40% Discount on GRAPHICS UNIX WORKSTATIONS." August 9, 1984. http://www.sgistuff.net/hardware/systems/iris1000.html.

Olson, Marisa. "Postinternet: Art after the Internet." *Foam Magazine* 19 (Winter 2011–2012): 59–63.

Ophir, Drora, S. Rankowitz, Barry J. Shepherd, and Robert J. Spinrad. "BRAD: The Brookhaven Raster Display." *Communications of the ACM* 11, no. 6 (June 1968): 415–416.

Panofsky, Erwin. "Jan van Eyck's Arnolfini Portrait." *Burlington Magazine for Connoisseurs* 64, no. 372 (March 1934): 117–119, 122–127.

Panofsky, Erwin. *Perspective as Symbolic Form.* Translated by Christopher S. Wood. 1927; New York: Zone Books, 1991.

Parikka, Jussi. *What Is Media Archaeology?* Cambridge, UK: Polity Press, 2012.

Parisi, David. *Archaeologies of Touch: Interfacing with Haptics from Electricity to Computing.* Minneapolis: University of Minnesota Press, 2018.

Parke, Frederic. *Computer Generated Animation of Faces.* Technical Report UTEC-CSs-72-120. Salt Lake City: University of Utah, 1972.

Parke, Frederic. "A Parametric Model for Human Faces." PhD diss., University of Utah, 1974.

Patterson, Zabet. *Peripheral Vision: Bell Labs, the SC 4020, and the Origins of Computer Art.* Cambridge, MA: MIT Press, 2015.

Patterson, Zabet. "Visionary Machines: A Genealogy of the Digital Image." PhD diss., University of California at Berkeley, 2007.

Perry, Tekla S. "PostScript Prints Anything: A Case History." *IEEE Spectrum* 25, no. 5 (1988): 42–46.

Peters, John Durham. "Mormonism and Media." In *The Oxford Handbook of Mormonism,* edited by Terryl L. Givens and Philip L. Barlow, 407–424. Oxford: Oxford University Press, 2015.

Pharr, Matt, Wenzel Jakob, and Greg Humphreys. *Physically Based Rendering: From Theory to Implementation.* Cambridge, MA: Morgan Kaufmann, 2016.

Phong, Bui Tuong. "Illumination for Computer-Generated Images." PhD diss., University of Utah, 1973.

Pierson, Michele. *Special Effects: Still in Search of Wonder.* New York: Columbia University Press, 2002.

Plant, Sadie. *Zeros and Ones: Digital Women and the New Technoculture*. New York: Doubleday, 1997.

Price, David. *The Pixar Touch: The Making of a Company*. New York: Vintage, 2009.

Prince, Stephen. *Digital Visual Effects in Cinema: The Seduction of Reality*. New Brunswick, NJ: Rutgers University Press, 2011.

Prizada, Usman. "Intel CREATE Event at SIGGRAPH 2019: New High Performance Raytracing Engine, Raja's Law, Xe GPU Collabs and More." WCCF Tech, August 1, 2019. https://wccftech.com/intel-create-event-siggraph-2019-rajas-law/.

Puglisi, Joseph J., Jack Case, and George Webster. "CAORF Ship Operation Center (SOC)—Recent Advances in Maritime Engine and Deck Simulation at the Computer Aided Operations Research Facility (CAORF)." Paper presented at the International Conference on Marine Simulation and Ship Maneuvering MARSIM 2000, Orlando, FL, May 8–12, 2000.

Randell, B. "On Alan Turing and the Origins of Digital Computers." In *Machine Intelligence 7*, edited by Bernard Meltzer and Donald Michie, 1–19. Edinburgh: Edinburgh University Press, 1972.

Rankin, Joy Lisi. *A People's History of Computing in the United States*. Cambridge, MA: Harvard University Press, 2018.

Redmond, Kent C., and Thomas M. Smith. *From Whirlwind to MITRE: The R&D Story of the SAGE Air Defense Computer*. Cambridge, MA: MIT Press, 2000.

Redmond, Kent C., and Thomas M. Smith. *Project Whirlwind: History of a Pioneer Computer*. Bedford, MA: Digital Press, 1980.

Reid, Brian, reid@Glacier. "PostScript and Interpress: A Comparison." [fa.laser-lovers], March 2, 1985. https://groups.google.com/forum/#!msg/fa.laser-lovers/H3us4h8S3Kk /-vGRDirzDV0J.

Reintjes, J. Francis. *Numerical Control: Making a New Technology*. Oxford: Oxford University Press, 1991.

Rentsch, Tim. "Object Oriented Programming." *ACM SIGPLAN Notices* 17 (September 1982): 51–57.

Resch, Ronald D. "The Topological Design of Sculptural and Architectural Systems." In *Proceedings of the June 4–8, 1973, National Computer Conference and Exposition*, 643–650. New York: Association for Computing Machinery, 1973.

Rickitt, Richard. *Special Effects: The History and Technique*. New York: Billboard Books, 2000.

Rippy, D. E., and D. E. Humphries. "Magic: A Machine for Automatic Graphics Interface to a Computer." In *Proceedings of the November 30–December 1, 1965, Fall*

Joint Computer Conference, Part I, 819–830. New York: Association for Computing Machinery, 1965.

Roberts, Lawrence G. "Machine Perception of Three-Dimensional Solids." PhD diss., Massachusetts Institute of Technology, 1963.

Roberts, Sarah T. *Behind the Screen: Content Moderation in the Shadows of Social Media*. New Haven, CT: Yale University Press, 2019.

Rodowick, David Norman. *The Virtual Life of Film*. Cambridge, MA: Harvard University Press, 2009.

Romney, Gordon. "First Rendering: A History of 3D Rendering through a Look at the Contributions of Gordon Romney, Alan Erdahl, Edwin Catmull and James Blinn." Accessed November 5, 2020. https://firstrender.net.

Romney, Gordon, Gary Watkins, and David Evans. "Real-Time Display of Computer Generated Half-Tone Perspective Pictures." In *Information Processing 68: Proceedings of IFIP Congress 1968, Edinburgh, UK*, 973–978. Laxenburg, Austria: International Federation for Information Processing, 1968.

Rosen, Margit, ed. *A Little-Known Story about a Movement, a Magazine, and the Computer's Arrival in Art: New Tendencies and Bit International, 1961–1973*. Cambridge, MA: MIT Press, 2011.

Rosen, Philip. *Change Mummified: Cinema, Historicity, Theory*. Minneapolis: University of Minnesota Press, 2001.

Rougelotand, R. S., and R. Shoemaker. *G.E. Real Time Display*. NASA Report, NAS 9–3916. Syracuse, NY: General Electric Company, 1969.

Russell, Steve, Nolan Bushnell, and Stewart Brand. "Shall We Play a Game?: The Early Years of Computer Gaming." Video recording and discussion at the Computer History Museum, Mountain View, CA, May 7, 2002. Accession no. 102695272.

Sabin, M. *Offset Parametric Surfaces*. Technical Report VTO/MS/149. London: British Aircraft Corporation, 1968.

Sabin, M. *Parametric Splines in Tension*. Technical Report VTO/MS/160. London: British Aircraft Corporation, 1970.

Sabin, M. *Trinomial Basis Functions for Interpolation in Triangular Regions (Bézier Triangles)*. London: British Aircraft Corporation, 1971.

Saxenian, AnnaLee. *Regional Advantage: Culture and Competition in Silicon Valley and Route 128*. Cambridge, MA: Harvard University Press, 1996.

Schoenberg, Isaac Jacob. "Contributions to the Problem of Approximation of Equidistant Data by Analytic Functions." *Quarterly of Applied Mathematics* 4 (1946): 45–99, 112–141.

Schröter, Jens. *3D: History, Theory and Aesthetics of the Transplane Image*. New York: Bloomsbury Publishing USA, 2014.

Schure, Alexander, dir. *Tubby the Tuba*. Los Angeles: Embassy Pictures, 1975. 35 mm.

Seymour, Mike. "Founders Series: Industry Legend Jim Blinn." fxguide, July 24, 2012. http://www.fxguide.com/featured/founders-series-industry-legend-jim-blinn/.

Shoup, Richard. "SuperPaint: An Early Frame Buffer Graphics System." *IEEE Annals of the History of Computing* 23, no. 2 (April–June 2001): 32–37.

Siegert, Bernhard. *Cultural Techniques: Grids, Filters, Doors, and Other Articulations of the Real*. New York: Fordham University Press, 2015.

Sito, Tom. *Moving Innovation: A History of Computer Animation*. Cambridge, MA: MIT Press, 2013.

Skinner, Frank D. "Computer Graphics: Where Are We?" *Datamation* 12 (May 1966): 28–31.

Smith, Alvy Ray. "The Dawn of Digital Light." *IEEE Annals of the History of Computing* 38, no. 4 (2016): 74–91.

Smith, Alvy Ray. "Digital Paint Systems: An Anecdotal and Historical Overview." *IEEE Annals of the History of Computing* 23, no. 2 (April–June 2001): 4–30.

Smith, Alvy Ray. "Tint Fill" *ACM SIGGRAPH Computer Graphics* 13, no. 2 (1979): 276–282.

Smith, Brian Cantwell. *On the Origin of Objects*. Cambridge, MA: MIT Press, 1996.

Smith, Douglas K., and Robert C. Alexander. *Fumbling the Future: How Xerox Invented, Then Ignored, the First Personal Computer*. New York: William Morrow and Company, 1988.

Sobchack, Vivian. "Afterword: Media Archaeology and Re-Presencing the Past." In *Media Archaeology: Approaches, Applications, and Implications*, edited by Erkki Huhtamo and Jussi Parikka, 323–334. Berkeley: University of California Press, 2011.

Spielberg, Steven, dir. *Jurassic Park*. 1993; Los Angeles: Universal Pictures, 2018. Blu-ray Disc.

Spinoza, Baruch. "The Ethics." In *The Ethics and Other Works*, edited and translated by Edwin Curley, part 1, def 5. Princeton, NJ: Princeton University Press, 1994.

Sproull, Robert F., Richard Lyon, and Stephen Trimberger. *The Caltech Intermediate Form for LSI Layout Description*. California Institute of Technology Silicon Structures Project, Technical Report 2686. Pasadena: California Institute of Technology, 1980.

Sproull, Robert F., and Ivan E. Sutherland. "A Clipping Divider." In *Proceedings of the December 9–11, 1968, Fall Joint Computer Conference, Part I*, 765–775. New York: Association for Computing Machinery, 1968.

Staiti, Alana. "What's in a Model? A History of Human Modeling for Computer Graphics and Animation, 1961–1988." PhD diss, Cornell University, 2018.

Starosielski, Nicole. *The Undersea Network*. Durham, NC: Duke University Press, 2015.

Sterling, Bruce. "War Is Virtual Hell." *Wired*, January 1, 1993. http://archive.wired.com/wired/archive/1.01/virthell.html.

Steyerl, Hito. "Too Much World: Is the Internet Dead?" *e-flux journal* 49 (November 2013), https://www.e-flux.com/journal/49/60004/too-much-world-is-the-internet-dead/.

Stine, Kyle. "Critical Hardware: The Circuit of Image and Data." *Critical Inquiry* 45, no. 3 (2019): 762–786.

Stockham, Thomas G., Thomas M. Cannon, and Robert B. Ingebretsen. "Blind Deconvolution through Digital Signal Processing." *Proceedings of the IEEE* 63, no. 4 (1975): 678–692.

Straßer, Wolfgang. "Schnelle kurven und flächendarstellung auf grafischen sicht geräten." PhD diss., Technischen Universität Berlin, 1974.

Sturgeon, Timothy J. "How Silicon Valley Came to Be." In *Understanding Silicon Valley: The Anatomy of an Entrepreneurial Region*, edited by Martin Kenney, 15–47. Palo Alto, CA: Stanford University Press, 2000.

Sutherland, Ivan E. "Computer Displays." *Scientific American* 222, no. 6 (June 1970): 73.

Sutherland, Ivan E. "Computer Graphics: Ten Unsolved Problems." *Datamation* 12, no. 5 (1966): 22–27.

Sutherland, Ivan E. "Computer Inputs and Outputs." *Scientific American* 215, no. 3 (September 1966): 86–99.

Sutherland, Ivan E. "Looking Back: The TX-2 Computer and Sketchpad." *Lincoln Laboratory Journal* 11, no. 1 (2012): 82–84.

Sutherland, Ivan E. "Oral History with William Aspray." Charles Babbage Institute, Pittsburgh, May 1, 1989.

Sutherland, Ivan E. "The Problem: How to Build Digital Electronic Circuits from Now to 1985." Letter to William. R. Sutherland, January 26, 1976. http://ai.eecs.umich.edu/people/conway/VLSI/BackgroundContext/IvanSutherlandLetter1-26-76.PDF.

Sutherland, Ivan E., dir. *Sketchpad*. Cambridge, MA: MIT Lincoln Laboratory, 1962. Film. https://youtu.be/3wrn9cxlgls.

Sutherland, Ivan E. "Sketchpad: A Man-Machine Graphical Communication System." PhD diss., Massachusetts Institute of Technology, 1963.

Sutherland, Ivan E. "Sketchpad: A Man-Machine Graphical Communication System." In *Proceedings of the AFIPS 1963 Spring Joint Computer Conference, May 21–23 1963*, 329–346. Baltimore: Spartan Books, 1963.

Sutherland, Ivan E. "The Ultimate Display." *Proceedings of IFIP Congress* (1965): 506–508.

Sutherland, Ivan E., and Gary W. Hodgman. "Reentrant Polygon Clipping." *Communications of the ACM* 17, no. 1 (1974): 32–42.

Sutherland, Ivan E., and Carver Mead. "Microelectronics and Computer Science." *Scientific American* 237, no. 3 (1977): 210–228.

Sutherland, Ivan E., Carver Mead, and Thomas E. Everhart. *Basic Limitations in Microcircuit Fabrication Technology*. ARPA Report R-1956-ARPA. Santa Monica, CA: Rand Corporation, November 1976.

Sutherland, Ivan E., and Theodore H. Myer. "On the Design of Display Processors." *Communications of the ACM* 11, no. 6 (June 1968): 410–414.

Sutherland, Ivan E., Robert F. Sproull, and Robert Schumacker. "A Characterization of Ten Hidden-Surface Algorithms." *Computing Surveys* 6, no. 1 (1974): 1–55.

Sutherland, Ivan E., and William Sutherland. "Mom Loved Him Best: Bert and Ivan Sutherland." Discussion moderated by Robert F. Sproull, Computer History Museum, February 3, 2004. https://www.computerhistory.org/collections/catalog/102695308.

Sutherland, William. *Management of Industrial Research: Exploring the Unknown Technical Future*. Menlo Park, CA: Sun Microsystems, July 2008. https://ai.eecs.umich.edu/people/conway/Memoirs/VLSI/Files/Management_of_Industrial_Research.pdf.

Sutherland, William. "The On-line Graphical Specification of Computer Procedures." PhD diss., Massachusetts Institute of Technology, 1966.

Sutton, Gloria. *The Experience Machine: Stan VanDerBeek's Movie-Drome and Expanded Cinema*. Cambridge, MA: MIT Press, 2015.

Swords, S. S. *Technical History of the Beginnings of Radar*. London: Institute of Engineering and Technology, 1986.

Taylor, Robert. "Accomplishments in Calendar Year 1967, Internal Memorandum for the Acting Deputy Director, ARPA." January 5, 1968, 2–3. National Archive Branch Division, Record Group 330-74-107, box 1, folder: "Internal Memoranda 1968 through 1970." FOIA Ref. 13-F-1248.

Taylor, Robert. "Oral History with Paul McJones." Computer History Museum, October 10–11, 2008.

"Toward a Machine with Interactive Skills." In *Understanding Computers: Computer Images*, 31–38. New York: Time-Life Books, 1986.

Turing, Alan. "On Computable Numbers, with an Application to the Entscheidungs-problem." *Proceedings of the London Mathematical Society* 2, no. 42 (1937): 230–265.

University of Utah Department of Computer Science records. Acc. 051. University Archives and Records Management. University of Utah, J. Willard Marriott. Salt Lake City, Utah.

VanderLans, Rudy, ed. *Emigre*. San Francisco, 1984–2005.

Vernon Russell Anderson Papers. M1222. Stanford University Library Special Collections, Stanford, CA.

Vierkant, Artie. "The Image Object Post-Internet." JstChillin, 2010. http://jstchillin.org/artie/pdf/The_Image_Object_Post-Internet_us.pdf.

von Neumann, John. "First Draft of a Report on the EDVAC." *IEEE Annals of the History of Computing* 15, no. 4 (1993; June 30, 1945): 27–75.

Walker, Gianna. "The Inception of Computer Graphics at the University of Utah, 1960s–1970s." Notes from the annual meeting of the Association for Computing Machinery's SIGGRAPH Special Interest Group, September 27, 1994. https://web.archive.org/web/20020827134354/http://silicon-valley.siggraph.org/MeetingNotes/Utah.html.

Warburton, Alan. *Goodbye Uncanny Valley*. October 2017, 14:38. https://alanwarburton.co.uk/goodbye-uncanny-valley.

Warnock, John. "Adobe Co-Founder John Warnock on the Competitive Advantages of Aesthetics and the 'Right' Technology." Interview with Knowledge@Wharton, January 20, 2010. http://knowledge.wharton.upenn.edu/article/adobe-co-founder-john-warnock-on-the-competitive-advantages-of-aesthetics-and-the-right-technology/.

Warnock, John. "A Hidden Surface Algorithm for Computer Generated Halftone Pictures." PhD diss., University of Utah, 1969.

Warnock, John. "The Origins of PostScript." *IEEE Annals of the History of Computing* 40, no. 3 (2018): 68–76.

Watkins, Gary S. "A Real Time Visible Surface Algorithm." No. UTEC-CSC-70–101. University of Utah School of Computing, Salt Lake City, June 1970.

Weber, Rachel N. "Manufacturing Gender in Commercial and Military Cockpit Design." *Science, Technology, and Human Values* 22, no. 2 (1997): 235–253.

Weisberg, David E. "The Engineering Design Revolution: The People, Companies and Computer Systems That Changed Forever the Practice of Engineering." 2008. http://cadhistory.net/.

Weiss, Ruth A. "Be Vision: A Package of IBM 7090 Fortran Programs to Draw Orthographic Views of Combinations of Planes and Quadratic Surfaces." *Journal of the Association for Computing Machinery* 13 (April 1966): 194–204.

Whissel, Kristen. *Spectacular Digital Effects: CGI and Contemporary Cinema*. Durham, NC: Duke University Press, 2014.

White, Kenneth. "Strangeloves: From/De la région centrale, Air Defense Radar Station Moisie, and Media Cultures of the Cold War." *Grey Room* 58 (2015): 50–82.

Whitney, John. *Digital Harmony: On the Complementarity of Music and Visual Art*. Kingsport, TN: Kingsport Press, 1980.

Williams, Frederic, and Tom Kilburn. "A Storage System for Use with Binary-Digital Computing Machines." *Proceedings of the IEE—Part III: Radio and Communication Engineering* 96, no. 40 (1949): 81–98.

Williams, Lance. "Pyramidal Parametrics." In *Proceedings of the 10th Annual Conference on Computer Graphics and Interactive Techniques*, 1–11. New York: Association for Computing Machinery, 1983.

Winthrop-Young, Geoffrey, Ilinca Iurascu, and Jussi Parikka, eds. "Special Issue: Cultural Techniques." *Theory, Culture, and Society* 30, no. 6 (November 2013).

Witt, Andrew, and Eliza Pertigkiozoglou. *Computation as Design: Ron Resch and the New Media of Geometry*. Montreal: Canadian Centre for Architecture, 2019.

Wylie, Chris, Gorgon Romney, David Evans, and Alan Erdahl. "Half-Tone Perspective Drawings by Computer." In *Proceedings of the November 14–16, 1967, Fall Joint Computer Conference*, 49–58. New York: Association for Computing Machinery, 1967.

Yue, Genevieve. "The China Girl on the Margins of Film." *October* 153 (Summer 2015): 96–116.

Zajac, Edward E. "Computer-Made Perspective Movies as a Scientific and Communication Tool." *Communications of the ACM* 7, no. 3 (1964): 169–170. https://techchannel.att.com/embed/index.cfm?mediaID=11107&w=560&h=315.

Zepcevski, Joline. "Complexity and Verification: The History of Programming as Problem Solving." PhD diss., University of Minnesota, 2012.

Zielinski, Siegfried. "Media Archaeology." Special issue, *CTheory*, edited by Arthur Kroger and Marilouise Kroker (July 11, 1996). http://www.ctheory.net/articles.aspx?id=42.

Zinman, Gregory. *Making Images Move: Handmade Cinema and the Other Arts*. Berkeley: University of California Press, 2020.

Index

Note: Page numbers in italics indicate figures.